Library of
Davidson College

Ben Hecht
Hollywood Screenwriter

Studies in Cinema, No. 27

Diane M. Kirkpatrick, Series Editor

Professor, History of Art
The University of Michigan

Other Titles in This Series

No. 25	*Jean Mitry and the Aesthetics of the Cinema*	Brian Lewis
No. 26	*The Left Side of Paradise: The Screenwriting of John Howard Lawson*	Gary Carr
No. 28	*American Film Acting: The Stanislavski Heritage*	Richard A. Blum
No. 29	*Hollywood and the Profession of Authorship: 1928-1940*	Richard Fine
No. 30	*The Political Language of Film and the Avant-Garde*	Dana B. Polan
No. 31	*Subversive Pleasures: The Reflexive Dimension of Literature and Cinema*	Robert Stam
No. 32	*Abstraction in Avant-Garde Films*	Maureen Turim
No. 33	*The Filmology Movement and Film Study in France*	Edward Lowry
No. 34	*The Free Years of the Italian Film Industry: 1930-1935*	Elaine Mancini
No. 35	*On the Kino Front: The Evolution of Soviet Cinema in the 1920s*	Denise J. Youngblood
No. 36	*Hitchcock and World War II*	Sam P. Simone

Ben Hecht
Hollywood Screenwriter

by
Jeffrey Brown Martin
Assistant Professor of Theater Arts
Emerson College
Boston, Massachusetts

UMI RESEARCH PRESS
Ann Arbor, Michigan

The author wishes to thank the following for permission to reprint material used in this book:

The estates of Ben Hecht and of Rose Hecht for material from *Child of the Century, Gaily, Gaily, Letters From Bohemia, Charlie, A Guide for the Bedeviled,* and *The Front Page*. Fred Lawrence Guiles for material from *Hanging on in Paradise*, 1975. *The Lubitsch Touch* by Herman G. Weinberg, 1977, Dover Publications, Inc., used with permission of the publisher. "Raising Kane" by Pauline Kael. Copyright 1971 by Pauline Kael. By permission of Bantam Books, Inc. All rights reserved.

Copyright © 1985, 1978
Jeffrey Brown Martin
All rights reserved

Produced and distributed by
UMI Research Press
an imprint of
University Microfilms International
A Xerox Information Resources Company
Ann Arbor, Michigan 48106

Library of Congress Cataloging in Publication Data

Martin, Jeffrey Brown, 1950-
  Ben Hecht, Hollywood screenwriter.
    (Studies in cinema ; no. 27)
    "A revision of the author's thesis, Indiana University, 1978"—T.p. verso.
    Filmography: p.
    Bibliography: p.
    Includes index.
    1. Hecht, Ben, 1893-1964—Moving-picture plays.
  2. Hecht, Ben, 1893-1964—Film adaptations.
  3. Moving-picture plays—History and criticism.
  4. Moving-pictures—United States. 5. Authors, American—20th century—Biography. I. Title.
  II. Series.

PS3515.E18Z76   1984   812'.52   84-16181
ISBN 0-8357-1571-X (alk. paper)

Contents

List of Plates   *vii*

Preface   *xi*

1   A Child of the Century   *1*

2   Screwball Comedy: A Background   *25*

3   *The Front Page*   *41*

4   *Design for Living*   *57*

5   The Screwball Comedy Vogue: *The Twentieth Century, Nothing Sacred, His Girl Friday*   *79*

6   Writer-Directors: *The Scoundrel* and *Crime Without Passion*   *109*

7   "My Tribe is Israel": World War II and the Irgun   *141*

8   Gaily, Gaily: 1945–1964   *161*

Appendix A: Filmography   *183*

Appendix B: New York Theatre Productions   *211*

Appendix C: Bibliography of Works by Hecht   *215*

Notes   *217*

Bibliography   *229*

Index   *235*

List of Plates

1. *Underworld* (1927). (Photo: Museum of Modern Art/Film Stills Archive courtesy Paramount Studios.)   *26*

2. *The Scarface* (1932). (Photo: Museum of Modern Art/Film Stills Archive courtesy United Artists.)   *35*

3. *The Scarface* (1932). (Photo: Museum of Modern Art/Film Stills Archive courtesy United Artists.)   *36*

4. *Viva Villa* (1934). (Photo: Museum of Modern Art/Film Stills Archive courtesy Metro Goldwyn Mayer.)   *43*

5. *The Front Page* (1931). (Photo: Museum of Modern Art/Film Stills Archive courtesy United Artists.)   *53*

6. *Design for Living* (1933). (Photo: Museum of Modern Art/Film Stills Archive courtesy Paramount.)   *64*

7. *Twentieth Century* (1934). (Photo: Museum of Modern Art/Film Stills Archive courtesy Columbia.)   *85*

8. *Twentieth Century* (1934). (Photo: Museum of Modern Art/Film Stills Archive courtesy Columbia.)   *88*

9. *The Front Page* (1931). (Photo: Museum of Modern Art/Film Stills Archive courtesy United Artists.)   *92*

10. *His Girl Friday* (1940). (Photo: Museum of Modern Art/Film Stills Archive courtesy Columbia.)   *93*

11. *Nothing Sacred* (1937). (Photo: Museum of Modern Art/Film Stills Archive courtesy United Artists.)   *97*

List of Plates

12. *Nothing Sacred* (1937). (Photo: Museum of Modern Art/Film Stills Archive courtesy United Artists.)   *99*

13. *Nothing Sacred* (1937). (Photo: Museum of Modern Art/Film Stills Archive courtesy United Artists.)   *101*

14. *Comrade X* (1940). (Photo: Museum of Modern Art/Film Stills Archive courtesy Metro Goldwyn Mayer.)   *107*

15. (1934). Charles MacArthur and Ben Hecht direct in Astoria, Long Island studios. Cinematographer Lee Garmes consults. (Photo: Academy of Motion Pictures.)   *114*

16. (1934). Hecht and MacArthur direct Claude Rains in scene from *Crime Without Passion.* (Photo: Academy of Motion Pictures.)   *118*

17. *Crime Without Passion* (1934). (Photo: Museum of Modern Art/Film Stills Archive courtesy Paramount.)   *124*

18. (1935). A duet during a break from the shooting of *The Scoundrel.* (Photo: Museum of Modern Art/Film Stills Archive courtesy Paramount.)   *127*

19. *The Scoundrel* (1935). (Photo: Museum of Modern Art/Film Stills Archive.)   *131*

20. (1934). On location shooting *Once in a Blue Moon.* (Photo: Academy of Motion Pictures.)   *135*

21. Rose Caylor, Hecht's wife, at work in Astoria, Long Island studio. (Photo: Academy of Motion Pictures.)   *136*

22. *Soak the Rich* (1935). (Photo: Academy of Motion Pictures.)   *138*

23. Hecht with co-director Lee Garmes working on scene from *Angels Over Broadway* (1940). (Photo: Academy of Motion Pictures.)   *144*

24. *Angels Over Broadway* (1940). (Photo: Museum of Modern Art/Film Stills Archive courtesy Columbia.)   *146*

25. *Spellbound* (1945). (Photo: Museum of Modern Art/Film Stills Archive courtesy United Artists.)   *165*

26. *Notorious* (1946). (Photo: Museum of Modern Art/Film Stills Archive.)   *168*

27. *Specter of the Rose* (1946). (Photo: Museum of Modern Art/Film Stills Archive.)   *170*

28. *Actors and Sin* (1951). (Photo: Museum of Modern Art/Film Stills Archive courtesy United Artists.)   *172*

29. *Actors and Sin* (1951). (Photo: Museum of Modern Art/Film Stills Archive courtesy United Artists.)   *173*

30. *Monkey Business* (1952). (Harry Carey, Jr. and Jerry Sheldon). (Photo: Museum of Modern Art/Film Stills Archive courtesy Twentieth Century Fox.)   *175*

31. *Roman Holiday* (1953). (Photo: Museum of Modern Art/Film Stills Archive courtesy Paramount.)   *177*

32. *Miracle in the Rain* (1956). (Photo: Museum of Modern Art/Film Stills Archive courtesy Warner Brothers.)   *180*

Preface

In the not too distant past, the twentieth century was dubbed the film age—a name that appeared apt since the motion picture seemed to symbolize the revolutions in art, technology, communication, and simply the pace of change that has characterized our time. But in the same way that Modern Art did not remain avant-garde but gave way to Post Modernism, so too has the film age given way to first the space age and now the computer age. What once seemed to be a breaking away from the past is now viewed as having continuity with preceding cultural traditions. What was once immediate and new has now become the topic of historical and critical study. The sound film in particular has become a battleground for two opposing crtitical attitudes: the one, producer and director dominated, based on the movies' own short experience in its silent days; the other, writer oriented, growing from the older tradition of the spoken drama which came into film with sound. The two traditions clashed on the sound stage and critical writing about film since dialogue was introduced over fifty years ago has continued the discussion. Recent critical attention has focused on the early days of talking pictures, and a heightened awareness of screenwriters has developed—an appreciation of those individuals who wrote the dialogue films that the contemporary public thought emanated from monolithic studios, or popped fullgrown from the imagination of directors, or were shaped by the personalities of their favorite stars.

The prototype for our idea of the Hollywood screenwriter was Ben Hecht, one of the most prolific, highly paid, critically acclaimed, and independent writers to work in film. Hecht and his friend and collaborator Charles MacArthur were so notorious for their skill and antics that it seemed natural when writing their comedy about Hollywood studios, *Boy Meets Girl*, that Bella and Samuel Spewack would use Hecht and MacArthur as models for their central characters—two screenwriters who run roughshod over studio bosses, bring lovers together, and manipulate everyone around them to fulfill their screen formulas in real life. Although his reputation has diminished, Hecht remains a symbol of both the talents and the foibles of his profession. Hecht died in 1964 at the age of seventy, but the legacy of his life and work persists as current event rather than merely as cultural artifact. When I began this study, the *Chicago Daily News*, where Hecht had done some of his early and best reporting, went out of business. His play *The Twentieth Century* opened in New York, recycled as a musical. Menachem Begin, former head of the Irgun, an organization Hecht had supported during and after the Second World War, became Prime Minister of Israel. More recently, the Hartford Stage Company revived Hecht and Gene Fowler's *The Great Magoo*, a play that had not been produced since it opened and quickly closed in New York in 1932 (and even as a piece of nostalgia the reasons for that initial failure were clear in the recent revival). Today in Astoria, Long Island, the studio where Hecht and Charles MacArthur made four independent films for Paramount Studios in 1934 and 1935 has been refurbished and is now the focus of the resurgence of filmmaking in New York. Most recently, Brian de Palma dedicated his remake of *The Scarface* to its original director and writer, Howard Hawks and Ben Hecht. These outcroppings of Hecht's work provided impetus to this work—an attempt to define Hecht's contribution to American film and to place that contribution into some biographical and historical context.

Although he was writing films until the time of his death, Hecht's films of the 1930s, particularly his screwball comedies, represent some of his most durable work. The screwball comedy is not usually the subject of critical veneration and when it is its success is often ascribed to its directors, such as Howard Hawks or Preston Sturges or to its stars such as Katherine Hepburn, Clark Gable, Cary Grant, or Carole Lombard. But the screwball comedy, along with other thirties genres such as newspaper and gangster films, represented something new and indigenously American in film, and Hecht contributed in a major way to each of these forms. The sound film was new, and every new script contributed to the growth of a genre and style since a great measure of their success can be traced to the freshness, spirit, wit, and originality of the writing. Focusing on the work of one individual such as Hecht makes it possible to trace changes and developments within these larger forms.

The critical groundwork for a study of Hecht's screenplays has been laid by the work of other writers and scholars: Richard Corliss in *The Hollywood Screenwriters* (1972) and the expanded *Talking Pictures* (1974) drew attention to the contribution of the author to the personality of various films; Fred Guiles in *Hanging On in Paradise* focused on the lives and careers of a number of writers in Hollywood; Pauline Kael's *Citizen Kane Book* dealt with both the work of Herman Mankiewicz and early sound film comedy cycles; and Andrew Sarris in an article on screwball comedy, "The Sex Comedy Without the Sex" (*American Film*, March 1978), outlined some of the characteristics of the genre. In different ways, each of these writers defined the issues and opened new areas for study. Working in a similar direction, Hecht's films of the 1930s form the focus of the present work. In order to understand Hecht's contribution in a fuller context, chapter 1 has been devoted to his background and early work. Chapter 2 discusses sources and characteristics of screwball comedy. Chapters 3, 4, and 5 discuss the development of Hecht's own mixture of melodrama, satire, farce, and romance, primarily in *The Front Page* (1931), *Design for Living* (1933), *The Twentieth Century* (1934), *Nothing Sacred* (1937), and *His Girl Friday* (1940). Chapter 6 deals with Hecht's collaboration as writer-director with Charles MacArthur in Astoria, Long Island in 1934–1935. The final two chapters discuss Hecht's movement away from the spirit of the thirties: chapter 7, his reawakening Judaism, his war activities and films during those years; chapter 8, his life and films in his last two decades, 1945–1964.

There are many alternate ways in which this study might have been organized. The seven films Hecht directed could conceivably have constituted the entire subject matter, but because some of these are not available for extended study and because they do not represent his best work, this seemed undesirable. Similarly, an approach by studio or by director was unsatisfactory because this would have grouped films of uneven quality and different genres, which were produced years apart, without a clearly defined cohesion. A genre study, handled chronologically, with its focus on one group of important films, seemed to make the most sense within the context of Hecht's life.

There are many other fruitful areas of study possible for the scholar interested in Hecht—such as a study of the collaborative process of writing and writing-directing. There are also a number of films I have either barely mentioned or ignored entirely. Certainty of authorship, appropriateness to the discussion, date of composition, and prior attention by other scholars have all been factors in these decisions. *Wuthering Heights* (1939), for instance, has not been discussed, in part because of George Bluestone's satisfying study of the film in his book *Novels Into Film* (1968) and in part because the film has little relevance to the basic study of comedy or any particular element or event in Hecht's life.

The problems of ascertaining writing credit for the films should also be mentioned. Writers in the studio system frequently worked without credit. One-half of the films to which Hecht is reputed to have contributed (this excludes films made from his original nonfilm material—story, novel, or play) do not list him among the credits. This does not mean, however, that he did not do a major share of the writing. There are also a few films that carry his name on which he did little or no work, such as *The Queen of Outer Space* (1958). Even among the films already listed, two are without his name, *The Front Page* and *His Girl Friday*. There is a certainty he worked on the first and a fair certainty he worked on the second. I have attempted to concentrate on the films for which clear authorship can be established. I have also included a filmography as an appendix which lists the films and includes other pertinent information.

Historical facts have also often been a problem. Hecht himself is not always a reliable source. Harry Selden, a journalist, friend of Hecht's, and fellow worker for Israel, has compared Hecht's concern for fact with that of a lapidary who is more concerned with the imaginative setting he creates than in the jewel of fact that the setting is intended to serve. Norman Mailer, frustrated by the fabrications in the Hecht-written Marilyn Monroe "autobiography" *My Story* (1974),[1] commented that the "Marilyn Ben Hecht" version was untrustworthy in part because "Hecht was never a writer to tell the truth when a concoction could put life in his prose."[2] Even beyond Hecht's own creative use of facts, Hollywood legends are the stuff of press agents, and often many different versions of the same story or riposte are ascribed to a number of likely celebrants. I have attempted to differentiate entertainment, my own and the reader's, from fact as much as possible.

One set of facts of which I am certain are those who contributed to this study. I enjoyed research privileges and the help of the staff of The Academy of Motion Pictures, The American Film Institute, The University of Southern California, The University of California at Los Angeles Film Archive and Theatre Collection, The Museum of Modern Art, The New York Public Library Theatre Collection, The Library of Congress Motion Picture Section, and The Lilly Library. I received a very useful Grant in Aid of Research from Indiana University while working on this study, and faculty development funding from Emerson College allowed me to continue work on the manuscript and ready it for publication.

In his autobiography, *A Child of the Century*, Hecht commented that "I can see now that any time I loved anything, friends bloomed magically around the thing loved."[3] I have been fortunate to have such friends whose encouragement and aid went far beyond the point where they would have been happy never to hear the name of Ben Hecht again; my parents for their love and support; Fran Snygg for her patience and help during the research and writing of the manuscript; Harry Selden for his insight into Ben; Jeffrey Alberts for his criticism of the manuscript; Lee Hotz, whose identification with Hecht the journalist has been an exciting stimulus; Ginger Davis and Robert Toombs, my typists at different stages; my advisors, Dr. Oscar G. Brockett and Dr. Harry M. Geduld for their indulgence and guidance; Alan Lebowitz; James Gelarden; my wife Barbara for her care and criticism of both the manuscript and me; and all the others who shared their homes, their time, or were otherwise forced to listen to yet another Hecht anecdote. Thank you all.

1

A Child of the Century

Ben Hecht's fifty-year career embraced a number of different professions. He was by turns a newsman in Chicago between 1910 and 1924 on *The Journal* and the *Daily News*; a novelist well known for *Erik Dorn* (1921) and prosecuted for *Fantazius Mallare* (1922); a success as both playwright and screenwriter during the Depression; a sufficiently visible propagandist for the Israeli guerilla organization, the Irgun Zwei Leumi, to be singled out by the British Empire as a national enemy in 1948; and finally, a memoirist of imagination and skill.

These were not a succession of activities for the protean Hecht: he worked at many of them simultaneously. He thought of himself as a writer and storyteller, and the medium in which he worked mattered less than the tale itself. Because he thought of himself as a writer working on a deadline, he was able to work without pretention and with great craft, although never with great modesty, in whatever form demanded his skills.

Hecht was quite comfortable with the twentieth century's increased life tempo—especially in travel and communication. His talents were both facile and diverse enough to always be appropriate to the immediate need. He boasted of his ability to turn a rough translation of Apuleius' *The Golden Ass* into rhymed verse as it was read to him, dictate a best selling novel in less than forty-eight hours on a bet, and, having never read the book but with the film already in production, write the first nine reels of *Gone With the Wind* (1939) in a week long nonstop session. His curiosity coupled with his diverse abilities as a writer put him in demand in any new medium. In this way, as in many others, he was "a child of the century," the title he gave his autobiography.

Hecht seemed to excel in almost every field. When Henry Justin Smith, one of Hecht's editors, disguises in his memoirs the men who worked around and under him at the Chicago *Daily News*, the Hecht persona is characteristically called The Star. With his publication of the Chicago *Literary Times*, his novels, his Dadaist antics, and his prosecution for obscenity in

Federal Court, Hecht was the leading light of the Chicago Renaissance, and when he left Chicago for New York in 1924, the rival Hearst newspaper, the *Herald-Examiner*, printed a front page article by drama critic Ashton Stevens mourning his departure and calling for the flags to be flown at half mast. Hecht's play *The Front Page* (written with another Chicago newsman, Charles MacArthur, in 1928) is ranked among the most durable American comedies, is constantly revived, and has been filmed three times. He was "The" Hollywood screeenwriter, according to Richard Corliss in his book on the subject, and by his own count Hecht wrote upwards of seventy or eighty films. With his pageants, such as *A Flag is Born* (1946), and his other publicity efforts he raised millions for the Irgun and helped them in their campaign for public support in this country for a Jewish state.

Today, however, Hecht's reputation is in eclipse. He has what Doug Fetherling terms in his Canadian study of Hecht only the history of a reputation.[1] His Chicago days are footnotes in American literary history. His novels are largely unavailable. His Irgun work, much like the Irgun itself, has been obscured by the official Haganah version of the struggle for Israeli independence. His movie work, on those films where he actually received screen credit, is usually discussed in terms of the *oeuvre* of the directors of the films. Reading the recent books on Howard Hawks, first a French and now a favorite American auteur, one is hard pressed to find more than a passing mention that Hecht had a hand in more than a half dozen of Hawk's films, including some of his best: *The Scarface* (1933), *The Twentieth Century* (1934), *Viva Villa* (1934), *Barbary Coast* (1935), *His Girl Friday* (1940), *The Thing (From Another Planet)* (1951), and *Monkey Business* (1952).

To a degree, the disappearance of Hecht, except for the numerous garbled anecdotes told about him and his friends, is understandable. Newsmen expect to write on water and be remembered only in their cohorts' reminiscences. The mainstream Labor Party, successor to the Haganah, was in control in Israel, and besides, guerillas are never very popular after the revolution has been won. Two dissertations[2] have been written on Hecht's novels, but both authors dismiss his fiction as a minor example of important trends, although they are not in complete agreement regarding which trends.

Hecht believed that the eclipse of his literary reputation was due to working in the film industry.

> It is difficult to praise a novelist or a thinker who keeps popping up as the author of innumerable movie melodramas. It is like writing about the virtues of a preacher who keeps carelessly getting himself arrested in bordellos.[3]

Although self-serving, there is a degree of truth to Hecht's judgment. Literary critics are more comfortable when their icons either disdain work in the films or fail at it. While it may be sad or even tragic that Fitzgerald was a failed movie writer it does no harm to his literary reputation, and although recent research has shown that Faulkner actually did passable journeyman work in Hollywood, his lack of interest in the medium and his desire to get back to Mississippi as soon as he could is considered a display of his integrity as an artist and a positive trait when his achievement as a writer is measured.

Hecht wrote films for almost forty years. While he heaped abuse on the heads of the employers who rewarded him, he enjoyed himself enormously. He was well paid, his work was in demand, and he was critically acclaimed (at least as far as he expected one's work in a lowbrow popular form could be). His very success seems to have worked to the detriment of his reputation. Perhaps most damaging, he was not romantically self-destructive. He survived intact while many of his contemporaries followed one of the two roads that, according to Fred Guiles in his book on Hollywood screenwriters, *Hanging On in Paradise*, was inevitably their route: "the one that leads to cirrhosis and an early grave or the way to the cross."[4]

To some extent, Hecht's work is obscured by his personal reputation and history. He was always at the center of the bright and witty people of his generation, whether it was the group in Chicago around the *Literary Review* or at Schlogl's Restaurant, in New York at the Algonquin table, or in the Hollywood writer's colony. In the fine tradition of newsmen everywhere, Hecht projected an image of himself as playing most of the time and writing only when he needed to and then very quickly. His two-day film script jobs, his ability to juggle three or four writing projects at once, his love of collaborating with his friends, and his own constant railing at the idiocies of the film industry all work against the traditional respect for hard work, diligence, and care which it is customary to attribute to an important and serious author.

It would be convenient if there was a positive correspondence between the seriousness and time that Hecht put into a project and the stature and worth of the result. His novels, on which he lavished much effort and care, would thus be more worthwhile than his newspaper work. His serious plays would be more important than his comedies. His carefully crafted film scripts for "class" adaptations, such as *A Farewell to Arms* (1957) or *Wuthering Heights* (1939), would be more effective than his offhand comedies and gangster films, such as *Nothing Sacred* (1937) or *The Scarface* (1933).

It would also be more convenient if Hecht's best work was displayed in films over which he had most control, either by writing the script in solitude or by functioning as a director, original author, or even producer. Our vision of the individual artist forging his work alone would thus be satisfied.

Unfortunately, where there is a correlation between these values, it is often a reverse one. Although there is much in Hecht that is slapdash and careless, and much that may have been spoiled by too many meddling hands, Hecht's best works are those that have least what he called "the glorious smell of Art."[5]

Many of the columns and short works of fiction hold up better than the novels. *The Front Page* and *The Twentieth Century* (1933) remain his lasting contribution to the theatre. His screwball comedies, newspaper, gangster, mystery and adventure films are still fresh and alive while the studio showpieces have dated quickly. His own films usually suffer from an overindulgence in language but an underuse of other important dramatic means. He appears to have worked better in collaboration with another friendly writer or director than when unrestrained. Hecht the newsman was often more effective than Hecht the artist.

The twists and turns of Hecht's life also seemed filled with contradiction. The man who for many years defined art as that which was not liked by the middle class became the highest paid screenwriter of his day, churning out scripts for an enormous popular audience. The man who continually declared any political movement or government corrupt, spent eight years as a propagandist and fund raiser. The man who seemed to forget he was a Jew and wrote a novel widely considered anti-Semitic, *A Jew in Love* (1931), became the Jews' most vocal defender before and during the Nazi holocaust when many other Jews were silent lest they offend and turn the war into a fight to save the Jews instead of merely one to save Britain or France. The sneering cynic who denigrated the public's taste for melodrama and low comedy spent forty years supplying it with those genres.

In writing about his friend Herman Mankiewicz, Hecht commented that he was not surprised that Mankiewicz never wrote a book of his own. "I knew that no one as witty and spontaneous as Herman would ever put himself on paper. A man whose genius is on tap like free lager beer seldom makes literature out of it."[6] There is a similar danger when dealing with Hecht. So much wit, so many anecdotes, so many different lives are there in the single man that his spirit threatens to overwhelm any study of his work, reducing it to a discursive meander through a charming man's life. But, Hecht's film writing was shaped by his training as a journalist, and a knowledge of his early experience and a sense of his personal style are essential to an understanding of his attitudes as they become manifest in the form and content of his subsequent writing.

Hecht's working career began in Chicago when at the age of sixteen he was employed by the *Chicago Journal*. In Chicago a whole new urban world, a pressurized job, and the society of the newsroom affected the impressionable Hecht deeply. Of the *Journal* Hecht said, "Many habits were formed by those days, and points of view which I have never outgrown or improved upon came to rest in my head."[7] These attitudes and habits were to be the marks of both Hecht's personality and work for years to come. Long before he became a professional memoirist he attempted to recreate his newsroom experiences either by surrounding himself with the working society of compatible men or through the creation of newsmen and news stories in his plays, stories, and films.

Until his arrival in Chicago, Hecht had enjoyed a rather pastoral and wholesome, although not uneventful, childhood. The precocious Benny had given a violin recital at the age of twelve in Chicago's Orchestra Hall, and at fourteen had spent part of a summer with Harry Costello's one-ring tent show as an acrobat. (Hecht always loved the circus and attempted to use his circus experience as source material a number of times [*Jumbo*, 1935; *Once in a Blue Moon*, 1935; *Circus World*, 1964], but the results lacked the cutting perspective he gained towards his later experiences and they degenerate into nostalgic sentimentality.)

Although he was born in the Jewish ghetto on New York's Lower East Side (February 28, 1894) and lived briefly in Chicago, Hecht was raised in Racine, Wisconsin, where his father, Joseph Hecht, was a tailor, designer of women's fashions, and unsuccessful entrepeneur. An only child, Ben was doted on by his father, mother (Sarah Swernofsky Hecht), and a multitude of uncles and aunts. Hecht said that their unjudging love for him shaped his later attitudes towards people. "I might never have known how to love anybody. I would have judged people by their thoughts, their expressions of opinion on foreign treaties and presidential candidates. And, who knows, I might have gone mad."[8] Cynicism and sentimentality are always the balancing forces in Hecht's writing. The crusty invective with which he attacked the institutions he knew most intimately usually hid a fondness for his targets that ultimately softened the attack. The compassion and faith in the possibility of love that balanced the pessimism in much of his work may have stemmed from the security and unquestioning love that Hecht received from his family throughout his life. When he undertook to defend Jews in Europe he said that he always envisioned them as having the faces of his family. It was his uncles and aunts who were under attack and needed defending and not an abstract religious group.

His parents appear to have been more ethnically Jewish than religious, although for an immigrant family the two strains were more closely connected than in modern bagel-and-lox American Judaism. He did not grow up in an overwhelmingly Jewish environment, however, but in midwestern, American, Racine, where he was a cheerleader and football player. Although not well read themselves, his parents fostered the love of literature in their son who lived an active fantasy life and while still in school began converting his ideas into stories and plays.

According to his own reminiscences, Hecht came to Chicago in 1910 after having narrowly escaped an education at the University of Wisconsin. He attended school for three days, decided it had nothing to teach him, and headed for the city. While entering a vaudeville theatre he was spotted by one of his distant uncles. His Uncle Moyses, a liquor salesman, took him to John C. Eastman, one of his customers and publisher of the *Chicago Journal,* who hired him, first as the writer of some obscene verse for a stag party he was attending that evening, then as an errand boy, and finally as a picture-stealer.

Chicago and his new profession had a great impact on the sixteen-year-old Hecht. Lacking an advanced formal education he became the protege of the more experienced, or at least the more outspoken, men around him. He aped their ways and attitudes long before he developed ideas of his own. He adopted their protective poses before he had experienced the need to protect himself, thus doubly saving himself from disappointment. The excitement of the newspaper profession, which he came to believe the highest possible calling, and the adrenal energy of being inside yet superior to every event intoxicated him. "I was young and indifferent to the inhumanities which I brought bird dog fashion to my city editor.... In those days I belonged to life as uncritically as a rain barrel belongs to the rain."[9]

Hecht was a bright compulsive worker and he advanced quickly. He first gained a reputation as a picture-stealer. Newspapers were not yet capable of easily acquiring spot photographs and therefore relied on finding portraits or drawings of the suicide or accident victim. These had to be coerced from the bereaved families and often sneaked past the police. This was Hecht's work, and his zeal touched on grand larceny. He gradually was allowed to do some reporting, partially in recognition of his good work, partially, Hecht said, to protect him from jail. His reputation for requisitioning such objects as large portraits in expensive frames prompted Walter Howie, editor of the rival Hearst paper and the model for Walter Burns in *The Front Page,* to offer Hecht a job. The idealistic Hecht refused, sending back word that he was "incapable of such treachery as he [Howie] proposed."[10]

Hecht gradually became a fulltime reporter but his naive zeal again got him into difficulty. When he could not find stories, he invented them using his relatives for models and names. Soon he was famous for his fortunate scoops, and no amount of complaint from the streetcar authority could convince Martin Hutchens, Hecht's managing editor, that the streetcar accident that Hecht had reported had never occurred. Hecht's career as a fantasist newsman ended abruptly when his story about a runaway Rumanian princess featured the picture of one of the busiest prostitutes in Chicago. A chastened Hecht confined himself after that incident to writing about actual events, or at least he kept names and professions straight.

At the *Journal* Hecht came under the tutelage of Sherman Duffy, the sports editor. Well educated and a bachelor, Duffy exposed Hecht to the various lives of Chicago from the opera and theatre to the bars and whorehouses. Hecht imitated Duffy's philosophy and his ability to move in any social circle. "Drunk or sober," said Hecht, "I trailed my Socrates through all his groves."¹¹ Through Duffy, Hecht was able to associate with his fellow newsmen at lunches or in drinking bouts. Hecht admired them all and took them as models. He copied the newsman's superior, cynical world view and tried to overcome his own novice status by adopting their pose as outsiders. "I contributed happily to the denunciations.... I, the least embittered young man on earth, sat and took gleeful part in the destruction of the world."¹² Hecht loved the idea that social pretense, human greed, and conventional behavior were beneath their concern. The worst that society had to offer was the prized raw material for a story. He discovered, too, that the most experienced reporter was an innocent when deprived of his protective coloring.

> They sat, grown and abuzz, outside an adult civilization intent on breaking windows. There was, I am sure, neither worldliness nor cunning enough among the lot of us to run a candy store. But we had a vantage point.... Around this table in King's restaurant we who knew nothing spoke out of a knowledge so overwhelming that I for one, never recovered from it. Morality was a farce full of murders, rapes and love nests. Swindlers ran the world and the Devil sat everywhere. These discoveries filled me with great joy. The waltzes played.... There were no thoughts yet in my head. But I was gay with bright pangs and drunk with a superiority that could flaunt no more than a soiled collar and an outlaw's guffaw.¹³

Hecht's innocence, his ability to live in a brothel without realizing it or to believe any story told him by a woman of easy virtue, gradually eroded, but his love for the life of men who formed their own group outside the mainstream never deserted him. Newsmen enjoyed a fierce independence, the security of the protection of their fellows, and the succor of their parent editors. They were allowed by their job, thought Hecht, to be the best of men. "No other profession, even that of arms, produces as fine a version of the selfless hero as journalism does."¹⁴

Hecht exulted in the pride and loyalty that was part of his profession. Since every other endeavor was corrupt, "A good newspaperman ... was to be known by the fact that he was ashamed of being anything else."¹⁵ Tied to his job and mercilessly ridden by his editor, Hecht's ideal newsman somehow managed to maintain a sense of his independence. He allowed himself to be harnessed only because he loved his work. "For the newspaperman, the most harried of employees, more bedeviled by duties than a country doctor, more blindly subservient to his editor than a Marine private to his captain, considered himself, somewhat loonily, to have no boss, to be without superiors and a creature always on his own."¹⁶

It was only a strong sense of individuality that allowed the newsman to remain superior in his own estimation to the outerworld and the demands of his job. His reporter status made him a celebrity and gave him power in a society that otherwise would ignore him. As Duffy pointed out, "Socially, a journalist fits somewhere between a whore and a bartender but spiritually he stands beside Galileo. He knows the world is round."[17] (In *Gaily, Gaily* Hecht attributes this statement to his fellow reporter Wallace Smith.)

"What I have become," Hecht said, "that youth who sat breathlessly in the *Journal* local room was what I was meant to be."[18] The statement is both nostalgic and insightful. The literary magazines in Chicago, the salons of New York, the movie studios, even to some degree the Irgun committees provided the common values and comaraderie Hecht found invigorating. Each group cast a baleful eye on the rest of the system and thought themselves the only ones who knew the world was round. At times they tried to spread the word. At other times they kept the secret as their source of strength.

The hint of perennial adolescence that attaches itself to each of these groups, no matter how serious their work, was part of their appeal for Hecht. The *Journal* was an adolescent experience for him; it was his college fraternity and he did not readily give it up. In these groups an individual could maintain a serious antiestablishment stance more easily than in isolation, and any group that disdains conventional wisdom will appear irresponsible and, therefore, adolescent.

Hecht's love for the club of workers (and usually of men) is significant because it became a favorite working habitat. As an attitude it informed much of his work. The male group of fellow workers, outsiders drawn together by common love and vocation, became a basic motif that had its roots in his newspaper career.

If Hecht blindly adopted the cynicism and unconcern towards murder and corruption, the badge of entry into the fraternity of newsmen, it was not long before he became aware that the sordidness he reported touched on his own life as a human being. It was not the hangings that affected Hecht as much as the last minute attempts by the doomed to gain another minute in asserting their innocence by throwing guilt onto the lovers, brothers and friends whom they had staunchly protected. "You'll find out that's the easiest thing people do," Duffy told him, "change into swine."[19] Hecht even found some of that swinishness in himself:

> Crime, murder, suicide, swindle, and perversion were my daily pickings. But they were outside my world, a storm that blew and rattled wildly beyond its snug windows. Now the storm was inside the windows, the wrong was around me. I had discovered a new fact; that injustice existed, and that everybody I knew was somehow a part of it.[20]

Hecht respected the criminal, the man committed to his actions, his loyalties, and his code of honor, but contempt grew in him for the graft that built a gallows higher and larger than necessary, for the hundreds of spellbound spectators allowed to be entertained through political favors, and for the sheriff's lovely seventeen-year-old daughter sitting in romantic moonlight softening up the rope for the hanging because her father would not "let me see the hanging, so I said, anyway, I ought to have some fun out of it. I mean, excitement."[21] When Hecht's editor wired him to "Keep story of hanging brief. Omit all gruesome details. The world has just gone to war." Hecht, who had little interest beyond "Chicago's thirty-two feet of intestines"[22] that made up his world, could only wire back "Will try to make hanging as cheerful and optimistic as possible."[23]

By this time, August 14, 1914, Hecht had moved out of his incubator of the *Journal* to the newsroom of the *Chicago Daily News* and under the guidance of Henry Justin Smith. If newspapers in the period of Hecht's training were more a form of entertainment than they were examples of the grey objectivity which we associate with newspapers today, the *Daily News* was one of the most diverting. Henry Justin Smith assembled in his newsroom a group of incipient authors and poets whose style he nurtured and developed. He had little interest, said Hecht, in circulation or editorial policy. "He saw the paper as a daily novel written by a score of Balzacs."[24] He hired writers such as Carl Sandburg and protected their copy from being edited by less sympathetic members of the editorial staff. Hecht describes their work as "remarkably fancy stories. No reader could find out who was murdered or how or why until he had waded through several moody paragraphs of high class prose."[25]

In his own reminiscences, *Deadlines*, Smith describes a thinly disguised version of Hecht, whom he calls The Star. He is given this name because "his nature is a lens from which drab colors of this earth are reflected in hues that fascinate one, confound one, and are yet real. He never sees things as anyone else sees them; we gave up long ago trying to make him do so."[26] Smith describes The Star as a happy, romantic, loyal, and honorable individual who would commit murder before admitting to any of these qualities. "He is death on pretenders, hypocrites, and optimists."[27] He scoffs at success and asserts that nobody is content, particularly himself. "This young man strolls through the world with a queerly bitter greeting for it, yet with an engaging smile. He asserts he hates the world, hates the human race, spurns its contrivances for being peaceable and joyous, and has no hope for it.... [But] See him enter a room; how his face lights up! Maybe he hates humanity, but he is himself human."[28]

Hecht was The Star for another reason. His beat was the lower reaches of the city, the police precincts and courts. He covered the trials and the hangings. In that period, the last flowering of the newspaper before radio made the hot extra edition and the scoop less sensational, Hecht was not only a top reporter but a colorful writer as well. He had attained a certain fame but only among his fellow craftsmen and in bohemian circles.

Fellow reporter Harry Hansen in his essay on Hecht written in 1923, remembers him best as a reporter:

> For there was a nonchalance, a recklessness, a boisterousness, and enthusiasm about his reporting that sat much better upon him than his later and more serious mood. He was always intensely interested in human foibles and life's trivialities, and seen through his eyes they became magnified and important. His ability to tell a story, to write quickly, to grasp the contents of a situation intuitively, to conjure up images in great profusion without apparent effort, made a newspaper career inevitable for him. He could make a situation alive, interesting and human, because he invariably drew on his imagination. A few words uttered by some one, a fragment of thought begun, but not completed, were enough to start trains of thought in his mind and to let loose the resources of his creative power. He therefore became a romantic reporter, one to whom the meticulous accuracy of a stenographic report was abominable and uninspired, and who loved to let the imagination play over the dull, prosaic routine of a commonplace event. He had the faculty for making a drab world seeem gorgeous and full of color; he had the dissector's skill for laying bare the sores of humankind in all their vileness.
>
> There are innumerable anecdotes extant of his proficiency, of his ability to "deliver." His "angle" on a story was always different from that of the conventional reporter.[29]

David Karsner, who was not a local reporter, came to Chicago to cover a trial and worked for two weeks at the press table with Hecht. He describes Hecht as an iconoclast who was unwilling to be content in mirroring the events with a conventional analysis as did most reporters. Hecht told Karsner that he was not interested in the import of the trial or in changing the government. He did not believe in crusaders, and expressed a contempt for humanity "a loathing for the protecting slave philosophies of the people, government, etc.; a determination not to become a part of the mind which the swine worship in their sty."[30] But Karsner, even with his scant acquaintance of Hecht, observed that "One finds Hecht working many hours past the union scale to become a determined iconoclast."[31] Hecht was willing to live within conventional morality but protested that "My manners don't reach into my mind."[32] The image of a man disdaining all structures but living within them, who expresses contempt for man yet is passionately involved with men is a picture of Hecht that recurs in the writings of his contemporaries.

Karsner worked with Hecht in the summer of 1918. Later that year Hecht became a foreign correspondent posted in Berlin working for a syndicate headed by his own paper.

In *Foreign Correspondent* (1940), an Alfred Hitchcock film on which Hecht is reputed to have worked, a crime reporter is taken off his beat and sent to Europe. His editor complains that foreign correspondents write like diplomats, and he wants his reporter to treat the European situation as if it were a crime story and really find out what was going on. Whether or not it was the intention of his editor, this was the attitude that Hecht, whose whole world up to that point had been circumscribed by the city limits of Chicago, took with him to Germany. He arrived in Berlin via London on December 30, 1918 and remained there more than a year. In *Child of the Century*, written after the Second World War, Hecht said this about the Germany he found and his attitude toward it:

> All the inhumanity I note today as history, I saw in Germany in 1918-20, except that I saw it then with a youthful delight for the preposterous. Political zanies, quibblers and adventurers—mindless and paranoid performed around me in that time in Germany as if I had blundered into a side-street Grand Guignol Playhouse. I had no notion that its humorless and macabre atmosphere was to become the air of the world. I considered the antics I witnessed purely German phenomena. And I reported them with the enthusiasm I had brought in Chicago to four-eleven fires, basement stabbings, love-nest suicides and all the other hi-de-do doings outside the norm of living.[33]

Hecht was soon out covering the revolutionary upheaval that gripped Germany after the abdication of the Kaiser. Hecht's first story was about the Spartacist Liebknecht's attempt to sleep in the Kaiser's bed in the palace. Liebknecht was scared away by a falling table and Hecht, in traditional Chicago style, opened his story with the lead "Kaiser Wilhelm returned to Berlin last night—"[34]

Always open to influence, Hecht became attached to Count Russworn von Gleichen who led Hecht to the crime story of his career. The German high command was using the Western fear of a Bolshevik government in Germany or of a Russian invasion to stave off the Allies at the bargaining table.

> My knowledge was skimpy, my political insights almost nonexistent and my sources of information limited at the time to drug addicts, nymphomaniacs and a waiter. But the Lie about Russia was as obvious as a sheiss house in a fog.[35]

His syndicate, Charles Dennis in Chicago, and Edgar Price Bell in London wanted stories about the Russian threat. Instead Hecht began to cable out stories about the farce going on in Germany, becoming something of a nascent propagandist. Like his later efforts at swaying public opinion, Hecht had no real program of his own. His propaganda was more preventive in the tradition of the crime beat, blowing the whistle on a vast swindle. It was "my first emergence as a political thinker, and I felt somewhat alone."[36]

Some of his more spectacular stories, such as the one about the massacre of two thousand Spartacists at Moabit Prison which Hecht witnessed from a tree beyond the walls of the prison, were printed, but a more common response to his dispatches was this cable from Dennis, "Your surmises both wild and dangerous to President Wilson's work for just peace. Confine yourself solid political facts." Hecht cabled back, "All my information solid not surmise,"[37] but another correspondent, Gordon Stiles, was sent to replace him. Before this occurred, however, Stiles barricaded himself in his room and started shooting at the Germans and had to be evacuated. Despite warnings to Hecht about the "cynical" nature of his dispatches, Henry Smith stood by him and said he was "Glad you're having good time."[38]

The whole process was disillusioning to Hecht. His own paper would not believe his reports. He watched a country fabricate a revolution and witnessed mass execution and betrayals. Even worse, he perceived an instinctive subservience in the German people which he later considered part of the cause of the massacres of World War II. In 1920, Hecht turned down Smith's offer to stay in Europe as a roving correspondent and asked to return to Chicago. "I was a youth of twenty-four when I entered Germany. When I emerged from it my young cynicism had lost much of its grin."[39]

If there was no political revolution in Germany, Hecht did find an artistic one. From the beginning of his stay in Berlin Hecht fell in with surgeon and poet Karl von Doehman and with George Grosz. Grosz, a caricaturist and painter, was at the center of the Dadaist movement in Berlin. The Dadaist principles as Grosz stated them were in tune with Hecht's social and artistic attitudes. "I am opposed to all politics and, naturally, politicians, also. You may say I am opposed also to art and any other so-called manifestation of beauty, including of course, music, toe dancing, and poetry."[40]

Dadaism was similar to other movements of the period in its opposition to any kind of convention, myth, formula, or concept of beauty. It was also an attack on German patriotism, militarism, idealism, and conformity. "What ever is more important than one human being we are prepared to revolt against,"[41] said Grosz. Unlike other movements, it had no program to replace the one it attacked. "Our final battle cry will be 'down with the Dadaists.' Also 'down with Dadaism.' At that time, I assure you, I will be proud to fight as a traitor which is the secret of progress."[42] Hecht was attracted to this sort of "personally adjustable revolution." Since conformity was absurd and aesthetically devastating the only logical response was Dadaism's combination of comic stance and bitter cynicism. Its attacks through ridicule and caricature, seen most clearly in Grosz's cartoons, complemented Hecht's own flip cynicism. Its antipolitical stance also appealed to the Hecht who when asked upon entering Germany what his politics were in the United States, replied: "I haven't any. I'm a reporter."[43]

He attended many of the Dadaist events, including the "First German Post-War Renaissance of the Arts. Admission, 20 Gold Marks. Formal Dress Required."[44] Here the best of Berlin's bourgeois and military society were confronted with a poetry competition where eleven poets and a bellboy read poems simultaneously, a race beteween a girl at a sewing machine and a girl at a typewriter, and a "Recital for the Eye of Modern Music" consisting of three girls in tights placing on an easel a succession of canvasses painted with single musical notes. The evening ended in a counter-revolution by the audience who fired pistols at the stage and demanded the arrest of the perpetrators of such a swindle and affront to German culture, but the Dadaists, heeding their own slogan for the evening, "Take your foot out of the butter before it is too late," had already disappeared. Hecht admired this Dadaist ability to elicit an outraged response, something difficult to do in the general mayhem of Chicago, as much as he did their artistic principles. Hecht enjoyed a good fight and often needed one to motivate his most energetic work.

The Dadaists were able to elicit violent reactions from their German audiences, Chicago was in the midst of a quieter, but equally important, cultural revolution. From as early as 1890 until the middle of the 1920s Chicago was involved in what Malcolm Cowley called "The Revolt Against Gentility"[45] or the Genteel Tradition which dominated American letters in the latter portion of the nineteenth century. This tradition insisted that America was a pastoral and simple society whose purity had been maintained even while it was transformed into an industrial society. More prudish than Victorianism in England, it idealized the Civil War rather than examined its brutality, which was the subject of the work of a few authors such as Stephen Crane and Ambrose Bierce. It ignored the realities and vulgarities of a metropolitan industrial society as well. Rural, Eastern, English-Scottish, Protestant, and firmly middle class, it defended the rich against the political rise of the lower middle class and could depend on a broad base of popular support. According to Cowley, the most fruitful years of revolt were those after 1910 "when almost every new writer was a recruit to the army against gentility, and when older writers like Dreiser and Robinson were being rescued from neglect and praised as leaders.... For a time every honestly written book was a foray against the conservative and some were resounding victories."[46]

The revolt was largely urban, midwestern, and politically left wing. It attacked prudery, and favored individuality in any form. Its reaction to the repression of the older tradition was a kind of "carnal mysticism," a throwing off of repression by enjoying the pleasures of life, particularly the flesh. It was a mixture of free love, simplistic Freudianism, sexual equality, and primitivism not to be achieved consciously but by giving over to the subconscious, the imagination, and the body. At its heart it was antimiddle class but as a reaction against traditions and because of its support of the individual rather than any organized movement, it was basically passive and reactive rather than constructive. In this way it had many similarities to Dadaism without the much more repressive European environment.

The revolt was centered in the Bohemian areas of Chicago. From his early days in Chicago, Hecht was involved in the city's artistic movements. He places the period of the city's greatest creativity between 1913 and 1922, but perhaps this is only because it was the period of his greatest involvement with the movement: "It contained days of brightness and an American literary renaissance—a small one, but our own. Burning its quick and vivid years—there were hardly nine (1913-1922)—Chicago found itself, mysteriously, a bride of the arts. Not gangster guns but literary credos barked."[47] Hecht frequented literary meeting places such as Floyd Dell's on 57th Street and became friends with the poet Maxwell Bodenheim and the sculptor Stanislau Szulaski. He was involved in Elizabeth Gingham's Players' Workshop and became a contributor to and, on occasion, editor of Margaret Anderson's *Little Review*, which was published in Chicago between 1914 and 1916. Experimentation and liberation were the cornerstones of these activities. *The Little Review*, published in the Fine Arts Building, which also housed Maurice Browne's Little Theatre, was, along with Mencken's *The Smart Set*, the first to publish sections of Joyce's *Ulysses* in this country. Despite the fact that it paid no fees, the magazine contained early work by such American authors as Eliot, Masters, Lowell, and William Carlos Williams, by Europeans such as Cocteau and Gide, and it championed the local work of writers such as Sherwood Anderson, Sandburg, Bodenheim, and Hecht. The *Little Review* never had a large following despite its reputation, but this was something of a vindication for Hecht and his fellows who held

> ...the approval of either the crowd or critics a mark of final failure.... Art was not a thing to sell or to offer for applause. It was the individual's lonely response to the mysteries of man and nature. It was to be enjoyed chiefly by the artist making it, and by a handful of other artists.[48]

From these lofty sentiments it should not be concluded that the work of the group was without humor. As with the Dadaists, ridicule was a weapon used to attack any bastion of convention. At one point Hecht and fellow literary rebel Alexander Kaun were given an issue of the magazine to edit. According to Hecht:

> We opened all the mail and whenever we spotted a manuscript that seemed to be just the ordinary conventional writing we sent it back with a caustic note. There was a whole box of poems from Vachel Lindsay and we fired it back with the memo, "Rotten." Then Dreiser sent a play which he explained had been knocking about in his desk. We wrote back that if that was the best he could do he might let it knock around another ten years. Finally a story from Galsworthy. We wrote something about "cheap stuff" across the face of it and mailed it back.[49]

In addition to recognizing the pace and variety of Hecht's activities, further insight into his character and philosophy is gained by knowledge of two of Hecht's heroes and why he admired them. The two men were Theodore

Roosevelt and H. L. Mencken. Hecht concedes they were an unlikely couple, but says:

> [I] hailed a quality they both had—although, if I remember rightly, they despised each other. This was the quality of exuberance, of bouncing up and down from sunrise to sunset like a pair of lads on a trampoline. One of them was a physical exuberant; the other an intellectual one.[50]

Hecht particularly admired Roosevelt's ability to embrace life and enjoy himself. In Mencken he valued the iconoclast. In his own mind he pictured Mencken as an isolated and lonely figure. Mencken liked Hecht, always printed his stories and gave him encouragement. Later in his life Hecht was to perceive many of his friends as this kind of solitary dreamer, and he would contend that the dream and the attempt at achievement were as important as success itself. He placed Herman Mankiewicz, John Barrymore, and Max Bodenheim in this group. This point of view is as much a comment on himself as on those he admired. He was himself a man of tremendous vitality, and he was always attracted by exuberance, charm, and a full enjoyment of life in men far more than he cared about their political, artistic, or social philosophies. He embraced failings in those he loved although his generosity did not always make him comfortable since it seemed to betray the true cynic he believed himself to be.

In the same way that Mencken and Roosevelt were united in Hecht's mind by a common spirit, his own newspaper work and his artistic endeavors were never as separate from one another as this chronological biographic account might suggest. The newspapers of the period contributed to the prose side of the liberation, both because so many writers made their living working on papers and because newsmen were also expected to be literary stylists. It was a period when literary writing and news reporting were not yet distinct disciplines. Nowhere was this more true than at the *Daily News*. Bernard Duffy in his book *The Chicago Renaissance in American Letters* describes the *Daily News* under Henry Smith as an "almost unique combination of city room and salon."[51] The members of Smith's staff thought themselves to be the heart of the renaissance, and in fact they "contributed to it more variously and as colorfully as any other single group."[52] It was the *News* staff that supported the Saturday lunches at Schlogl's Restaurant which Duffy calls a "show window" of the movement. Here:

> Ben Hecht dazzled the company with what almost succeeded in being corruscating tirades against modern civilization and letters. Sherwood Anderson enlarged his reputation as a master story-teller. Carl Sandburg, with a square cap pulled over his eyes and his coat hung over his shoulders, maintained a dogged pursuit of populistic and proletarian values. And Maxwell Bodenheim spoke the same artificially elaborate language that characterized his verse.[53]

Schlogl's was not an inexpensive restaurant or a bohemian hangout. It was known for its German cuisine and exotic dishes such as "owls to order." It was a treat the reporters could only afford once a week, but unlike the Algonquin lunches, which were essentially publicity affairs, the Schlogl meetings were special events for the enjoyment of the participants.

Nor did this group despise money or the spending of it. Hecht's definition of an "artist" may differ slightly from the conventional. He says his friends were not artists as the public pictured such men.

> In addition to being impoverished zanies who were often found frozen to death in their garrets, "artists" were also people who were enormously overpaid for playing the fiddle, piano, or cornet, for making faces in front of movie cameras, for cracking jokes on coast-to-coast programs, and so forth.[54]

Hecht contends that his artist friends would be touchy about being described in such a manner.

> They worked like cart horses to become artists but insisted on being regarded as solid citizens. Artists are often like that; in fact, I have known no other. However violent their protests against society, they are always eager to shine as well-mannered, pleasingly clothed members of the community. Nonconformity is as embarrassing to the "true artist" (meaning one of genuine talent and such productivity) as nudity. His mind may be fearless of attracting attention, but his person shies from it as from a head cold.[55]

This definition, written late in life, must be taken with a bit of skepticism since it comes from a man who, although he always wanted to be loved and accepted, reveled in public noncomformity and bickering. It is true, however, that Hecht never thought of poverty as essential to creativity. He merely wanted the freedom to choose his own styles. In his Chicago period, his clothing habits would vacillate from lowlife to dandy depending on his mood. He always had an ambivalent attitude towards wealth. Early in his career he did not mind earning little money—as long as he could live well. Later he consistently needed vast sums of money but spent them almost before he reached the bank. He did not mind earning it, but he did not want to have to protect it, and he even gave a great deal of it away. Whenever he found himself in a financial hole, some new scheme would turn up and he would become solvent again. Consequently, although he knew both poverty and wealth and the awareness of economic problems was always in him, it was rarely an obsessive concern. In later years he trapped himself into a life style which proved financially demanding. He reached a point of maintaining three households: homes in Nyack (New York) and in Oceanside (California) and a flat in New York City. At times it was a struggle to support them. This was particularly true when there was a British embargo on his films which resulted in less work for less money. For the most part, Hecht wrote his way out of financial difficulties. A reporter trained to write to order, Hecht simply turned to his literary craft whenever he needed money. The first time was in 1917. Deeply in debt to the butcher, among others, he sat down and in two hours jotted off a story for H. L. Mencken's *The Smart Set*. He had hoped to receive as much as a thousand dollars for his labors but was disappointed to find a check for only forty-five dollars. Unperturbed, he went back to his study and in the next few months wrote twenty-five stories to earn the money he needed.

Hecht, a compulsive writer, started writing stories after his parents moved to Chicago in 1911. He would write novels and short stories and then burn them. He did so not because the writing was bad but because it had only been done for his own amusement. The joy in writing for himself and to please himself served as both a wellspring of his talent and a protection against the hostile world. What he called his "juvenile distaste for authority"[56] led naturally to his wanting to write because in writing he was subject only to the authority of his own mind.

> When I came to write books and stories intelligent enough to merit publication, my delight in putting words on paper remained unchanged. The desire to please others and become famous was (unfortunately) never strong in me. I continued to write because writing pleased me, because it enabled me to remain "independent" and because it kept always fresh the quality I had most enjoyed in childhood—the talent for diverting myself with my own imagination.[57]

Hecht's departure for Germany took care of one set of money problems. He used the money intended to set up the Berlin office to pay his debts and simply never opened the office. Within six months of his return to Chicago, however, he was twenty thousand dollars in debt again and was forced to leave the paper and go into advertising to pay his way. He engaged in some highly questionable activities, including convincing the local Baptist synod to run a contest offering $5,000 for the best "life of Christ" essay, then writing an essay and winning the contest himself.

The period between his return to Chicago and his departure for New York was among the happiest and most productive in Hecht's life. During this period he published *Erik Dorn*, an expressionistic novel about a newsman's search for a positive outlet for his energies; *1001 Afternoons in Chicago* a selection of sixty-two essays from the over four hundred he wrote between June 1921 and July 1922 for his column of the same name in the *Daily News*; *Gargoyles* an attack on hypocrisy in American life centering on a man's rise to a judgeship; *The Egoist*, a comedy acted on the stage by Leo Dietrichstein; *The Florentine Dagger*, a murder mystery based on the Borgias; *Fantazius Mallare* an erotic psychopathic study that landed him in federal court for obscenity; and *The Chicago Literary Times* (later called *Ben Hecht's Chicago Literary Times*) founded and edited by Hecht with the backing of Pascal Covici, principal publisher of the Chicago Renaissance. He was also busy leaving his first wife, Marie Armstrong Hecht, a fellow reporter on the *Journal* whom he had married in 1915, and falling in love with Rose Caylor, soon to be his second wife. It was in this period that Hecht's fame transcended Chicago and he took on national stature, first with *Erik Dorn*, then with his obscenity trial.

The diversity of his work in this period displays many of the different aspects of Hecht's talents and concerns. *1001 Afternoons* may be what Harry Hansen in his *Midwest Portraits* calls: "the apogee of his reporting experiences." Here he wrote the "conglomerate mob life of a big industrial city."[58] Henry Justin Smith in his preface to the work says that Hecht would have everyone believe that the writing is "hack-work, done for a meal ticket," and says that Hecht would come in, fling each day's manuscript on his desk, and say, "Here's a rotten story."[59] But, he concludes, "They must have had the momentum of a strictly artistic inspiration and gained further momentum from the need of expression, from pride in the subtle use of words, from an ardent interest in the city and its human types."[60] Smith describes here the attitude that years later Hecht would consistently maintain towards his movie work—hack-work done for a large meal ticket—a rotten story produced for a deadline yet marked with a momentum, capturing the energy of his subjects, usually urban, and the pride of playing with words and dialogue. These are the reporter's skills finely honed, that would serve and protect Hecht in Hollywood: to care about his work while he was doing it and deny its importance and forget about it once it was done. David Karsner also believes the book contains some of Hecht's best work, and his description of newspaper writing versus novel writing is particularly apropos to Hecht's film work.

> In my opinion Ben Hecht wrote literature in his newspaper pieces if he ever wrote it anywhere.... Good writing, it seems to me, is the sole criterion, regardless of its form. The notion that the covers of a book makes the man who has written between them a *writer* is the bunk. I know plenty of newspaper men who daily write *literature* in two or three sticks of type, and repeat the performance half a dozen times a day.[61]

The short sketches range from invective, to lean stories, to mood pieces and descriptions. They show not only the cynical Hecht capable of verbal acrobatics but a man in love with his city, even romantic about it. This is Henry Smith's description of the column as written by The Star (Larry):

> The city never knew it was like Larry's pictures of it. The city fancied itself busy, or noisy, or prosperous, or admirable, or monotonous; it never knew it was complex, impulsive, romantic—gorgeously romantic. It thought its buildings were handsome; it did not realize they were beautiful, beautiful with a stunningly futurist design. It thought its people were

"interesting," but it never delved into the millions of variations of type brought here by the People of Fifty Lands. The city laughed at hundreds of "freaks," it vaguely pitied thousands of unfortunates, it flung dimes to innumerable beggars, it dreamed about scores of young lovers, it revered many a millionaire, it shrank from jails full of criminals—but it never realized any of them. Not until Larry was "turned loose."[62]

Erik Dorn (1921) takes the reporter who had often appeared in Hecht's short sketches as a filter for settings or mood and turns him into the central character he was to remain in Hecht's serious novels. The book is semiautobiographical telling the story of a reporter (now an editor) slightly older than Hecht was when he wrote the book (he was twenty-seven). Both Marie Armstrong and Rose Caylor appear as the wife who has put up with him and the young artist who attracts him. Dorn's central adventures are a retelling of Hecht's Berlin experiences. There is also a character called Hazlitt who represents forces of Puritanism at their most repressive. Dorn's problem is an overabundance of brilliance and verbal dexterity without a creative outlet either in his life or in his work although he catches glimpses of happiness in moments of intense emotion. He is dedicated to a kind of self-actualization that has no focus. He finishes in the newsroom where he started but without either woman.

The work again shows Hecht's love of the urban environment, epigrams, and the energetic use of verbal flourish. His portrait of Dorn is intense and largely unattractive in its honesty. The unsympathetic protagonist was to become common in Hecht's work even when the figure was what could be called the Hechtian man—urban, witty, cynical, cold but often with a touch of sentiment or love which is his saving grace. *Erik Dorn* gains maturity from Hecht's ambivalance towards his protagonist.

The portrait of Dorn also reflects Hecht's interest in Kraft-Ebbing and forms of psychology and sexual motivations. His characters are more driven psychological types than representative of philosophic polarities. When Hecht began writing, he protested to Mencken that "I had no program in me, nothing to tout. I just had a skepticism that was born of nothing; it simply existed and wanted to get out. Mencken replied: 'Go ahead anyhow. That will be the new start for a novel.'"[63] The writing is subjective, taking on the point of view and emotions of the focal character. Hansen believes the work was influenced both by Huysman's decadence and love of verbal craft and by Dostoevski's preoccupation with abnormal and subnormal minds. "There is only one plot in the world after all and that is the human mind,"[64] Hecht had said. But Hansen felt these influences were more acquired than innate. Hecht, he said, had too much energy and joy in life to be a true decadent regardless of his artistic stance and had gained his understanding of pathology through observation rather than through self-dissection as Dostoevski had.

Gargoyles (1922) is an extension and compilation of two unpublished earlier works, *Moisse* and *Grimaces*, both written before *Erik Dorn*. Here Hecht eschews subjective emotionalism and florid prose and attempts to write objectively of the realities of commonplace people. The book is based on a vice commission investigation that Hecht covered as a reporter. Hecht was disgusted by the insincerity and the opportunism of the commission's work. His method in the book is to take groups of people and then strip away their facades and reveal the hypocrisy, sexual perversion, and insincerity beneath. Hecht had censorship trouble with his publishers but eventually agreed to edit his copy. The incident prompted him to write an essay on literary repression.

Fantazius Mallare (1922) was more troublesome for Hecht because of his preface, in which he denounced every censoring force that came to mind, than for the work itself. Hansen says that Hecht "himself an admirer of subtlety and cleverness, failed to discern any difference between frankness and vulgarity."[65] It was neither the first nor the last time the charge would be made about a work of Hecht's. The story deals with an artist, Mallare, and his attempt to rise out of slavery to his senses and to distance himself from the physical world. The result, unfortunately, is hallucination and madness. Having similarities to Huysman's *Against Nature*, the work is as close to a Dostoevskian case study as Hecht would ever come.

The book was never widely read, however, because most of the copies were seized by the Post Office and Hecht was charged with sending obscene material through the mail. His lawyer, Clarence Darrow, suggested that Hecht, by now a celebrity, rally some important artists and critics for his defense. There was no rally on his behalf. Only Mencken, unbidden, volunteered to come to Chicago and testify for Hecht. Hecht lost his case and was disillusioned by the affair. The book became something of an underground classic and was reprinted in 1978.

The Florentine Dagger (1923) was written on a wager. Alfred MacArthur, insurance magnate and brother of Charles, accused Hecht of writing the way he did because he could not write "popular stuff." A two thousand dollar bet was made stipulating that Hecht would write a book in less than the two days it took MacArthur to read a popular novel and that it would sell twenty thousand copies. Hecht says that he dictated the book in thirty-six hours and did not enjoy it, although he won the bet. Like many Hecht anecdotes this one varies from source to source, but whatever the actual details, it was a prodigious display—although Hecht surely planned the novel before he actually dictated it.

Whatever its genesis, *The Florentine Dagger* is a fairly successful detective story. It involves the last of the Borgias, now a Broadway playwright, whose fiancée's father is murdered. Suspicion goes from him to his fiancée. The murderer is actually the maid, in reality the victim's demented wife who has been in hiding for a number of years. She killed her husband while they played the last act of their favorite drama. The work is carefully plotted, and suspense is maintained. The central character, a romantic and morbid version of the Hechtian man, at times believes himself to be guilty of the murder (the same ploy used in Hecht's script for Hitchcock's *Spellbound*, 1945). The use of the Borgias as a base combined with the theatrical background supplies the grotesque and heightened atmosphere that Hecht connected with decadence. The plot turns on madness rather than on a premeditated motive and a psychologist is present to explain matters. As is common with authority and educated figures in Hecht's work, such as the doctor in *The Front Page* who allows himself to be shot, the doctor is wrong in thinking the girl is guilty. The book ends with a chapter entitled "Hearts and Flowers" with the lovers riding away together using the accepted happy ending of the genre with both élan and a touch of cynicism. It shows the kind of dexterity and cynicism about form and audience expectations that made the best movie comedy and adventure films work when made with absolute conviction.

The Chicago Literary Times was almost totally a Hechtian enterprise. Other local writers contributed, but often an entire issue, printed on various shades of brightly colored paper, was written by the editor himself. Hecht got involved with the idea when publicity over his trial forced him to leave the *Daily News*. It was Hecht's most sustained attempt at pure Dadaism, and he used the paper as both a satirical weapon and as a means of support. He claimed that advertisers paid him to keep their business out of the paper, although at one point, the circulation reached 10,000.

As Hecht put it, "The policy of my paper was to attack everything. I enjoyed myself perhaps more than my readers."[66] It was in the *Literary Times* that Rose Caylor's review of the Moscow Art Theater's production of *The Brothers Karamazov* appeared in garbled Russian resulting in numerous congratulatory notes, none of which mentioned that the review was totally incomprehensible. Bodenheim was the New York correspondent, and it was in the *Literary Times* that *Cutie—A Warm Mama* (1942) appeared. Written by Bodenheim and Hecht, it was a slangy attack on censors in episodic form. As broad satire and for its own use of urban dialogue, the story, later published separately, was very successful.

These three extracts may give an impression of the tone and stance of the paper:

Progress in Art:

In 1913 Americans thought that Art was men who wore long hair and talked like sissies; naked women in a garret; something J.P. Morgan was interested in; a Chinese Kimono thrown over a chair in the vestibule; something they had in Europe; any statue in a public park.

> In 1923 Americans think Art is something that doesn't look like a photograph; marrying a negro in the South Seas; anything a Russian does; turning colored lights on the orchestra in the movie palace; a rape scene in a moving picture.[67]

On Journalism:

> Trying to determine what is going on in the world by reading the newspapers is like trying to tell the time by watching the second hand of a clock.[68]

A last note is interesting for both the slant it gives on the Chicago attitude towards foreign countries (such as New York) and for the differentiation Hecht makes between art and entertainment.

> New York Art Note:
>
> A lowbrow renaissance is being drummed up by the lads who do the heavy aesthetic thinking in New York. The pages of the art enfevered periodicals are full of hallelujahs for Ring Lardner, Joe Cook, Rube Goldberg, Ann Pennington, jazz ballads, Jack Dempsey, Charles Chaplin, etc.
>
> I find in these eastern essays small enthusiasm for the subject under discussion, but a large boast of the writer's ability to enjoy things you might think out of his line—he being so fancy minded and high falutin' a fellow.
>
> I am annoyed at these falsetto cheers set up by our eastern cognoscenti for rough-and-tumble entertainment. They are certain to hurt the robust talents by identifying them as art.[69]

Of the theatre, Hecht said that although he was in love with it from the age of eighteen, he did not look to the drama for his fame. The theatre, which he defined as "half an art and half a get-rich-quick operation,"[70] did not hold the fascination for him that he found in writing prose. "In my cubicle room over the city's river, I never secretly towered beside Shaw or Ibsen. It was in Montaigne's and Dostoevski's company that I dreamed myself."[71] The greatest pleasure he received from the theatre was in the collaboration with his friends. Throughout his life, his best plays were ones of dual authorship. In his Chicago days he worked with Max Bodenheim, Sherwood Anderson, and Kenneth Sawyer Goodman. Later in New York he would collaborate with Charles MacArthur and Gene Fowler.

At least according to Hecht, his first Chicago production, however, was of a play he wrote alone after the style of Maeterlinck's poetic plays. It was a rhymed parody of *Mona Vanna*, and was performed by the prostitutes at Queen Lil's between two and four in the morning after the "trade" had left the house:

> Instead of one Mona Vanna offering her naked body to the hostile general, I had three sisters nobly ready to sacrifice their virtue for their country—

> We bring you milk-white groceries to sup,
> And flame-tipped breasts to light your feasting up.
>
> Queen Lil, in a policeman's uniform, played the bedeviled general.[72]

Less intimate was Hecht's first public production of a play entitled *Dregs*. The play told a story related to Hecht by a derelict. In it a drunk mistakes his own reflection in a store window for a vision of Christ. It was accepted as one of four one-acts on a bill at the Players' Workshop, but Hecht had to find his own cast. The prostitute from Lil's did very well, but Max Bodenheim, in the role of the drunk, insisted on adding a musical performance to his debut.

Hecht wrote several one-act plays with Bodenheim, including *The Master Poisoner* and *Frenzied Fricassee*. Hecht described their composition this way: "Bodenheim used to sit around, say a sentence full of color and charm, and I would reply. Then we would write this down."[73]

Sherwood Anderson suggested that he and Hecht collaborate. For three weeks they worked on a play about Benvenuto Cellini, with whom Anderson identified. The first act was already three times the length of an act in a traditional play, but Anderson insisted on adding speeches to it. "He maintained," said Hecht, "a play could be as long as we wanted it to be and that people who went to the theatre were all pernicious idlers and would be grateful for a drama that ran eight hours."[74] Their partnership was short-lived.

Hecht worked with Kenneth Goodman at night in the board of directors' room in his lumberman millionaire father's office. Goodman had gone to Princeton and had studied some playwriting technique. They wrote a number of comedies including *The Wonder Hat* (a little play about Pierrot and Pierrette) and *The Hero of Santa Maria* which was eventually produced in New York by the Provincetown Players. They also wrote a number of other plays about derelicts and some about Jews such as *An Idyll of the Shops*, *The Homecoming*, and *The Poem of David* which had the virtue of calling for the use of a Yiddish dialect which Hecht contends was a "hallmark of artistry as Southern dialect is today."[75]

The Hero of Santa Maria is very similar to some of the plots Hecht was later to concoct for the movies. A man has, he thinks, been unjustly denied his Civil War pension. When his son is supposedly killed in the Mexican campaign and the local politicians want to capitalize on the death by making a great show of his funeral, he bargains with them to receive his pension before he will allow it. His son has actually switched identities with a man who wanted to go to war. It is this man who has been killed, and the son stands listening in the next room. He reveals himself and makes a deal with his father for half the pension in return for his silence and disappearance. As in later Hecht films, *Nothing Sacred* (1937) in particular, there is no innocent character. The only real patriot is dead and unidentified while the politicians, father and son, are hypocritically attempting to profit off his corpse.

This was not the sum of Hecht's playwriting during this period. He wrote a commercial play, *The Egoist*, which toured the country but closed shortly after it reached New York with Leo Dietrichstein in the lead. Hecht said he also wrote twenty or thirty plays with which he was dissatisfied, and he destroyed them.

In the spring of 1924 Hecht moved to New York. Although he had gained prominence in Chicago, the city itself had been diminishing for years as a cultural, bohemian, and publishing center. His national reputation now made Chicago somewhat claustrophobic, and Hecht was ready for new challenges. He settled in New York with Rose Caylor, soon to be his wife, and continued writing. He published *Humpty Dumpty* (1924), a continuation of his earlier novels with the artist hero Kent Savaron in anguish over his inability to fit into middle class society and live up to his own aesthetic aspirations. Savaron ends as a suicide. *Count Bruga* (1926) was another mystery written to pay debts. Here the murder victim turns out to be a suicide. Hecht used Bodenheim as a model for the central figure, Count Bruga, named Jules Ganz in the novel, and used a number of actual incidents. Bodenheim was not amused by the satire and answered with *Duke Herring* in which Hecht was caricatured. Even in *Count Bruga*, a rather slick story, Hecht uses the death not as a focus but as an excuse to write about his central artist figure and to attack contemporary morality, politics, and marriage. He also continued to publish short fiction.

Hecht enjoyed the literary life in New York and in an attempt to make money got involved in the Florida land boom. The boom deflated quickly and Hecht was again left close to destitution. It was at this point[76] that he received the now famous telegram from Herman Mankiewicz that was to start him on his movie career.

> Will you accept three hundred per week to work for Paramount Pictures. All expenses paid. Three hundred is peanuts. Millions are to be grabbed out here and your only competition is idiots. Don't let this get around. Herman Mankiewicz.[77]

2

Screwball Comedy: A Background

Hecht went to Hollywood and spent the rest of his life shuffling back and forth from coast to coast. Following Charles MacArthur's lead, he bought a home in Nyack, New York. He always considered New York his base and perceived his trips to California as forays into the jungle of the studios. Here he would work long enough, from two weeks to four months, to replenish his bank account and then flee back east. He continued to write short stories, novellas, and newspaper articles, but published only one more novel, *A Jew in Love* (1931) until the Second World War. He also began to assault the New York theatre with plays. Although he made a great deal of money from his successful plays, *The Front Page* (1928) and *The Twentieth Century* (1933), in general, his Hollywood capital bankrolled less remunerative enterprises. Hecht says his salary was often between fifty thousand and one hundred and twenty-five thousand dollars for jobs that varied from two to eight weeks.

Hecht contends that he looked on movie writing as "an amiable chore. It was a source of easy money and pleasant friendships. There was small responsibility. Your name as a writer was buried in a flock of 'credits.' Your literary pride was never involved."[1] Pride may not have been involved, but that did not mean the work required any less attention. Hecht said he did not mind writing hack scripts, but it took no less energy than doing good work: "It's just as hard to make a toilet seat as it is a castle window. But the view is different."[2]

Hecht's attitude towards film must be understood in his historical context. He had been born in an age when there were no mass systems of communication other than print. Radio had not developed out of its experimental phase and print was the highest possible aspiration for a writer. In his early life he saw film go from nickelodeons to silent movie palaces. As a form it became and remained a mass entertainment. No matter how highly developed the art of the silent screen might have been it was beyond the realm of any of Hecht's literary aspirations. His first experience with Hollywood was in writing for silent films (*Underworld*, 1927). The addition of sound to the screen did not come until after he had formed his opinions of the studio world. To him the films were merely a fantastic money-making activity, and the success of a film was probably due more to the publicity department than to the director.

1. *Underworld* (1927). Bull Weed (George Bancroft) at gangster's ball. Hecht said his first film story was filled with "moody Sandburgian sentences." Von Sternberg credited himself with converting a popular melodrama about Chicago gangsters into "an experiment in photographic violence and montage." Both were correct as this gauzy, stylized image suggests.
(Photo: Museum of Modern Art/Film Stills Archive courtesy Paramount Studios.)

These attitudes are clearly delineated in an article Hecht published in *Theatre Magazine* in June 1929 entitled "My Testimonial to the Movies: The Frank Confession of a Literary Man Who Puts Into Words What Others Have Only Dared Think." In the article Hecht says that he is chiefly interested in how much money he can get out of the movies, and he feels little responsibility for the success or failure of a movie he has written. He says that although there is no need for the studios to hire literary men, it flatters the ego of "a group of uncultured and almost untutored gentlemen [who] found themselves at the head of what was being called a 'New Art Form.'" The bigger the sum a writer demands the more integrity and importance the studio head feels for himself. Hecht says he is being "invited to participate in a species of hoax," and he does not mind doing it. Although he says that the introduction of sound has confused the issue somewhat, after seeing a half dozen talkies he still believes films will never be the medium for the literary man. He concludes: "When the gentlemen who create movies with a camera and a megaphone acquire enough confidence in themselves to know that these and not the condescending pen of a 'literary artist' are the tools of their trade, the movies will begin to improve and take on integrity."[3]

While Hecht's attitude towards the importance of writer and director to the final production would change over the years, his basic attitude towards the movies as a species of entertainment and not an art would barely alter. In many ways this was fortunate for him both personally and professionally. Because he thought of himself as a hired lackey making enough money to move on to something he cared about, and because he had the discipline to leave when he was able, Hecht never invested too much of his considerable ego in his work. This is not to imply that he did not care about it. He worked with all the craft of his hired pen creating good "toilet seats." He would argue and defend his script the entire time he worked on it, but like the newsman he was trained to be, he realized that once the piece was finished and handed in, it was out of his hands and likely to be butchered by his producers, fancied up by his directors, or rewritten by another set of writers who were "following" him. In fact one of Hecht's own specialties was as a script doctor, patching up the scripts of other writers.

Because he was doing a workman's job, Hecht was able to fit his work to the job required. Hecht's newspaper work is looser, more lively, more personal, and in many ways superior to his more serious novel writing, and his cynical, urban, slangy journalistic style was suited to the movies in a way his more literary approach was not. His best films, *The Scarface* (1933), *Nothing Sacred* (1937), and *Twentieth Century* (1934) have this urban exuberance where his more serious adaptations, *Wuthering Heights* (1939) or *Farewell to Arms* (1957) suffer from being overwritten even while they may be well structured and crafted.

Hecht also brought to his movie work a newsman's condescension towards his audience and the realization of the ephemerality of his work. What was written today would tomorrow be used to wrap a fish by a semi-literate workman (or be seen by the movies' unwashed millions). There was a duality in the newsman's work, particularly in Chicago. On the one hand the newswriter aspired to the respect of his peers by writing the best he could. In the newsrooms of the *Journal* and the *Daily News* there was some appreciation for good, even "literary" writing. But the newsman could only hope to be noticed by his cohorts because his job was essentially anonymous. He rarely was honored with a by-line, and when he was it was seldom valued by the public. As Hecht recalls, even the praise of his fellows was often backhanded as was this reaction to one of his stories: "That was a fine circus story you wrote. Several people spoke to me about it. They all had the same reaction—pains in the lower abdomen followed by nausea. I took an enema before going to bed and feel all right this morning, fully able to continue as a reader of the *Daily News*."[4]

The newspaper was not a place to achieve widespread fame, reach an elite audience, or leave a lasting literary legacy. Writers who wanted those things had to promote themselves as critics or columnists. In much the same way, working as a Hollywood scriptwriter would not bring importance or acclaim. Those who sought it there, particularly the pundits and critics, were sorely disappointed. Power was in the hands of the producer or the director. But Hecht, who expected no more from the job than its ridiculous monetary bounty, could work, relatively content, with the same attitudes that made him a good newsman. Admittedly, Hecht did protest vociferously that he was unconcerned with his assignments, but this was also consistent with the newsman's cynical denigration of everything around him, including his own work. Besides, his complaints always made good copy and would often be answered by a raise in salary: "My own discontent with what I was asked to do in Hollywood was so loud that I finally received a hundred and twenty-five thousand dollars for four weeks of script writing."[5] Hecht merely added the studio and its bosses to his list of execrable forces of repression and greed and continued to rail and continued to write.

The producers only put up with the kind of squawking that Hecht did because they valued his work. He was, first of all, fast. While they were looking for genius in their writers they did not want to have to wait for it. For instance, when David Selznick contracted with Hecht to do the final script for *Viva Villa* (1934), he stipulated that Hecht receive ten thousand dollars, fifteen thousand if he completed it within fifteen days. He explained the provisions to Louis B. Mayer this way:

> On the quality we are protected not merely by Hecht's ability but by the clause that the work must be to my satisfaction. It may seem like a short space of time for a man to do a

complete new script, but Hecht is famous for his speed, and did the entire job on *Scarface* in eleven days. I do not think we should take into consideration the fact that we are paying him a seemingly large sum of money for two weeks' work, because this would merely be penalizing him for doing in two weeks what it would take a lesser man to do, with certainly infinitely poorer results, in six or eight weeks.[6]

Hecht's claim that he wrote his movies in two weeks or dictated them in two days served two purposes. It showed how far above the work he placed himself, but it also was good publicity in an industry that valued speed and thus helped to keep his writing in demand.

But, as Selznick's memo also indicates, it was the quality of his writing as well as his speed that allowed Hecht the freedom of working when he chose. Hecht was one of a generation of screenwriters who did not flourish in Hollywood until after the demise of silent films. They specialized in supplying the contemporary dialogue that sound films called for. The best of them, according to Harry Geduld in *The Birth of the Talkies*, wrote screenplays which "were full of brief, vivid scenes and characters who spoke a language that was concise, racy, and dynamic, echoing the ceaseless, teeming vitality of America's burgeoning cities."[7] Of the many films that were produced in this period, newspaper films, screwball comedies, and gangster films, utilized this kind of speech and character most fully. They were urban-based, contemporary, and fast-paced. While the generic roots of these films may be traced into the silent era, it was only with the addition of sound, both as effects and as dialogue, that the genres fully developed. At their best there was a balance in the film between the visual action (violence, slapstick, character nuance) and the snappy dialogue.

These were the kinds of films that Hecht's skills and experience perfectly suited him to produce. Although he only wrote one undiluted gangster sound film (*The Scarface*, 1933) in the 1930s and only worked on a few unadulterated newspaper films (e.g., *Roadhouse Nights*, 1930), he was constantly combining elements from these genres in his comedies. His comedies of the period (including *The Front Page* [1931] and *Topaze* [1933] have among them a number of screwball comedies (*Design For Living* [1933], *The Twentieth Century* [1934], *Nothing Sacred* [1937], *It's a Wonderful World* [1939], *Comrade X* [1940], *His Girl Friday* [1940], and *Roxie Hart* [1942]), although always adapted to a Hechtian world view.

Screwball comedy was a form indigenous to the early American sound movie. A combination of technical advancements, social forces, and unique talents coalesced for a few years, roughly 1933-1941, to produce a style of film that has rarely been equalled in its enjoyment of language, its spirit, or its good-natured satire. It did not appear suddenly in a mature form but developed over the years from a number of different theatrical strands: the tradition of sophisticated comedy in English going back to the sixteenth century, the gangster and newspaper plays and films of the late twenties and early thirties, and the tradition of carefully synchronized gag comedy perfected by playwrights like George Kaufman and his collaborators. It was written by a particular fraternity of writers (veterans of city rooms, the Algonquin table, and Kaufman's studio) who brought their love of wit and their artistic frustration to their joint efforts. It was affected by the social forces of the period as well. Although not a revolutionary genre socially or sexually, it reflects an anticonventionality sharpened by the Depression. It had sexual energy, but because of the restrictions enforced by the Legion of Decency and the Production code, this sexuality was channeled into verbal duels and physical slapstick. The combination of these disparate traditions and forces resulted in a kind of film lacking in false sentimentality and produced in an unadorned visual style that remains fresh and popular with modern audiences.

Broadly defined, screwball comedy is a form of romantic comedy, firmly rooted in American urban dialogue as a souce of humor, contemporary in its settings, tough in its sentiments. The verbal weight and sophistication of the dialogue is balanced by a measure of slapstick. The films espouse an informed lightheartedness towards the very real evils of the world, an insular escape, and they vacillate in tone from the cynical to the merely liberated.

Examples of the genre are *Design for Living* (1933), *Twentieth Century, It Happened One Night,* and *The Thin Man* (1934), *Ruggles of Red Gap* (1935), *My Man Godfrey* (1936), *The Awful Truth, Nothing Sacred, Easy Living,* and *Topper* (1937), *Bringing Up Baby, Holiday,* and *Joy of Living* (1938), *Midnight* and *It's a Wonderful World* (1939), *The Philadelphia Story, His Girl Friday, Comrade X, My Favorite Wife,* and *Too Many Husbands* (1940), *The Lady Eve* (1941), and *Roxie Hart* (1942).

The films usually center around a love story, but often there is a secondary plot. *The Thin Man,* for instance, is a murder mystery, yet the relationship between Nick and Nora Charles, their sophisticated humor, their enjoyment of each other, and their playful bickering rivals the discovery of the body and the solution of the crime for attention in the film. At times the lovers are kept apart by self-imposed obstacles or a lack of awareness. Often a duel of wit and personality between the two partners develops as in *The Thin Man, Philadelphia Story,* or *Twentieth Century.* The lovers also handle some of the slapstick and physical humor in the films, and this may develop into an actual fight, as it does at the end of *Nothing Sacred.* Even though they are love stories, the films are antisentimental. The attitude of the characters is always that to have the emotion is fine but that to voice it would be insincere or show a lack of toughness.

Morally the films honor the goodhearted but disdain the innocent. The victors are those who know the score and are able to win by any means, although they may have momentary lapses into virtue caused by love as Clark

Gable does at the end of *It Happened One Night*. He is unscrupulous enough to trick his news story (Claudette Colbert) into traveling with him but finally too sincere to use it. The sharp and the witty deserve each other, as Cary Grant does Katherine Hepburn in *Philadelphia Story*, not by virtue of better talents or sentiments or a higher social class but by wit and appreciation of high spirits. As in *Philadelphia Story*, the films often involve one individual liberating the spirit of the other as Grant does for Hepburn. Quite frequently the woman liberates the man, as Hepburn does Grant in *Bringing Up Baby*.

Although the films are basically satires, they nibble rather than bite at their targets. The world view of the films is not of a benign universe which will be improved by love and understanding, as is common in the schmaltzy films of the thirties (typified by those starring Shirley Temple). The movies take place in a world where smart operators, hypocrites, and disappointments are inevitable. The protagonist conquers this world by a clear-sighted recognition of its baseness and by rising above it with superior wit, an unchained soul, and by having as equally clear-sighted lover. The couple becomes a basic unit of defense against the outside world. Protected by their relationship, they could ignore larger political or social concerns.

The films swipe at the inadequacies of the world but are basically unconcerned with them. The targets are usually any complacent, smug, self-satisfied group and any kind of establishment. The wealthy, newspapers, film studios, government, law enforcement, the complacent rebel as well as the complacent rich are all targets. Triumph over these groups is always personal rather than political; escape and self-actualization are more common than social change. Anything natural is positive; anything constricting is negative. Sex is very positive, but since most of the films under discussion were made after the Production Code exorcised the demon of overt sexuality in 1934, sexual energy is usually subverted into other channels. In *Bringing Up Baby* for instance, it is clear that Hepburn is more sexual than Grant's fiancée and assistant (who plans to have no children). The contrast between Hepburn's lively leopard and Grant's dessicated dinosaur bones clearly symbolizes their positions. Grant may come to know that his romp with her is the best time he has had in his life and a life of spirit may be in the offing for him with her, but in the film there is nary a kiss between them.

Even though the films were loaded with dialogue, they were fast-paced and farcical. Often they began with an improbable incident, such as in *Easy Living* in which a mink coat is thrown out of a window and lands in a car many stories below, and then are logically developed out of that improbability. If the pace was fast and the plot tight enough, the film was over before the incongruities and coincidences became too apparent. The element of license, allowing the characters to indulge themselves in anti-social or unconventional behavior such as tossing the coat out the window, is the characteristic that

Donald McCaffrey, in his study of thirties comedy,[8] isolates as a determining one for the genre and an important social attitude for a Depression audience. It provided a kind of wish fulfillment by denying the power of the forces that closed in around them.

Screwball comedies were similar to other contemporary genres of movies. The more vaudeville-oriented comedies of the Marx Brothers and W.C. Fields share many elements in common with screwball comedy, but are largely *tour de forces* for the comic stars rather than romantic comedies. Although screwball comedy shares a common bond of wit, pace, and irreverence with vaudeville comedy, screwball comedy is grounded much more firmly in a realistic environment than the vaudeville comedy world of Freedonia or Huxley College. There is also a similarity between gangster films, murder mysteries, and especially newspaper films on one hand and screwball comedy on the other. They are all urban, hard edged, cynical and they often contain the same melodramatic elements. The difference lies in the tone. The same material can be played for laughs or for excitement and suspense. *The Thin Man* could easily have been merely another crime film, as *Philadelphia Story* could have degenerated into social melodrama. These genres share a belief in the existence of evil in the universe which must be met with intelligence. In fact, screwball comedy relied heavily on these less comic genres, especially newspaper films, for its structure and environment. It should also be remembered that during this period even the films of these more serious genres were peppered with humorous elements such as the comic relief of Tony Camonte's secretary shooting at the telephone in *Scarface* (1933) or the undercurrent of wit and humor throughout *Citizen Kane* (1940).

While the roots of the genre were not deeply embedded in the cinema before the addition of sound, there is a history of sophisticated comedy and comic duels of wit between lovers that can be traced as far back as the sixteenth century in the English theatre. *Much Ado About Nothing,* for instance, has many similarities with screwball comedy. The duel of wits between Beatrice and Benedick in which Beatrice is often superior and in which only their own obstinacy keeps them apart, is very much like the duel between Grant and Hepburn in *Philadelphia Story* or between Nick and Nora Charles. If *Much Ado* were rearranged slightly by bringing the low comic scenes of Dogberry and his crew slightly closer to the sophistication of the central lovers and integrating them more into the action, and by adding the kind of physical fighting that takes place between Petruchio and Kate in *Taming of the Shrew* (another play sharing common elements with screwball comedy)—the result would not be distant in shape from the later film genre.

Restoration comedy is even closer to screwball comedy with its attack on false sentiment, its emphasis on wit, and particularly its battles of wit between lovers. The duel between Mirabel and Millamant in *The Way of the World* is comparable to the romantic pairings of screwball comedy. In both genres the witty realists rather than the Innocents are attractive and sympathetic. The cynicism about human nature that pervades Restoration comedy is also consistent with the world view of the thirties.

The immediate roots of screwball comedy are in the Broadway trends of the 1920s. Screwball comedy drew on the traditions of Broadway comedy best exemplified by the work of George Kaufman. Kaufman was a genius at exploiting the comic possibilities in any situation provided him by his many collaborators. Although the humor of the plays was ostensibly aimed at business, Hollywood, government, or any other popular target, the satire was always secondary to the laugh. With plays such as *Dulcy* (1921), *Merton and the Movies* (1922), *Beggar on Horseback* (1924) all written with Marc Connelly; *The Butter and Egg Man* (1924); *The Cocoanuts* (1925) with Morrie Ryskind; *June Moon* (1929) with Ring Lardner; and *Once in a Lifetime* (1930) with Moss Hart, he helped create a tradition of topical satire and impudent irreverence which was absorbed into the movies both through adaptations of his works and through the movie writing of his collaborators, a group which also included Dorothy Parker, Alexander Woolcott, George Oppenheimer, Nat Perrin, Laurence Stallings, and Herman Mankiewicz. As Pauline Kael expresses it:

> Kaufman fathered a movement that is so unmistakably the bastard child of the arts as to seem fatherless; the gag comedy was perfectly suited to the commercial mass art of the movies, so that it appears to be an almost inevitable development. It suited the low common denominator of the movies even better than it suited the needs of the relatively selective theatre audience, and the basic irresponsibility of this kind of theatre combined with the screenwriter's lack of control over their own writing to produce what some might call the brothel period of American Letters.[9]

The cynicism and the antiromanticism of other plays—such as *They Knew What They Wanted* (Sidney Howard, 1924), with their realistic dialogue and their mixture of lightness and seriousness—were also among the theatrical trends that were transferred to sound films. Still other forces shaped the form. The writers of the genre came not only from the Algonquin table and the studio of Kaufman but from the pressrooms as well. Most were former newsmen or critics, among them, Dudley Nichols, Gene Fowler, Billy Wilder, Hecht and MacArthur. They had been lured to Hollywood by the fast and easy money and the fun of collaboration. They disdained the work they did, but they attacked it with exuberance and wit. Many never freed themselves from the trap of the studios but, as Kael says:

> They did wonders for the movies. In New York they may have valued their own urbanity too highly; faced with the target Hollywood presented, they became cruder and tougher, less

tidy, less stylistically elegant, and more iconoclastic.... Though their style was often flippant and their attitude toward form casual to the point of contempt, they brought movies the subversive gift of sanity. They changed movies by raking the old moralistic muck with derision.[10]

The attitudes of the New York theatre were also transferred to the screen through adaptation. A number of the most popular films of the genre, including *Holiday* and *Philadelphia Story* (both by Philip Barry) had been on the stage (1929 and 1939) prior to their screen production, as had *Twentieth Century* and *His Girl Friday* (as *The Front Page*).

Screwball comedy may have gestated in the theatre of the twenties, but it was raised in the Depression world of the thirties. The critic Lewis Jacobs analyzes the period in his work *The Rise of the American Film* (1939). He points out that when box office receipts began to fall movies tried to change their subject matter and attitudes to cater to the concerns of their audience. In part, this was reflected in an increased interest in American middle class characters and problems. The gangster film, which had been a minor genre in film, became an enormously popular form. The hard bitten realistic texture and the violent cynicism of these films, epitomized by *Little Caesar* (1930), *Public Enemy* (1931), and *The Scarface* (1933) fascinated audiences with their images of the American dream gone sour.

As is often the case in the movies, these films were popularizing a trend already established in another medium, in this case a kind of urban realism that had become popular on the stage. Edward G. Robinson, for instance, had played a gangster role similar to his part in *Little Caesar* in Bartlett Cormack's *The Racket* (1927). On the stage, Elmer Rice's play *Street Scene* (1929) was praised for its realistic background noises and urban dialogue, as well as for Jo Mielziner's massive urban brownstone facade. Robert Littel, writing in *Theatre Arts Monthly,* was impressed with new technical devices: "a combination of phonograph and amplifiers... that give to *Street Scene* the vast, roaring loneliness of New York."[11] Motion pictures soon outstripped the theatre's ability to produce a realistic texture in sound effects and settings. These elements became distinguishing marks of the urban movie.

When public enthusiasm for what had been popular films—"bedroom farces, illicit adventures, and sinful tales of the sophisticated women of the world,"[12] which according to Jacobs reached their climax with *The Last of Mrs. Cheney* (1929), *Paris-Bound* (1929), *The Divorcee* (1930), and *Merrily We Go To Hell* (1932)—began to wane, sexual attitudes in films also began to change to meet the public's interests. As films became more domestic in their background—moving away from the exotic and romantic—they moved towards an acceptance of sex as part of everyday life. Approached as healthy, funny, and even enjoyable, sexual material no longer had to be excused as low

2. *The Scarface* (1932). Tony Camonte (Paul Muni), center, with his gang. Although ostensibly about the rise of a gangster in Chicago, the major psychological conflict concerns Camonte's incestuous feelings for his sister. His downfall comes through her betrayal. Similar to *Underworld* in plot and character conflict, *The Scarface* had a sharp, hard-edged visual style that helped set the style for 1930s gangster films. (Photo: Museum of Modern Art/Film Stills Archive courtesy United Artists.)

3. *The Scarface* (1932). The final shootout. "The City is Yours" sign in *Underworld* becomes "The World is Yours" in *The Scarface*. In the 1983 remake it appears on a blimp. (Photo: Museum of Modern Art/Film Stills Archive courtesy United Artists.)

or illicit passion. Love could be enjoyed rather than suffered over; a greater equality between the sexes developed. "Sin was taken out of sex; fun put in its place."[13]

Jacobs believes the films of Mae West and Jean Harlow epitomize the new attitude towards sex. West asserted her right to control relationships and enjoy sex openly, as the titles of her films suggest: *She Done Him Wrong* (1933), *It Ain't No Sin* (1934), *Belle of the Nineties* (1934), *I'm No Angel* (1933), *Goin' to Town* (1935), and *Every Day's a Holiday* (1937). Women could change men, and even marriage could be fun as in *The Thin Man* where Myrna Loy and William Powell could be sexy, funny, sharing, sophisticated, and still married.

Changing attitudes and public censorship eventually combined to muzzle West and Harlow, and screwball comedy became the vogue. Less outwardly lascivious or illicit than earlier forms, screwball comedy retained a healthy attitude toward sex, love, and romance, extended it more deeply into a domestic context, and combined it with witty dialogue and slapstick humor. Drawing room comedy was pushed closer to knockdown farce and often the central lovers fought physically as well as verbally. But even the fighting was part of a central attitude of play that undergirded the films. Conformism and empty gesture were ridiculed, and the nonconformist became the protagonist.

> In these films the rebel, the individual, is once more respected. The artist, the eccentric, the unaccountable, who was once a poor and lazy good-for-nothing in films, now is the sane person in a chaotic world. *Bringing Up Baby, Merrily We Live*, and *Nothing Sacred* accordingly exalted individuality and painstakingly avoided conventionality.[14]

Within the protection of marriage or a romance the lovers in these films desert the problems of the outside world and build a fantasy world of good spirits in their own relationship. Marriage in these films thus becomes a protective frame rather than a trap to be escaped. The cynicism is redeemed by the charm, kindness, gaiety, and goodwill of the central characters.

Jacobs sees the development of the genre as a positive form of self-criticism and realism:

> The loss of credibility in former values, the breakdown of the smugness and self-confidence of the jazz age, the growing bewilderment and dissatisfaction in a crazy world that does not make sense, has been reflected in the revival of comedies of satire and self-ridicule. These are best epitomized perhaps in the title of one of them, *Nothing Sacred*.[15]

Other critics, however, perceive the genre as an intellectual and moral retreat rather than as the development of a healthy indigenous form. Both Robert Sklar in his book *Movie Made America* (1975) and Molly Haskell in *From Reverence to Rape* (1974) hold this more negative point of view—that screwball comedy marked the abdication of greater freedom, both sexually and socially, found in the films of the early sound era.

Socially oriented, Sklar sees the early thirties as the only period in which the industry produced films which, while popular, were not in tune with American middle class values. In an attempt to maintain their audience in the midst of a worsening depression, studios turned to a social realism that exploited gangsters, violence, sex and politics to titillate or shock its audience. They circumvented the existing codes by paying lip service to poetic justice by allowing the gangsters and demimondes to enjoy all the illicit activities before being punished at the end of the film.

According to Sklar, screwball comedy represented the retreat of the film industry from any real social criticism, while as a form it reaffirmed social values.

> Screwball comedies were the last refuge of satire, self-mockery and sexual candor of early 1930's filmmaking, but their iconoclasm was used, overtly at least, to support the status quo.[16]

The films celebrated marriage, reaffirmed class distinction and the dominance of men over women. Built on the logic of farce where improbability becomes a base for incongruous but reasonable action, the comedies never disturbed the social order but tended instead to show how well it worked. Rather than focusing on society as a whole, the comedies withdrew into a safe domestic/romantic circle that abjured any social concern.

Haskell, concerned primarily with the presentation of women, notes that at least in the films of the early thirties sex was open and stated. The women could admit sexual as well as romantic desire and, even though many of the films had a pronounced machismo, they at least were open about their misogyny. Jimmy Cagney, shoving a grapefruit in Mae Clark's face in *The Public Enemy* (1931), was "surely a cleaner and less generalized expression of hostility than rape and the more insidious modern forms of misogyny in which women characters are drawn as bitches to be blotted out."[17] The enforcement of the Production Code, taking hold in 1933 and 1934, stripped some of the sex from the films. Women could still be aggressive, but now they became working girls, professionals and comrades. The *femme fatale* was exorcised.

Even to Sklar and Haskell, however, there were redeeming characteristics to late 1930s comedy. The women could be aggressive. Although they could not be sexual and businesslike at the same time, they could be romantic, playful, and sharp tongued. Even though screwball comedy did not present a revolutionary attitude towards society it did present a different conception of social purpose and human endeavor. If there was no political solution to the Depression or the great problems of the world, then the answer was to ignore them and have fun.

> The pictures gave audiences a whole new vision of social style, a different image of how to be a person: it was okay to be pleasure-loving, even if it made you look sexy or odd; it was good to puncture stuffed shirts and be lively, gay, and carefree; it was good to throw decorum to the wind.[18]

Screwball comedy was the result of these conflicting attitudes and pressures. It supported the status quo while bringing American speech, characters, and problems to the screen; it drew back from the truly open sex of the early thirties—it was less illicit and less talked about—but it allowed women to be aggressive companions.

Screwball comedies have remained popular with audiences and socially oriented critics but are usually ignored by more abstract theorists. Their popularity stems from their wit, hardheadedness, and modernity of attitude; they are dismissed because, even though the best of them were directed with craft and astringency, they lack the "artistic" flourishes that many critics find comforting. Visually the films center on character and dialogue rather than on atmosphere and setting. Gerald Mast's description of the technique of Preston Sturges can be extended to include the values of many screwball comedies. "The Sturges emphasis on dialogue determines his film technique, which relies on the conventional two-shot to capture the faces and features while the characters talk, talk, talk. But it is such good talk—incredibly rapid, crackling, brittle."[19]

Film critics, whether of the montage school of Eisenstein or of the photographic school of Bazin and Kracauer, have in common the belief that at its base "film is a visual medium.... For sound films to be true to the basic aesthetic principle, their significant communication must originate with the picture."[20] If appreciation of film is limited to the visual, screwball comedy, and indeed much of the studio production of the thirties, the decade of the talkies, will be judged inferior because such a judgement will ignore by choice the best features of the films—the writing and the acting. Pauline Kael suggests that part of the reason for this judgment may be that the dialogue is so American in its frame of reference and satire that European critics never fully related to the humor. "But it's a bad joke on our good jokes that film enthusiasts here often takes their cues on the American movie past from Europe, and so they ignore the tradition of comic irreverence and become connoisseurs of the 'visuals' and 'mise en scene' of action pictures."[21]

Screwball comedy was not the only kind of film made in the thirties, but it may be the genre that captures best the spirit and the texture of the period. It embodied that rare combination of optimism and self-criticism, exuberance, and joy in language that, like the wit and license of Restoration England or the expansionist energy of Elizabethan drama, flourished for only a few years before it was smothered by changing events and different moods.

3

The Front Page

In the first mad rush to supply dialogue to the new sound film the Hollywood studios looked for writers with practical experience. As a result, many of Hecht's collaborators in Hollywood in the 1930s were other former reporters. The films they wrote and which came into vogue were only one step away from the kinds of stories they had written in the newsroom. The audience enjoyed the urban subjects these reporters knew best because, according to Pauline Kael: "It was eager for modern American subjects. Even those of us who were children at the time loved the fast-moving modern-city stories. The commonplace—even tawdriness—of the imagery was such a relief from all that silent 'poetry.' The Talkies were a great step down."[1] Hecht excelled at writing this kind of story, particularly in the context of a newspaper film.

Until the introduction of sound, the newspaper film was a minor variation of other genres. Although the *American Film Institute Catalogue* for 1921-30 lists over sixty feature films about newspapers, films such as *The Star Reporter* (1921), *Headlines* (1925), *Freedom of the Press* and *Telling the World* (1928), these films were, in general, only crime stories, romances, melodramas, or comedies which happened to involve newspapers or newsmen. The newspaper setting was often little more than a source of expositional devices—headlines and dates showing the passage of time and events. When the newsman gained a voice he also gained a distinct character. In early sound newspaper films, such as *Gentlemen of the Press* (1929), *Night Ride* (1929), *Young Man in Manhattan* (1930), and *Roadhouse Nights* (written by Hecht in 1930), the paper and its workers moved to the center of the story. As a distinct genre, the newspaper film had its first great vogue in 1931 when the film version of Hecht and Charles MacArthur's play *The Front Page* was released. With *The Front Page* the melodrama, scandal, or crime story the paper was reporting became secondary to the newsman's fight to get the story and his relationship with his girl, his editor, or his fellow reporters. The silent newspaper film had focused on plot turns, but with sound, the emphasis could shift to the dialogue and the irreverent character of the reporter.

Once established, the form proved a durable framework for many dramatic uses ranging from *Citizen Kane* (1941) to television's *Lou Grant* (1977). All refer back to the types established by Hecht and MacArthur in the way Steven Scheuer does in his comments about the recent popular newspaper film, *All the President's Men* (1976): "This updated version of *The Front Page* is more tantalizing than any of them, but no contemporary Ben Hecht or novelist would dare dream up such a preposterous, farfetched plot line."[2] The newsman character has remained a commonplace participant in the most unlikely places—in Mexico with Villa (*Viva Villa,* 1934), in the drawing room (*Philadelphia Story,* 1940), in the arctic with *The Thing* (1951), in the desert with *Lawrence of Arabia* (1962), and in Vietnam with *The Green Berets* (1968). Although he may at times be foolish or venal the fictional newsman has with some consistency remained the cool professional with a tough hide protecting his soft and patriotic heart.

In his many films Hecht, himself, varied the form by changing the mixture of crime, romance, and comedy to suit his needs. *Roadhouse Nights, Let Freedom Ring* (1939), and *Foreign Correspondent* (1940) all tend towards action and melodrama. Romance is most prominent in *Roman Holiday* (1953), while comedy dominates *The Front Page,* and each of *Nothing Sacred* (1937), *Comrade X* (1940), *His Girl Friday* (1940), and *Roxie Hart* (1942) use large quantities of both. The newsmen characters also appeared in many films by Hecht in other genres. Their prominence in these films was often disproportionate to their importance to the plot. Hard drinking cynics with good hearts, they always reveal their selflessness in a moment of need, whether it is helping Fred MacMurray force the studio to release the film of a dead girl in *Miracle of the Bells* (1948) or writing an editorial to expose Edward G. Robinson in *Barbary Coast* (1935). At times the character gets out of hand, unbalancing the sense of the film. In *Viva Villa,* for instance, Stuart Erwin's newsman, Johnny Sykes, convinces Pancho Villa to attack a town because Sykes had already mistakenly reported it captured;[3] he first convinces Villa that he must start a revolution and later persuades him to leave the presidency; finally he writes Villa's dying words. All of this takes place in a film that purports to document actual events.

The Front Page created a new strain of newspaper films in which the melodrama and suspense were used as a backdrop for comedy. The infighting between editor and newsman or between newsman and his fellows, already irreverent and tough, became the arena for exuberant comic badinage. The reduction of crime scandal to comic fodder was part of the jaded world view that informed urban comedy in the thirties. Newspaper films were an easily recognizable type, as Kael describes:

> A newspaper picture meant a contemporary picture in an American setting, usually a melodrama with crime and political corruption and suspense and comedy and romance. In 1931, a title like *Five Star Final* or *Scandal Sheet* signalled the public that the movie would be a tough modern talkie, not a tearjerker with sound.[4]

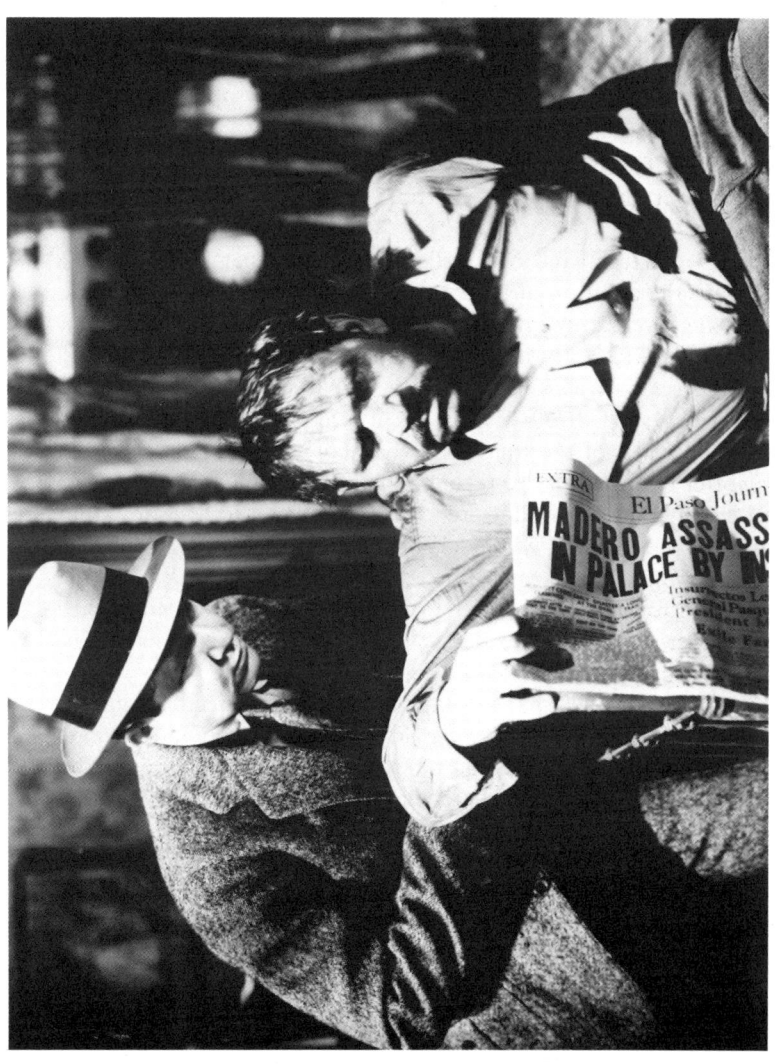

4. *Viva Villa* (1934). Johnny Sykes (Stuart Erwin), the American reporter, brings the drunken Pancho Villa (Wallace Beery) the news of President Madero's death. Although about the life of Villa, the film is dominated, often comically, by the ability of the reporter to force events and reshape the past through his stories.
(Photo: Museum of Modern Art/Film Stills Archive courtesy Metro Goldwyn Mayer.)

In *The Front Page* Hecht and MacArthur mixed Broadway farce, newspaper melodrama, and a great deal of wit. They helped mold the newsman into an identifiable "type." As Alex Barris comments in *Stop the Presses,* a study of newspaper films: "Ben Hecht and Charles MacArthur may not have invented the movie newspaperman, but they were largely responsible for his proliferation and longevity."[5] According to Barris, Hecht and MacArthur created a newsman who was the most hardboiled of cynics ready to kill to meet a deadline or get a story; they also made him human, heroic, and outrageously funny. That this "realism" was an exaggerated dramatic type a good distance removed from actual life seemed not to bother the audience or the newsmen who began to adopt the fictional hyperbole of Hecht and MacArthur's newsmen.

In the hands of Hecht and MacArthur, the newspaper film became a comic genre. With the addition of an extra measure of romance to the plot, newspaper comedies were only one step removed from screwball comedy. *It Happened One Night* (1934), for instance, often considered the first screwball comedy, is at base a newspaper film with Clark Gable yelling at his editor and falling in love with his story. In 1940, with very little alteration, *The Front Page* itself was to become one of the finest screwball comedies when as *His Girl Friday* the reporter role was changed from a man to a woman thereby setting up a romance between editor and reporter. Another Hecht-MacArthur collaboration, *The Twentieth Century* (1934), created an effective screwball comedy by transferring the newspaper film conventions to another profession, in this case, the theatre. Hecht's best films in the thirties were those that worked off of his newspaper characters and the newspaper farce conventions that he and MacArthur first used in *The Front Page.*

The elements of the newspaper film are borrowed directly from the theatre, and the success of *The Front Page* on Broadway, where it opened on August 14, 1928, may have influenced the newspaper genre even before the film version was released in 1931. All the characters and conventions which were to become basic ingredients of the newspaper film were firmly established in the stage play.

The newspaper film is often discussed without reference to its strong theatrical base, but, especially in the early sound era, film was indebted to the theatre for many of its innovations. On the stage, dialogue and character were essential in a way that was not even imagined for film in 1928. When the film had achieved the technical capabilities for adequate sound, theatrical models were available to be quickly absorbed.

The Front Page provides an good example of this transference. The play was the happy result of mixing urban realism, newspaper melodrama, and Broadway farce to achieve breathless comedy. It appealed to those looking for realism in the theatre with its frowzy single set of the pressroom of the Criminal

Courts Building in Chicago, its gritty, swearing language, and its lowlife characters. It crystallized a set of newspaper stereotypes that journalists, both fictional and actual, would be measured against for decades. At the same time, the play was a carefully constructed melodrama with simple characters, contrived coincidences and reversals, replete with a crooked mayor, an impending execution, and a whore with a heart of gold. The comedy and melodrama did not alternate but were combined throughout. The realistic texture and tight melodrama were used as a basis for the play's central concern, the comic struggle between reporter Hildy Johnson and his editor Walter Burns. It was as a wisecracking American laugh machine that the play had its greatest influence. It helped establish the pattern for early sound movie comedy, the parent of screwball comedy. What might have been an acid picture of human malfeasance gave way to nostalgia that lent the most callous action a measure of admirable chutzpah.

The play was kind to the people involved with it. It launched George Kaufman's third career (after dramatist and critic), that of a director, and many of the actors in the production (particularly Lee Tracy, who would continue to play newsmen roles in such films as *Bombshell* (1933) and *Power of the Press*, 1943), thereafter were regularly employed in the theatre and in the movies.

The play was also the first tangible literary result of the Hecht-MacArthur partnership. Their friendship, which manifested itself in plays, films, and comic antics of all sorts, often dwarfed their individual reputations. They were an unlikely pair. MacArthur, son of a minister and educated in a private school, was tall, elegant, and charming. Hecht, streetwise and Jewish, was broad and brash. What they had in common was their nostalgia for their lost youth as newsmen in Chicago and their interest in reliving those years. They were both about thirty-four years old when they wrote *The Front Page*. Working together they were able to create something fresh out of their past. It was a constructive use of their memories and it reinforced Hecht's tendency to use his own experience as a source of attitudes and materials.

Although they had known each other in Chicago where they worked for rival newspapers,[6] it was not until they met one day on the street in New York that their friendship really developed. Hecht said that when they became bored with telling stories of their youth to each other, they settled down to writing.

> Our friendship was founded on a mutual obsession. We were both obsessed with our youthful years. I had no more interest in Charlie's past than he had in mine. But for twenty-five years we assisted each other in behaving as if these pasts had never vanished. We remained newspaper reporters and continued to keep our hats on before the boss, drop ashes on the floor and disdain all practical people.
>
> But it is difficult for two grown men to continue playing games and palavering as if they were marking time in some pressroom. Thus, since MacArthur (the nonreporter) was hotly in love with the theatre and I was ready to work on anything, we added playwriting to our relationship and later movie writing.[7]

They wrote *The Front Page* in MacArthur's New York apartment, establishing a work pattern they were to follow for twenty years. Hecht would write in longhand on a lap board; MacArthur would wander about, doodle, or stare. According to Hecht, they never argued over ideas. If either man shook his head "no," then the other would trust that judgment without question.

The pairing was useful for both. Hecht wrote of himself, "[I] needed somebody else's love for the stage as a stimulant. The success the theatre had to offer appealed to me less than the satisfaction I found in writing books."[8] As for MacArthur: "The stage was his homeland. But he lacked the discipline for lone expression. He needed a monitor to hold him to a task, however much he loved it."[9] Hecht says that he usually supplied more of the dialogue and plot turns than MacArthur did but that MacArthur was the playwright of the two. Comedy was their mutual love.

> We had the same eye and ear for the innocent oddities of humans. So alike were out tastes and inventiveness that I have seldom been able to tell, after a work was done, which lines he or I had written.[10]

For their second play (the first, *The Moonshooter,* had been lost on a commuter train after a drunken evening in the city) and their first memory work, MacArthur needed no extra discipline.

> Charlie worked like a house afire. We were both writing of people we had loved, and of an employment that had been like none other was ever to be. Also, of a city we both called Avalon.
> There were no bandages on Charlie's soul for this job. The explosive went off. I remember of the collaboration chiefly the fact that I have never known since in anyone the inventiveness and certainty, the burst of creation, Charlie brought to *The Front Page*.[11]

As productive as they considered themselves, Hecht and MacArthur seemed to project a lack of dedication. Kaufman, nervous about his first directing effort, complained to his wife, Beatrice, that they were madmen who took nothing seriously. When Kaufman would send them out to rewrite some lines, he would find they had wandered off and started to play rummy. Eventually they would get the right words written but not until Kaufman had taken the cards out of their hands and pointed them towards their typewriters.

The action of *The Front Page* (as a play) takes place in the newsroom with the reporters in the pool forming a chorus as they sit playing cards and talking over the phone to their respective papers. Hildy Johnson, star reporter, is resigning to leave for New York with his girl to get married and go into advertising. He has waited until the last moment to resign in order to leave his editor, Walter Burns, in the lurch on the eve of the execution of Earl Williams. The execution is a great story: the city government is using it to win votes; the newspapers are using it to boost circulation. Hildy comes to the newsroom to say goodbye to his friends and gets caught up in the excitement when Williams escapes while being examined by an alienist (psychiatrist). Hildy uses the money intended for the trip east to buy the story of the escape but has to wait for Burns to send payment to him. Pincus, a messenger, arrives with a reprieve from the Governor but the Mayor attempts to bribe him into disappearing until after Williams can be shot or hung. While the reporters are out covering the story, Williams drops through the window into the pressroom. Hildy and Molly Malloy (a hooker and Williams's girlfriend) hide him in a roll top desk. The other reporters press them for information, but to protect Williams, Molly jumps out a window. Burns arrives, and he and Hildy contrive to get Williams and the desk to the newspaper office. Hildy's girl, other reporters, and finally the sheriff intervene and Williams is captured. Just when Hildy and Walter are about to be jailed themselves, Pincus reappears with the Governor's reprieve for Williams. Walter and Hildy are in control and free. Walter, pretending to be surprised that Hildy sincerely wants to leave, nevertheless gives him his blessing and his own watch inscribed "To the Best Newspaperman I know"[12] as a present. After waiting for Hildy to get out the door, he has Duffy, his copy editor at the paper, wire ahead to the first stop on the rail line to have Hildy arrested for stealing his watch.

In *The Front Page,* character types, interpersonal dynamics, themes and ideas are developed that were to reappear consistently in Hecht's work. It is not my intention to ignore the contribution of MacArthur, or for that matter any of Hecht's collaborators (Hecht needed collaborators to exercise a judicial sanity). But in much the same way that Kaufman's plays may vary in collaborator but consistently reflect his own style and attitudes, so, too, do the plays and screenplays of Hecht bear the unmistakable mark of his concerns.

The basic dilemma found in *The Front Page* had already appeared in Hecht's novels. There, the Hechtian man, artist or newsman, is caught between his drive for self-actualization and the demands of the world around him: between his work and his home, between his soaring spirit and possibilities and the encroachments of age and the bourgeois civilization that always threatens him. In the films, the conflict is usually externalized into concrete forms. The inner torment that dominates the novels is minimized and more dramatic elements are emphasized. When they do appear, as for instance Cary Grant's dark ambivalence towards women and love in *Notorious* (1946), they remain attitudes and a source of conflict rather than central concerns to be explored.

In *The Front Page,* Hildy Johnson is the Hechtian man. He is acknowledged to be the best reporter both at his own paper and in the entire pool of newsmen. He is brash, fast talking, and streetwise. He knows who to bribe, where to get a drink, and assumes on principal that any government official or person in a position of authority is corrupt and should be treated like a two dollar whore. On the other hand, two dollar whores, cleaning women, and any other persons working for a living deserve a measure of respect. For all his brashness, Johnson is a rank sentimentalist, easily touched for loans, and in love. He is loyal in the manner of his profession. He loves his work and is caught by the excitement and the danger of being close to important events. When his fiancée, Peggy, complains: "It's always a big story—the biggest story in the world, and the next day everybody's forgotten it, even you!"[13] Hildy can only answer with the name of an obscure murder that only confirms her point. He is also something of a child. Any resemblance between Hildy and young Ben is intentional.

Being a newsman means being part of a professional group. While the profession of the group may change from film to film (actors, soldiers, gangsters, spies), the group itself reappears. The group has its own conventions and morality. It will protect its members from their wives or editors. The group is usually all male or male-dominated.[14] They are involved in their stories because it makes good copy, not because it affects them. As newsmen, they live outside of society with their own conventions, interests, and aesthetic sensibilities (usually ostentatiously hard-boiled). They are somewhat adolescent, escaping middle class domestic demands and entanglements. The deadline of one form or another generates an energy and tension for members of the group distinct from the tensions and drives felt by the uninitiated.

Group members are more bourgeois than they would like to admit. They are both proud and embarrassed by their nonconformist status. Journalists, as Hildy says:

> Peeking through keyholes! Running after fire engines like a lot of coach dogs! Waking people up in the middle of the night to ask them what they think of campanionate [sic] marriage. Stealing pictures off old ladies of their daughter that got raped in Oak Park. A lot of lousy, daffy, buttinskis, swelling around with holes in their pants, borrowing nickels from office boys! And for what? So a million hired girls and motormen's wives'll know what's going on.[15]

The group's unconvinced response is: "Your girl must have handed you that line." Hecht's "girl," Peggy, is the source of tension between Hildy and the group. As in many of Hecht's films, Peggy represents a number of forces: security versus the hand-to-mouth existence of the group; maturity rather than the adolescent values of the group; the threat of loss of integrity or manliness in the eyes of the group; abandonment of the profession and all it represents in terms of self-image and excitement; entering the bourgeois life; love and happiness. These are both positive and negative values, just as the exciting life of the group has its drawbacks, as Hildy's list indicates. Hildy is ambivalent about his decision, and the issues as they are presented to the audience are never totally clear-cut.

This ambivalence gives the play a complexity that rescues it from becoming juvenile. In *The Front Page,* the newspaper profession, group allegiance, the drive to get the story, and the excitement of the moment all pull Hildy to stay. At the same time, the callousness of Burns and the knowledge that there is no future in his profession and that his friends will "all end up on the copy desk—gray-haired, humpbacked slobs, dodging garnishees when you're ninety,"[16] push him to leave. His love of Peggy, his new, well-paid job (even if it is in advertising) and the secure easy life are incentives to leave, just as the claustrophobia of a life "writing poetry about Milady's drawers,"[17] and living a middle class life with his mother-in-law in New York all repell him. (If the reporters there are all "lizzies," and working for the *New York Times* is like working in a bank, what can life for a normal citizen be?)

If the reporter is loyal to his cohorts, he is even more loyal to his editor and his paper. Walter Burns adds this dimension to the conflict. Burns is the scoundrel who manipulates anyone within his reach, especially his employees. He revels in his own nastiness, and although he talks about responsibility, civic duty, and freedom of the press, his single goal is the scoop. He is even more irresponsible than Hildy because he lacks the cautionary grace of Hildy's sentimentality. All concerns are secondary to the story. Burns is Hildy's mentor and nemisis. Goaded by his fellows, Hildy tells Burns off but admits he has enjoyed all the stories Burns has tricked him into reporting and would never work for anyone else. Hildy's bravado, and his relationship with Burns, as well as the use of slang in the play is conveyed in this interchange in which Hildy talks to Burns on the telephone:

Murphy:	What's the matter? Scared of him?
Hildy:	I'll talk to the maniac. I'll talk to him with the greatest of pleasure.... Hello, Mr. Burns.
...	
Hildy:	What's that, Mr. Burns?
...	
Hildy:	Why your language is shocking, Mr. Burns.
...	
Hildy:	Now, listen, you lousy baboon. Get a pencil and paper and take this down. Get this straight because this is important, Mr. Burns. It's the Hildy Johnson curse—
...	
Hildy:	The next time I see you, no matter where I am or what I'm doing I'm going to walk right up to you and hammer on that monkey skull of yours till it rings like a Chinese gong—
McCue:	Oh boy—
Endicott:	That's telling him.
...	
Hildy:	Listen to him!
...	
Hildy:	No I ain't going to cover the hanging—I wouldn't cover the Last Supper for you—if they had it all over again in the middle of Clark Street—

Hildy: Never mind the vaseline, Jocko! It won't do you any good this time because I'm going to New York like I told you—and if you know what's good for you, you'll stay west of Gary, Indiana. A Johnson never forgets.

Hildy: (He hangs up) And that, boys, is what is known as telling the managing editor.
McCue: I'll say it is.[18]

Although the dialogue in the play is not offensive by modern standards, at the time of its initial production the play drew criticism for its use of profanity, its reference to peeping toms, policeman midwifing births, the Last Supper, sex, prostitutes, and for the final line of the play, "The son of a bitch stole my watch."[19] Brooks Atkinson, for example, remonstrated that Hecht and MacArthur's "insistence upon thrusting bespattered conversation down the throats of the audience is as superfluous as it is unpleasant."[20] The production was frequently visited by censors, and Jed Harris, the producer, found it necessary at times to run a sanitized version. Occasionally it was even necessary to invite a visiting dignitary backstage and sidetrack him with a few drinks.

The differences between Hildy and Burns are crystalized in their attitudes towards women. If Hildy is essentially a sentimentalist; Burns is a misogynist. It is not exactly that he does not like women, it is just that they cannot be trusted. (Of course, Burns does not trust men either.) When Hildy begins to realize that in the rush of events he has sent his fiancee away, Burns expresses his feelings about women as he tries to straighten Hildy out:

Walter: Listen, Hildy. Let me tell you something. *I* was in love once with my—with my—with my third wife. I treated her white—let her have a maid and everything! I was sweet to her!
Hildy: Never mind!
Walter: I trusted her. (pause) Then I let her meet a certain party on the *Tribune* and what happened? One night I came home unexpectedly—I let myself in through the bathroom window, and there they were!
Hildy: I don't want to hear about it.
Walter: The very next morning, what do I find in the *Tribune,* all over the front page? My traction story, I'd been saving for two months!
Hildy: You know a lot about women! You and your stable of tarts! You never met a decent woman! You wouldn't know what to *do* with a pure girl!
Walter: Oh, yes I would!
Hildy: You take that back!
Walter: Say, Hildy, listen! What do you think women are? *Flowers?* Take that dame that shot the dentist! And Mrs. Verymilya! Husband comes home all worn out, hungry, takes a spoonful of soup and falls dead! *Arsenic!* And Mrs. Petras! Burning her husband up in a furnace! When you've been in this business as long as I have, you'll know what women are.[21]

The audience is also ambivalent about what it wants Hildy to do. It admires Burns for his wit and cavalier control of any situation yet recognizes the selfishness and callousness that are also part of his character. Sympathy shifts back and forth during the play as the audience first hopes Hildy will get away and then hopes Burns will stop him. Burns's energy carries the audience as well as Hildy along with him. When Hildy starts to leave, Burns catches his imagination with the size and importance of their story; Hildy, as impressionable as ever, buys the whole ploy:

Walter: I...listen, Hildy, if I didn't have your interest at heart would I be wastin' time now arguin' with you? You've done somethin' big—you've stepped into a new class—
Hildy: Huh?
Walter: Listen, we'll make such monkeys out of those ward heelers that nobody will vote for them—not even their *wives*.
Hildy: Expose 'em huh—
Walter: Expose 'em! Crucify 'em! We're gonna keep Williams under cover till morning so's the *Examiner* can break the story exclusive—Then we'll let the Senator in on the capture—share the glory with him.
Hildy: I see—I see.
Walter: You've kicked over the whole City Hall like an applecart. This ain't a newspaper story—it's a career.
Hildy: Gee, I—I wasn't figuring it that way, I guess. We'll be white-haired boys, won't we?
Walter: Why, they'll be naming streets after you. You and I and the Senator, are going to *run* this town—do you understand that?
Hildy: Yeah—yeah![22]

Gradually Hildy realizes what he has thrown away in his excitement and under Walter's influence. At this point audience sympathy swings back to hoping that Hildy will meet his new deadline, the time of the train's departure. The ending of the play, with Hildy gone but Burns calling ahead to have the train stopped, leaves the issue unresolved. Since Hildy and the audience have never been sure what he should do, this suspended state is appropriate and satisfying.

To some degree, audience sympathy will vary in reaction to how the part of Hildy is interpreted. Pat O'Brien in Lewis Milestone's 1931 film version of the script played Hildy as not really wanting to leave his friends and job. Jack Lemmon in Billy Wilder's 1974 remake of the film, made it clear from the outset that his desire to leave was stronger than his will to stay.

The effectiveness of the play is built on more than slang, however. The humor of the piece is built on a lightning pace. The pace is structured into the play with overlapping dialogue, a verbal equivalent of visual montage, which constantly comments on the action and gives it texture. When the room is filled with people there are often two or three activities going on at once. Suspense is carefully maintained and action and entrances prepared for. Walter Burns's entrance is indicative of the way the play is constructed. Like Tartuffe, with whom he has much in common, Burns does not appear until halfway through the play. All the other major characters have been introduced and Burns's reputation has preceded him. When Molly Malloy throws herself out the window, everyone except Hildy rushes out. When they do, Burns is revealed standing in the doorway. Walter Kerr, in a discussion of what made the play "like a watch that laughed," says that this underplayed disclosure of Burns is:

> ... immaculate. Walter Burns has been so built up that finding him an adequate entrance is next to impossible. He can't just come on and declare himself. Furthermore, he's two of a kind. He's mean and he's funny. He's got to walk into a tough situation in order to be brutally nonchalant, which is what we think is funny about him. The machinery has not only given him and the play the right punctuation, the change of pace that refreshes even as it moves on. It has also *covered* him, kept him from being obvious while exploiting the one most obvious thing about him. You might say that the machinery has covered itself, has perfectly squared itself. We are delighted to have the man on, we are delighted to have him on at this time, we are aware that it is sleight-of-hand that has got him on, and we are as delighted by the sleight-of-hand as by the man.[23]

This ability to create and cover his technique made Hecht what Alfred Hitchcock called a "good professional." In *The Front Page,* plot contrivances are doubly covered: first by suspense and action, then by laughter. When Hecht relied on action alone to maintain audience interest he was less successful. In *Roadhouse Nights* (1930), another newspaper film, story is the most important element, but plot points by themselves can not make the film interesting. Charles Ruggles plays the newsman who, when sent off to find his recently murdered fellow worker stumbles instead on his old girlfriend, Helen Morgan, and a gang of bootleggers. Although Ruggles has a few comic scenes and Morgan and Jimmy Durante (in his first film) sing, the film is, in reality, merely a crime melodrama with a reporter and his editor thrown in. It is an opportunity for Ruggles to do a drunk routine, and the routine is amusing, but the film is contrived and lacks the energy and smoothness of *The Front Page* or others of Hecht's comedies.

While the discussion of *The Front Page* has focused on the text of the play, the observations about Hecht's work apply equally to the 1931 film. Produced by Howard Hughes and directed by Lewis Milestone, the film is more than fair adaptation of the play text with few changes of substance. The dialogue is shortened, although not laundered. The action remains very largely confined to the pressroom, which has a marvelous gritty feeling to it. The movie is considered an important early sound film, not only because of the influence of the play on comedy and newspaper films, but because Milestone incorporated great visual fluidity into the production. The camera moves easily around the room getting many shots in depth, catching levels and changes of action. Numerous reaction shots of the different newsmen at their places help maintain

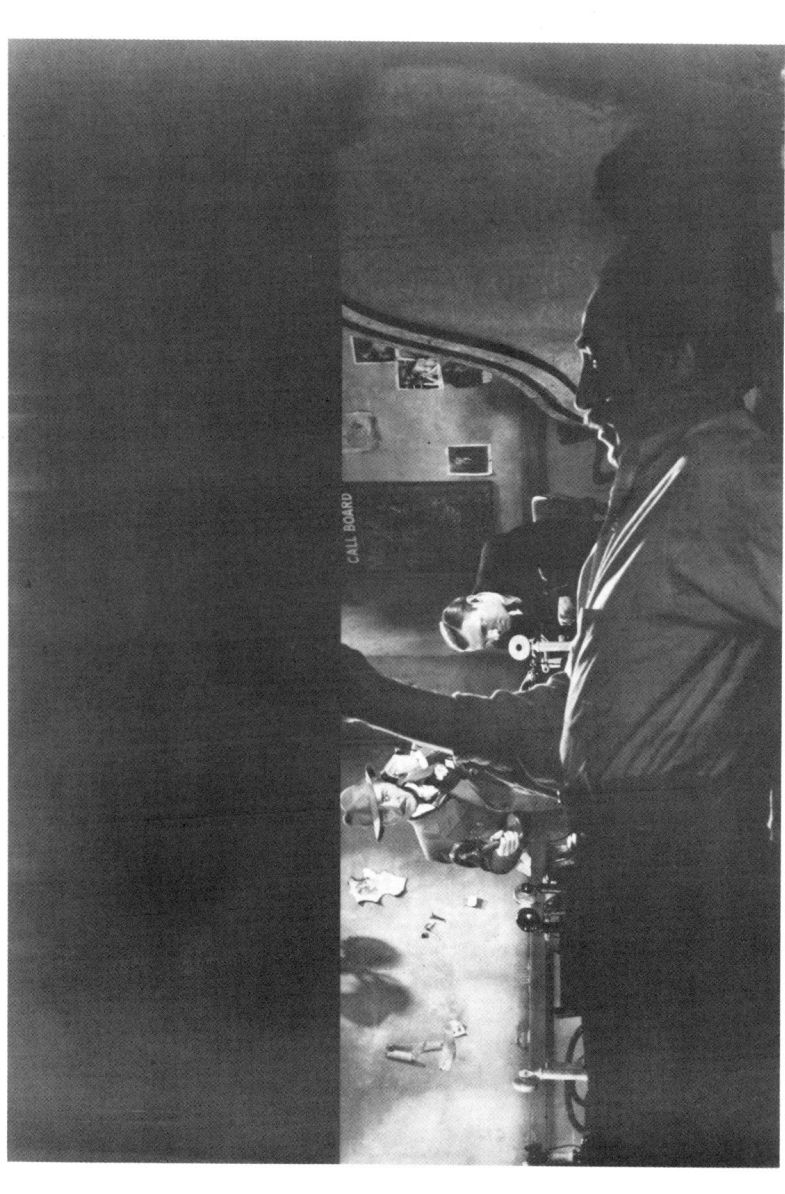

5. *The Front Page* (1931). Editor Walter Burns (Adolph Menjou) and reporter Hildy Johnson (Pat O'Brien) hide escaped murderer Earl Williams (George Stone) in a desk. *The Front Page* was one of the first sound films to free the camera and shoot from interesting subjective angles, as in this shot from inside the desk. (Photo: Museum of Modern Art/Film Stills Archive courtesy United Artists.)

a feeling of the layers of action in the room, without relying on long static shots. Milestone uses a number of low angle or oddly placed camera positions for effect, such as below the trap door on the gallows to catch the sandbag coming through it toward the camera. Usually these shots are positive additions to the film and help sustain visual interest and tempo, although at times, such as when he bounces his camera up and down to keep time with a song, his straining for effects shows. Adolph Menjou is a slick Burns and Pat O'Brien has a nice sense of innocence. The dialogue is delivered at a rapid but effective pace and the overlapping dialogue is retained. The film was nominated for the Academy Award for Best Picture and Best Director, and Menjou was nominated for Best Actor.

Most of the changes in text have to do with cuts, paraphrases, or insertions of different names (such as the addition of Mr. Benchley who is still at the bar, Judge Mankiewicz, or George Kid Cukor) but the delayed entrance of Burns has been cut. Burns is seen in the opening scene trying to find Hildy. He and Hildy have a scene mentioned in the text, drinking at Pollack Mike's after Burns catches Hildy by turning in a false alarm knowing that Hildy will always turn out to cover a fire. While the effect of the anticipated entrance is lost, the establishment of Burns and his relationship with Hildy earlier in the film provides a safer structure for the action. *Design for Living* (1933), *Twentieth Century* (1934), and *His Girl Friday* (1940) all vary from their original sources by starting at an earlier point in the plot allowing for more action and lessening the need to provide lengthy exposition. Starting with Burns also allows the audience to see his office, the presses, a speakeasy entrance and a brothel where Burns owes two dollars. (The entrance to the brothel is ingeniously hidden behind a three-way mirror.) Most of the cutaway shots from the pressroom are to action mentioned in the text.

The film retains the tone of cynicism edged with sentiment found in the play. Athough *The Front Page* has been cited as a fine attack on the technique of yellow journalism, ultimately it glorifies the newsman. Hecht and MacArthur were writing about their first great love and they honor the hard-boiled attitudes of the newsmen, who become slightly heroic, more dedicated, faster talking and wittier than mortals. While they may be callous enough to demand that the hanging be moved up from seven to five in the morning so they can make the early edition, they are against the corruption of the government. This makes their cynicism appear to be a healthy dose of reality rather than misanthropy.

The authors also admire Burns. He is such a perfect scoundrel that he is more to be marvelled at than judged. In the same way, Hecht and many other screenwriters admired studio heads like Irving Thalberg who did the most to destroy the writer in Hollywood. Hecht and MacArthur had a love for any true Machiavellian character who could wield power without scruples. Their judgment was suspended in such cases.

There are other reasons Burns is respected in the play. Even though he is an editor, and therefore Hildy's nemesis, he is still a newpaperman and a part of the initiate group. He is still opposed to authority and to any establishment, even as he himself represents a position of authority. While he manipulates the reporter, he is working towards the same goals and deadlines. The authors create a sympathetic villain by attacking him without judging him. It does not matter whether the target is the newspaper business, the theatre (*The Twentieth Century,* 1933), the army (*Gunga Din,* 1939), or Mexican revolutionaries (*Viva Villa,* 1934), good will, if not humor, will be maintained in the face of callousness and cupidity as long as no judgments are made about the character. For instance, Oscar Jaffe in *The Twentieth Century* is just as unscrupulous as Walter Burns in trying to get his star working for him again, but Jaffe is never compared with anyone better in the film and so his antics are accepted as inspired rather than evaluated as dangerous. There is also the comfort of knowing that despite their realistic texture, the characters are essentially comic creations and, therefore, distanced from the audience.

In fact, there are very few innocents in Hecht's films. It is a callous world the characters inhabit, and, at best, the hero is a half-innocent like Hildy. He thinks he is as cynical as Burns, but his sophistication is a facade that hides his sentimentality. Burns can shrug off Molly going out the window, but Hildy is shaken by it. Even Hildy's love of his tough profession has a sentimentality about it.

Hildy is an admirable character compared with other Hechtian heroes. What Hecht manages to do in his best work, in *Erik Dorn* as in *The Front Page* and *The Twentieth Century,* is to make the audience sympathetic to a protagonist who is essentially an unsympathetic individual. He does this in part by making him the best person in the universe of the work. Walter Burns and Hildy Johnson may be callous individuals but there is no one on stage who is more sympathetic. The possible exception is Peggy, but the audience is so ambivalent towards the life she represents, and she is so thinly drawn and is on stage so briefly that she does not have the weight given to Burns or even the other reporters.

Love can be a redeeming value in Hecht's works, but there are two kinds of loves. The first is the love that draws the individual out of the group and into the trap of middle class domesticity. There is a suggestion of this in *The Front Page.* It is more clearly stated in *Gunga Din* where Joan Fontaine is literally wrapping up Douglas Fairbanks, Jr. in a bolt of fabric which clings to him as he follows his friends. Her love will eventually destroy his manhood. The conflict in this film between the group and love and home is clearly weighted towards the camaraderie of the soldiers and the good times to be had fighting an enjoyable battle. Uncomplicated by an ambivalence towards an unscrupulous boss, the conflict is stated in simple terms: honor, friendship, excitement, youth, adventure, and fun versus helping make the curtains. If the choice were not clear enough, there is the native boy, Sam Jaffe in a napkin, who aspires to nothing more than to achieve the position that Fairbanks is so foolishly ready to give up. In *The Front Page,* as in many of the comedies, the ambivalence towards the male virtues saves the film from adolescent wish fulfillment.

At times there is the possibility of finding love within the group. The lover could be a fellow worker or at least someone who shares the same spirit (but always of the opposite sex). While this type of woman does not appear in *The Front Page* (with the possible exception of the minor character Molly Malloy as a match for Williams), *The Twentieth Century, Design for Living,* and much of the screwball comedy mode is based on this kind of coupling. Bringing the lovers together within the protection of an unconventional group, even if that group comprises only the two lovers, is the solution to the protagonist's need to mature while maintaining his credentials as a jaded cynic and initiated outsider.

This enlargement of the exclusive male group to include a female comrade and lover is the development from *The Front Page* to *Design for Living* or *The Twentieth Century.* The story evolves by combining the love interest into the plot as a positive rather than a negative force. If *The Front Page* is melodrama played as comedy, then *Design for Living* or *The Twentieth Century* is comedy taken to romance. If *The Front Page* is a love story about Hildy trying to leave Walter, a peer group adolescent love story, then *Design for Living* or *The Twentieth Century* is a heterosexual love story, with the exclusivity of the adolescent group incorporated into the love affair. The result is a movement from urban newspaper comedy to hardball screwball comedy.

4

Design for Living

In 1933 Hecht collaborated with Ernst Lubitsch on an adaptation of Noel Coward's *Design for Living*. Originally a dry drawingroom comedy, in Hecht's hands it became an antic romantic farce, a screwball comedy. The infusion of Hecht's cynical wit, American energy, and slangy dialogue even affected Lubitsch's style of polished light European sex farces. The continental characters and situation of two artists in love with the same girl became a story about American Bohemian artists. *Design for Living* establishes the same situation Hildy Johnson faced in *The Front Page*. At first the choice for the men seems to be between love and friendship, but eventually, by including the girl as a comrade, their conflict disappears without sacrifice. That the girl is the lover of both men only makes the solution more satisfying.

Unfortunately the film is usually compared to Coward's original play or to Lubitsch's other films as patterns which it fails to equal. On the rare occasion when it is praised, it is as an oddity rather than as one of the first screwball comedies. Although Robert Sklar suggests it may be the first, Donald McCaffrey is more typical of scholars in not even mentioning the film in his discussion of the genre.

When the film is compared by critics to the play it is said to be: less sophisticated in its wit and milieu, less mature in its thought, less adult or erotic in its tone, and less tightly constructed. Although the film was written specifically for Gary Cooper, Miriam Hopkins, and Fredric March, their performances are downgraded in favor of the stagework of Alfred Lunt, Lynn Fontanne, and Noel Coward, for whom Coward tailored the play.

Lubitsch was known for his superb control of dramatic irony (in visual and aural detail as well as in basic structuring); he approached his comedies with an amoral, nonideological, bemused understanding of human frailty. His comedies and musicals, such as *The Love Parade* (1929), *The Smiling Lieutenant* (1931), and *Trouble in Paradise* (1932), set a style at Paramount and in the film industry. Because *Design for Living* deviates from this old world mold and is instead broadened into an "inevitably inferior" American idiom and context, it is thought to lack the delicate "Lubitsch touch." Although their styles and interests actually differed widely, Coward's play was thought to be perfect material for Lubitsch, and this expectation further added to the misunderstanding of the film's point of view.

These critical preconditions have become aesthetic biases which prevent a more balanced evaluation of the film. If approached as a screwball comedy, *Design for Living* shows Hecht's characters, dialogue and attitudes (such as his reversal of Coward's class snobbery or his greater use of economic tensions) to be positive rather than negative factors. The balancing of Lubitsch's world-weary cynicism and visual skills with Hecht's flare for language and antiauthoritarian cynicism animates the film without the nastiness that marks some of Hecht's solo efforts.

Because, unlike *The Front Page*, Hecht adapted *Design for Living* from a work by another author, his contribution to the film is difficult to measure, although with the exception of one line (a toast to "Our Immortal Souls") all of the original dialogue was discarded. (Hecht said he also inserted lines from two plays by Coward, *The Vortex* (1923) and *Hay Fever* (1924), but if he did, they do not stand out.) An understanding of the changes in characterization, tone, and attitude wrought by Hecht can be clarified by comparing the film with the original play.

Although they differ widely in construction and attack, the basic situation remains the same. In Paris in the early thirties two artists (a painter and a playwright) are in love with and are loved by the same girl. She has an affair with one, then the other, and finally leaves them both to marry an older friend and confidant. The artists, who had been fighting over the girl, are reconciled in a long drinking scene. They tour the world by freighter and arrive in New York to rescue the girl from her middle class life and her straightlaced husband. At the end they are reunited and laughing immoderately. The major difference in plot between play and film is that while the play has a late point of attack, beginning when the girl leaves one artist for the other, the film traces the relationship from the moment the girl meets the two men. The play takes place in six long scenes while the film is made up of a number of short episodes.

The characters in the play are Otto Sylvus (Alfred Lunt) the painter, Leo Mercure (Noel Coward) the playwright, Gilda (Lynn Fontanne) an interior decorator, and Ernest Friedman (Campbell Gullan) an art dealer. The action moves from Paris (Act I) to London (Act II) and finally to New York (Act III) in increasingly affluent surroundings, although the first act set is already comfortable since both artists are relatively sucessful when the play opens.

The play premiered in Cleveland on January 2, 1933, and in New York on January 24, where it ran for 133 performances. Although it was well received it was not the unqualified success that critics of the film remember. The play was criticized both for its writing and for its subject matter. Those who questioned the writing observed that for all its laughs there were long stretches of idle chatter and exposition. Act I and much of Act II were over before the real comic set pieces, the love scene and the drinking bout, began to propel the play. Prior to this point only expert acting and burlesque of lower class characters and institutions carried the play. Act III also had its weaknesses, as Brooks Atkinson noted:

> Unfortunately for the uses of artificial comedy, establishing this triangular situation involves considerable sobriety. All through the first act Mr. Coward writes as earnestly as a psychologist. Through a long stretch of the third act he surrenders to the patter of ordinary folk and incidentally, to ordinary actors who can make little of the wrangling impertinence of the lines.[1]

The thematic content of the play was also criticized. A few agreed with Ernest's comment in the last act: "a disgusting, three-sided erotic hotchpotch,"[2] and were disturbed by the morality of the triangle. Others were annoyed by the bitterness and the sophisticated superiority of the trio to the world around them. *The Times* commented when the play opened in London in 1939 that the play "remains, in the aggregate of its parts, good entertainment, though with a bitter taste and sometimes with a callow 'daring.'"[3]

Although the morality of the triangle of lovers was touched on and the topic of marriage earnestly discussed, these issues were left unresolved. The laughter that ends the play leaves open the problem of the lovers' future. For that matter, the secondary theme which occupies much of the second act, the responsibility and problem of success and continued growth, is more talked about than explored or developed.

Atkinson and others were willing to overlook script weaknesses, which were apparently made up for in the playing. While he comments, "Occasionally Mr. Coward appears to be asking you to look upon the volatile emotions of his characters as real, and that—if it is true—would be a pity," Atkinson ventured that although it might be decadent it was "a play of skill, art, and clairvoyance, performed by an incomparable trio of comedians."[4] While Coward did not want the design taken seriously, neither did he want the play dismissed as mindless entertainment. In Frank Swinnerton's *The Georgian Scene,* Coward protested:

> I do resent very deeply, on my own behalf and on the behalf of those young writers who are sincerely attempting to mirror contemporary life honestly and truthfully... that this weight of bourgeois ignorance and false sentimentality should not be allowed to force those in authority to crush down rising talent for the sole reason that its outlook doesn't quite conform with the moral traditions of twenty-five years ago, but that it should be encouraged in every possible way by the Press.[5]

In a more recent evaluation of the play, Milton Levin in his study of Coward's work comments that this is Coward's most serious comedy, one in which he "raises and discusses questions about morality in more than a passing light hearted way."[6] Levin goes on to point out that although Coward wants his characters to be taken seriously he does not "intelligibly" resolve the issues he raises, either of the sexual triangle or of the problems of success.

By far the most scathing attack on the play was George Jean Nathan's. In an essay, "Several Writers for the Theatre,"[7] he says that although he has heard for years of Coward's wit his own analysis of the play shows only rehashed vaudeville humor elevated by namedropping masquerading as sophistication, and trivialities dressed up as philosophy. Nathan provided sixteen examples of dialogue from Coward's play and their antecedents in vaudeville. And although Nathan's comments may seem extreme, they have a particular relevance to the history of the play. According to Fred Guiles in *Hanging On in Paradise,* it was this article that turned Lubitsch against the play after he had purchased it for £7000, leaving him to adopt the opinion that Coward was nothing more than a "cheap vaudevillian."[8]

Because Lubitsch usually developed a script with his writers, the final product was more than dialogue and plot, it was a detailed blueprint for the film. Camera angles and the particular abilities of the actors already engaged for the picture were considered. Lubitsch knew what he wanted from his actors, and, in rehearsal as in story conference, he would invariably act out their parts for them, male and female.

Always asking "Is it hilarious? It must be hilarious!"[9] Lubitsch and his collaborators would totally transform the original source material. Samson Raphaelson says that of the original play used for *The Shop Around the Corner* not a scene or a line remains.[10] Although this was a common practice, when Lubitsch and Hecht left only one line of *Design for Living* in the final film, it caused some consternation among the critics who seemed to care for the reputation of British playwrights but were not at all concerned about the sanctity of the work of Eastern European writers.

Hecht wrote a piece on working with Lubitsch which was released by Paramount's publicity department. In it he describes Lubitsch as "having the look of a creditor" and of "giving one the impression of a kangaroo on a pogo stick" when he danced, and of pirouetting, leaping, or bursting into tears when contradicted during collaboration. Hecht reports that when Lubitsch does not like a line "His elfin face fills with reproach and he lies tossing for sometimes as long as several hours, moaning, 'Dull, dull, oh so dull...! No good, Ben... terrible! Oh, how dull it is!" If Hecht sneered at him he would take to his bed. Finally, after noting that Lubitsch was the best director in films, Hecht finishes with an account of Lubitsch's genius as a collaborator. Hecht offered a plot turn and Lubitsch asked: "'You think that's good?' I said I did. 'That's the kind of suggestion people send me in the mail.'"[11] The piece is a delightful concoction intended as whimsy but Weinberg had to convince Raphaelson that Hecht was only being playful. Raphaelson offered Lubitsch's version of working with Hecht:

> I had asked him, "How did you get along with Hecht?" And he said, "Oh, fine, fine, Sam, fine—he's very able, very able." "No problems?" I said. "Vell, in the beginning," he said, "you know, ve vasn't used to each udder. I'd say to him, 'Look, de vay I usually vork, Ben, is ve get together, ve meet in the morning at a reasonable hour, we have a secretary and ve vork together." And Hecht replied, "Not me, I'm not going to sit around and have you tell me how to write my stuff. I go home and I write the stuff and I bring it to you. Then, if you don't like it, we fight it out." "So I say, 'O.K., Ben.'" said Lubitsch, "'Go ahead. Dis is de general feeling how I vant, how I feel, de opening scene.'" And he explains it. "'You agree?'" "'Sure,'" said Hecht, "'I'll work on it.'" "So he came two days later vit de scene," says Lubitsch. "And you know, how can a man, in two days... do anything... anyway I vas interested so I read it and I say, 'Now come on, Ben, for God's sake, you don't call dis writing.' And he says, 'What's the matter with it?' He gets sore. So ve talk a little bit, and ve talk a little bit more, and den ve talk a little bit more, and pretty soon Hecht and I are working every day from ten o'clock in the morning."[12]

Raphaelson thinks that Hecht became intrigued by Lubitsch and enjoyed the collaboration. The give-and-take of conference writing was one Hecht preferred when writing with friends he respected. In the publicity release Hecht said that working with Lubitsch had taught him "something very vital about films. What it was, I don't remember—maybe it was how to write them. It's a pity I've forgotten, but on the other hand, Mr. Lubitsch hasn't, you may be sure." Even beyond the publicity bravado of the statement, a fondness and respect of Lubitsch is apparent. Weinberg feels that the Hecht-MacArthur producer-directorial collaboration that closely followed *Design for Living* and produced *The Scoundrel* and *Crime Without Passion* was in some way the result of the lessons Hecht learned from Lubitsch. The latter film, Weinberg says, was brilliant and "would certainly have earned for him the approving smile of the master."[13]

Design for Living was filmed at an awkward period in Hollywood censorship. The Legion of Decency was not formed until 1934 but the bowdlerizing forces were already at work on what were considered the more blatant offenders such as Mae West. *Design for Living* is considered by some, such as Herman Weinberg and Fred Guiles, to have been affected by the enforcement of the production code. Others, such as Molly Haskell and Ed Lowry (in his program notes for a film showing at the University of Texas)[14] believe the film instead to have maintained the open attitude towards sex of the earlier period. Haskell believes it to have been more defined by Lubitsch's general approach than by external censorship. Lowry suggests that *Design for Living,* with its wholly sexual subject matter, was actually one of the films that provoked the pure of mind to take action against the movies. Lubitsch rarely had trouble with censors because his style and approach to material artfully suggested sex without stating it. His ability to use visual metaphor in lieu of verbal statement, his distancing of material into a foreign and often fairytale milieu, and his assumption of amorality as a basic condition on which the films were based, sidestepped the censors rather than met them head on. This approach may have made *Design for Living* seem outwardly less open than the play while it was as suggestive and even more positive in its sexual attitudes. The divergence in attitude between play and film, however, stems not from censorship but from a difference in world view. The film is not merely a bowdlerized version of the play nor does it lack the play's sophistication. The film has a sophistication that springs from its adult attitudes towards reality, language, and relationships rather than from self-conscious wit or naughtiness, and these differences in perspective are consistent with the elements of screwball comedy.

Although still based in Paris, and, therefore, slightly exotic in its setting, the characters of the film are all Americans mirroring American attitudes and realities as firmly as if the play were set in Chicago. (Richard Corliss argues that, in fact, it is set in Chicago.[15]) The language of the play is discarded and replaced by hard edged colloquial American patter. The social attitudes in the play—that artists are part of an upper class elite; that lower classes should be the butts of jokes; that the cardinal sin is to lack taste and be a bore—are replaced by Hecht's Bohemian viewpoint—artists are the sniping enemies of the bourgeois; the upper class is merely the middle class in a tuxedo: stodgy, puritan, and infantile; the poor are usually sharp enough to swindle the heroes. The lucky characters in the play who always seem to have a private source of funds are thrust into the more realistic world of the Depression where the money for dinner may only buy frankfurters. Sex is not sinful, dirty or dangerous, but fun and healthy. To be eccentric and unconventional is the proper way to live because it is more fun and not because those who possess eccentricity are morally or artistically superior to the rest of society. The character relationships change from those of a play dominated by Gilda's predatory femaleness to a more balanced set of male relationships that are extended to include her. Rather than a cold interior decorator of the soul she is a practical commercial artist able to work with the men as well as love them, and is thus included as a comrade as well as a lover. These attitudes, particularly towards sex and sex roles, were essential to the world of screwball comedy.

The film is carefully structured to underline these perceptions and attitudes. The male relationship, for instance, is strengthened through the telling of the story from the meeting of Gilda rather than from the moment of crisis when they are estranged from one another. The film's variant concerns are displayed in a vastly different comic stance rooted in its social attitudes. Balanced and compact, it grows organically with little wasted movement. The visual style of the film, where the attitudes of Lubitsch are most clear, works in concert with the dialogue to achieve a unified effect. Since the film was a collaborative effort, to isolate the contributions of Lubitsch and Hecht into visual and verbal categories would be simplistic and misleading. However, by noting the changes made in the material in bringing it to the screen and by comparing these changes with the habitual thrust of Lubitsch's style, a rough understanding of how Hecht's attitudes and skills affected the film can be made.

Only approximately one-third of the scenes from the play survive the transposition to film and each of these is compressed to a fraction of its original length. Although this is due in part to the shorter length of the film as compared to the three-act play, the differences are more the result of dissimilar approaches to plot, thought, and character. In contrast to the play's late point of attack, the film begins with Gilda Farrell (Miriam Hopkins in the Fontanne role—the film supplies her with a last name) meeting Thomas Chambers (Fredric March in the Leo Mercure/Coward role) and George Curtis (Gary Cooper in the Otto Sylvus/Lunt role) on a train bound for Paris. The film traces the development of the triangle relationship and only reaches the confrontation with which the play opens at a point more than half way through the film's overall length.

Lubitsch explained that he started so early in the story because:

> I think the cinema should not talk about events in the past. That is why I have changed completely the beginning of the stage play. On the stage it was dull. One was told where they met, what they had done for many years, how they had loved. I must show these things but in their proper order.... The cinema should have nothing to do with the imperfect tense.[16]

More than the simple telling of the story in immediate terms is achieved by this arrangement, however. At the same time the love relationship is developed, the relationship between the two men is also explored. In the play the two men are only on stage in moments of confrontation until the drinking scene at the end of the second act. One is asked to accept their love for each other on faith since they are only seen in acrimonious quarrels. In the film the rivalry still provides a basic tension, but it is strongly rooted in a friendship that can be observed from the first sequence.

The opening scene contains many of the elements that define these relationships. Tom and George are sleeping in a compartment, feet propped up on the opposite bench. Gilda comes in and sits facing them. She takes her pad out and sketches them; she props her stockingclad legs between them and goes to sleep. George's hand falls on her leg; he dreams. George wakes up to find a pair of legs next to him and an attractive woman asleep in front of him. He awakens Tom. They look at her sketches. With increasing interest they see sketches of Napoleon, Napoleon in his suspenders, Napoleon with his trousers off. They are looking forward to the next picture but find only the sketch of themselves. They are disappointed. She awakens and in the first dialogue of the scene they argue in French about the sketches. She tries to explain that Fredric March's face is distorted because it is a caricature. Finally, in exasperation she says, "Oh, nuts." The men look at one another and begin to hum the "Star Spangled Banner." They introduce themselves. Gilda recognizes George's name from an exhibit of his paintings:

Gil: Oh, let me see, Lady Godiva wasn't it.... I saw it with a friend of mine. She loved it. We haven't spoken since.
Tom: I wouldn't consider her one of your greatest admirers.
Gil: Are you a painter, too?
Tom: Oh, no, not me. I'm a playwright. I write unproduced plays. Very good of that kind.
Geo: Why didn't you like my picture?
Gil: It's smart aleck. You're wise-cracking with paints. It simply reeks of originality. Lady Godiva riding a bicycle.
Tom: I know what she means. It is a little hard on Lady Godiva's historical background.
Geo: Shut up. I see.... Lady Godiva doesn't belong on a bicycle, but it's O.K. to put Napoleon in a Kaplan and McGuire two-fifty non-wrinkling union suit.
Tom: Quite right. That's not history. And, if I may say so, they do wrinkle.
Gil: I'm a commercial artist. I'm being paid for telling the world that if Napoleon were alive he would wear Kaplan and McGuire two-fifty non-wrinkling underwear.
Geo: Pure hooey.
Gil: You're wasting your time painting for art galleries. You should get in contact with some bicycle manufacturer. You'd clean up. I'll give you a slogan. "Join Lady Godiva on our tandem."
Tom: Don't say nuts. Not to a lady.
(Dissolve to the three of them moving down the platform.)
Geo: Hurry up Gilda. Shake a leg.
Tom: It's amazing how a few insults can bring people together in three hours.
Gil: It was certainly good to hear all the names you called me. I haven't heard them since I left father and mother.
Geo: What we want to know is, do you like us better than Kaplan and McGuire.
Tom: Let me tell you, Curtis and Chambers deliver the goods.

At the station she meets Max (Edward Everett Horton). The men decide that he is not Kaplan, McGuire or Napoleon.

Much is accomplished in this brief scene. First, the initial meeting is fixed in our minds. The insulting playful tone of their conversation establishes the way they deal with one another. Tom and George's easy banter establishes their closeness and familiarity. The dialogue itself establishes all three as firmly American, colloquial and idiosyncratic in their speech. There is a playfulness that undercuts the possible pretension of the lines. They are not trying to be more witty and sophisticated than one another as in Coward's play but instead

6. *Design For Living* (1933). Director Ernst Lubitsch (with cigar) and his cast: Gary Cooper, Miriam Hopkins, and Fredric March. (Photo: Museum of Modern Art/Film Stills Archive courtesy Paramount.)

there is a self-mocking attitude which displays an understanding that sophistication is merely another empty pose.

The scene is not conveyed totally through dialogue, however. The use of the stockingclad legs between the two men is a perfect visual metaphor for the action of the film, a "Lubitsch touch." Lubitsch commonly withholds information from his audience to set up an expectation. By undercutting the moment he creates humor. Here this is accomplished in dialogue as the opening of the film in French is immediately undercut by Gilda's, "Oh, Nuts." Tom and George's pleasure in finding a compatriot abroad is shared by the audience whose expectation of a certain rarified tone (set up by the French) is also undercut by the switching not only to English but to a relaxed vernacular. That Gilda says "Nuts" (something Tom cautions George not to do in front of a lady) is particularly important in making her a comrade rather than merely a sexual object. This is the thrust as well of the final conversation on the platform. She has enjoyed trading insults, and they want her to team up with them. There is not only a quality of expatriots banding together here but also a recognition of kindred souls that does not extend to Max (even though he is another American abroad).

The nature of their work is also quickly and deftly explored. Gilda is a commercial artist. She is practical, knows the angles, and immediately begins to give advice. Tom writes unproduced plays, a fact that he seems to take some pride in. George paints seriously, but his mixing of Lady Godiva and a bicycle speaks more of the playfulness of the Dadaists than of either the serious intentions of Coward's Otto or of our image of the American painter abroad seriously pursuing his art.

In the next scene, Max, who is one of Mencken's Booboisie, visits Tom in an attempt to dissuade him from seeing Gilda. Tom greets him with a hearty, "Plunkett Incorporated! Welcome to Bohemia." The only result of the meeting is that Tom uses Max's carefully wrought aphorism, "Immorality may be fun, but it isn't fun enough to take the place of one hundred percent virtue and three square meals a day," as a curtain line in his new play, *Goodnight Bassington*. The statement, used throughout the film as a comic device, perfectly encapsulates Max's philosophy.

Tom's "Welcome to Bohemia" can be taken as more than just a flippant greeting. It is also consistent with his personal philosophy, as is his reference to Max as "Plunkett Incorporated." It is not merely in nationality and speech habits but in artistic viewpoint that Tom and George differ from Leo and Otto. For Leo and Otto, success is defined as adulation, respect, and cash returns. If they were once Bohemians, that time is past when the play begins and their problem is how to handle success and the loss of youth. Tom and George are still youthful and unrecognized, but even if they were older the recognition they would seek would come from different quarters than Leo and Otto's.

George and Tom think of themselves as Bohemians. The meaning of this in the film is as vague as it became for Hecht. Hecht thought of himself as a Bohemian and a Dadaist. His experience of European artistic life was not Paris in the thirties but rather George Grosz and Berlin in 1919 at the height of the Dadaist surge. Above all he appreciated the Dadaist's ability to laugh and make fun of all cultural and artistic stuffiness. As journalist and author in Chicago, he attempted to follow the Dadaist example: holding a literary debate with Max Bodenheim on the topic, "Anyone who attends literary debates is an imbecile"; or wanting to dedicate a work "To Warren Gamaliel Harding, with the affectionate hope that its reading will afford him the keen diversion that the reading of his speeches has afforded the author."[17] It would not be hard to imagine Hecht, had he been a painter, putting Lady Godiva on a bicycle.

Bohemia for Hecht became a general concept, not a particular set of ideas or an historical locale or period. It was an iconoclasm, an antiauthoritarian urge in which the gesture, the thumbing of the nose, was more important than the motivation as long as the target was well entrenched, powerful, and humorless. When Hecht entitled a book of his reminiscences *Letters From Bohemia* (1954), he could include such diverse figures as George Grosz, George Anthiel, Gene Fowler, Charles MacArthur, H. L. Mencken, Max Bodenheim, and Sherwood Anderson without any question of basic terms although they are united only in their sometime, and often very quiet, attack on authority.

An inherent part of the Bohemianism of Tom and George is their chronic lack of funds. This immediately separates them from Coward's elite and connects them with the reality of the Depression (and with the reporters in *The Front Page*). They are forced to live on a diet of frankfurters, with little left over for extras. When George is looking for a few francs for the laundry, Tom itemizes their expenses:

Tom: Two cans of sardines, 5 francs; Madame Paparino, blackmail, 7 francs 50; no laundry.
Geo: That's fine, I haven't got a clean shirt to my name.
Tom: Clean shirt? What's up, a romance?
Geo: I'm not talking about pajamas, I'm talking about a clean shirt. I don't want to go around looking like a ragpicker.

Later, when Tom receives the one hundred pound advance on his play, the money is equally as important as the success it symbolizes. Gilda supports herself only by her living as a commercial artist. When she gives up her work to live with Tom and George, she gives up that income.

By comparison, Coward's characters are well off. Leo and Otto's years of scrimping, however dire they might have been, are only referred to, never demonstrated, and Gilda has no money problems because she has a small private income. Money is never an issue. People are assumed to have it. In the film, the characters' endemic lack of money is integral to character and action. This continual concern for funds would have been familiar to a Depression film audience. Since everybody is well off in the play, characters are defined by personal taste and creativity. Ernest is not worse than Leo or Otto because of his wealth but is scored for his lack of creativity, mercenary way of life, and middle class morality and life style. So, too, are the characters in New York. Their sin is that they are boors not that they are the idle rich.

George and Tom's actual work is less important than their attitude about their work, which is consistently a playful one. It is also germane that Tom dominates the conversation with Max not by being more sophisticated, but merely by making fun of Max's stuffiness, clothing, and attention to social convention.

Tom and George finally realize that they have both been seeing Gilda. After an argument in which Tom tells George, "It's quite apparent beyond any question that you have behaved in this question as a common ordinary rat," they decide they should not let a "little bit of feminine fluff" come between them:

> Geo: I've been listening to these halfwitted dramas of yours for eleven years.
> Tom: And I've grown cockeyed looking at those humpty-dumpty pictures of yours.
> Geo: We should give up all this on account of some girl we met on a train?
> ...
> Tom: No more clean shirts?
> Geo: We ignore her fifty-fifty.
> Tom: Fine.
> Geo: Sacrifice helps an artist.
> Tom: Exactly. The sorrows of life are the joys of art.

They agree not to see Gilda and if they must mention her to refer to her as Miss Farrell, but when the phone rings, they both race to answer it. Gilda will come the next day. They busy themselves cleaning the apartment, each trying to display his own work prominently.

The next day Gilda controls the interview by playing the roles of sultry seductress, indulgent mother, innocent victim of love and comrade in arms, all with equal relish. She dramatically throws herself onto a couch only to have clouds of dust destroy the intended effort. She confesses.

> Gil: I'm so nervous. Couldn't we all be a little more (pause) nonchalant.... I came here to make a confession, a confession hard to make at eleven o'clock in the morning.
> ...
> A thing happened to me that usually happens to men. You see, a man can meet two, three, or even four women and fall in love with all of them and then by a process of an interesting elimination he is able to decide which one he prefers, but a woman must decide purely on instinct, guess work, if she wants to be considered nice. Oh, it's quite alright for her to try on a hundred hats before she picks one out....

Tom:	Very fine, but which chappeau do you want madame.
Gil:	Both. You see, George, you're sort of like a ragged straw hat with a very soft lining. A little bit out of shape. Very dashing to look at, very comfortable to wear. And you, Tom, piquant, perched over one eye, and has to be watched on windy days. And both so becoming. Oh, I'm the most unhappy woman in the world.
Tom:	(to George) Poor girl, she's in a rather tough spot.

Tom and George agree that it's a "pitiful situation." They argue about which of them is more sincere in his proposal of self-sacrifice. Gilda stops them and suggests they discuss it as if it were a "disarmament conference." While they munch hungrily on rather phallic frankfurters (the only thing they can afford), Gilda, her mouth stuffed, says:

Gil:	Well, boys, it's the only thing we can do.
Geo:	O.K.
Tom:	Agreed.
Geo:	It may be a bit difficult in the beginning....
Tom:	But it can be worked out.
Gil:	Oh, it'll be grand.
Geo:	Save lots of time.
Tom:	And confusion.

She proposes that she manage their work, giving up her own job. She is going to force them to do better work. She will be a "Mother of the Arts." Her children agree, and she kisses each on the forehead. "No Sex. It's a gentlemen's agreement."

The problem of choosing between love and friendship has been circumvented, but the truce does not last long. One source of humor in this scene and throughout the film is this reversal of normal roles: Gilda is the aggressor, a gentleman, "Mademoiselle D'Artagnan." She takes a Margaret Anderson role, telling the boys their work is "rotten" but promoting it well. Tom's play is accepted for production in London and his departure throws George and Gilda together. The inevitable occurs, and Tom is left with a successful play but no lover. Some time later he returns to Paris and finds George away in Nice. He has forgiven George but not Gilda. When she asks why, he explains: "George betrayed me for you. Without wishing to flatter you, I understood that. I can still understand it. But you betrayed me for George— an incredible choice." Ego and not morality is at issue. They are drawn to one another, and the inevitable happens again.

It is only at this point, halfway through the film's ninety-minute length that the opening of the play has been reached. George returns; Gilda, distraught, slips out the back way leaving a note for each. She leaves them for a number of reasons, not the least of which is her desire not to break up the men's friendship. Her real confusion, however, is romantic. Unable to decide between them, she is also unable to accept the morality of loving both. In the note she asks them to "be nice, and let me be nice."

In the play, a great deal of time is spent emphasizing that they all love one another. The scene in the film is much shorter since it enjoys the luxury of having established the relationships over the course of the story up to that point. There is also a sense in the film that it is bad form to be overly sentimental. In the play, the scene takes place in London, and Gilda also suffers from a general malaise. She is leaving, she tells Ernest, because she is being drowned by the frivolous life and needs to regain her roots. To do so, she intends to go to Berlin. Instead, she goes to New York with Ernest. How Ernest's mercenary business and society life style is superior to the one she is fleeing is never pointed out.

Tom takes his second loss of Gilda philosophically. George does not. Tom had tried to point out the dramatic possibilities in the scene and suggested that George's furniture breaking habit would not help.

Tom: That's one way of meeting the situation. Shipping clerk comes home, finds Mrs. with boarder. He breaks dishes. It's pure burlesque. Then there's another way. Intelligent artist returns unexpectedly, finds treacherous friends, both discuss the pros and cons of the situation in grownup dialogue. High class comedy, enjoyed by everybody.
Geo: There's a third way. I'll kick your teeth out and tear your head off and beat some decency into you.
Tom: Cheap melodrama, very dull.
(George slugs Tom.)
Tom: Still very dull.

Eventually George calms somewhat, and the men get down to serious drinking.

The drinking scene in the film is much shorter and much less maudlin than Coward's, particularly because in the play it is the first time the two men are seen together when they are not battling over who is sleeping with Gilda. For that matter, it is the first time they are alone on stage. In part, the difference between the two scenes is owing to the society that the men inhabit. Coward's men are going to lose themselves in their celebrity status, letting the mad gay life salve their sores. Tom and George are merely "two slightly used artists in the ash can." Otto and Leo will miss Gilda and end up crying on each other's shoulders.

Otto: We shall always want her, always, always, always—
Leo: (miserably) We shall get over it in time, I expect, but it will take years.
Otto: I'm going to hate those years. I'm going to hate every minute of them.
Leo: So am I.
Otto: Thank God for each other, anyhow!
Leo: That's true. We'll get along, somehow—(his voice breaks)—together—
Otto: Together—
Leo: (Breaking down completely) But we're going to be awfully—awfully—lonely—.[18]

George and Tom, who we already trust will be together, would rather not mention Gilda's name at all, a discussion of smallpox (which they toast) would be superior. The differences in reaction define the two attitudes towards masculinity. The film, more identifiably American in attitude, opts for a closemouthed, don't-talk-about-your-troubles set of reactions. The play accepts a more open attitude about the expression of love between the men, as well as that of sorrow and loss. Tom's idea of a "high class" reaction to the situation is much the same as George's, only less violent and more verbal. The two sets of men drink for different reasons. Leo and Otto drink to remember Gilda and wallow in their sorrow. Tom and George drink to forget Gilda and wallow in their sorrow.

Gilda goes to New York and marries Max. The differences between Max and Ernest indicate different social attitudes in the play and film. Ernest is a figure of sophistication—an art dealer capable of arbitrating disputes of authenticity. Although he may be staid and colorless, "a respectable little old man in a jet bonnet," as Gilda describes him, he is not to be dismissed easily.

Max shares with Ernest a lack of humor and creativity, and both possess a mercenary spirit that affects Gilda. Max's morality is based primarily on discretion, and while he is Gilda's friend he does not hold Ernest's position of confidant and is, therefore, seen less frequently.

The most important difference, however, is that Max is a Babbitt figure and as such his tastes are scorned rather than honored. He is in advertising, which is considered no better in this film than it was in *The Front Page* ("Writing poetry about Milady's drawers"). He represents the grey middle class and is provincially American rather than cosmopolitan. The film may take place largely in Europe but, through Max and his friends, bourgeois taste and morality remain a ready target. Except in the last scene, Ernest is not a target of humor; Max, particularly as personified by Horton, is consistently ludicrous.

Gilda marries Max for a respite. After the ceremony when Max asks how it feels to be Mrs. Plunkett, Gilda replies "peaceful" and "secure," and when asked if she loves him, Gilda gently replies: "Oh, Max, people should never ask that question on their wedding night. It's either too late or too early. I'm your wife, Max." Max's expectations from marriage, however, are not the most torrid. He wants to retire early (it is 9:30) but not for amorous reasons—he has an important 10:15 appointment in the morning. Although Gilda tries to be a socially useful wife, she is too much like Tom and George to be content with Max's values. For her husband's sake, she professes interest in the personal affairs of Strump and Eaglebauer, manufacturers of cement, planners of a large ad campaign, and socially important to Max. She and Max give a party, and, although she is tired of playing Post Office, Drop the Handkerchief, and Going to Jerusalem, and would rather hide, she agrees to play Twenty Questions with Mr. Eaglebauer.

72   Design for Living

Returned from China, passing themselves off as police officers, and unexpected ("Not exactly expected. Anticipated. Hoped for. And dreamed of."), Tom and George arrive at the party. They wait upstairs hiding behind a screen on their knees and surprise Gilda, who is quite relieved to see them. While Max and Gilda argue about her returning to their guests, the boys go downstairs and turn the party into a brawl. (This is another of Lubitsch's scenes where the camera stays on the closed door and suggestion, sound effects, and later, description, convey the information.) Gilda tells Max she is "sick of being a trademark married to a slogan." She has doubled his business since she married him, which was all he really wanted. She is sorry about the fight, but she says that after she leaves him he will be a very big and very successful martyr. Max is caught between Gilda leaving and a disgruntled Eaglebauer on the phone. He chooses the phone, happy to have the chance to placate his client.

In their taxi, Tom, George, and Gilda resolve to head back to Paris, burn their tuxedoes and get their old studio back. She will again tell them their work is "rotten." They each kiss her, concur solemnly that "It's a gentleman's agreement," and dissolve into laughter.

In the play, partially because the laughter follows directly on Ernest's stumbling, wrathful exit, the meaning of the laughter and thus of the ending is unclear. Coward attempted to defend and define its meaning:

> Different minds found different meanings in this laughter. Some considered it to be directed against Ernest, Gilda's husband and the time honoured friend of all three. If so, it was certainly cruel, and in the worst possible taste. Some saw in it a lascivious anticipation of a sort of triangular carnal frolic. Others, with less ribald imaginations, regarded it as a meaningless and slightly inept excuse to bring the curtain down. I as the author, however, prefer to think that Gilda and Otto and Leo were laughing at themselves.[19]

The film avoids confusion on this point. Because the laughter directly follows the gentleman's agreement it is clear that the trio is laughing at their own naivete in thinking such an unnatural solution could work. From this it might also be inferred that there is included a note of anticipation, but if so it is firmly based in the self-knowledge they have gained, however slight.

The amorality of the ending extends deeply into the film, however, and the assumption that the film is more chaste than the play can be seriously questioned. Richard Corliss suggests that the basic relationship in the play is between Otto and Gilda (Lunt and Fontanne) and that the relationship will eventually revert to their coupling with Leo as a continued friend. In the film there is no such tidy suggestion. Although in the film Gilda has affairs with both George and Tom, in the number of sexual acts performed the play still outdoes the film. But the number of sexual acts is less important than how they are perceived. If in the film sex is healthy and "inevitable" and to be celibate is trying to fool nature, in the play Gilda's living unwed with either man is willful egocentricity. Throughout the play she is asked, usually by Ernest, to justify the fact that she is unmarried. In the first act, this question raises her ire, and she seems compelled to justify herself at length:

> Gil: (calming down) The only reasons for me to marry would be these: to have children, to have a home; to have a background for social activities; and to be provided for. Well, I don't like children; I don't wish for a home; I can't bear social activities; and I have a small adequate income of my own. I love Otto deeply, and I respect him as a person and as an artist. To be tied legally to him would be repellant to me and him, too. It's not a dashing bohemian gesture to Free Love: we just feel like that, both of us. Now, are you satisfied?
> Ern: If you are.[20]

Nor is it only Ernest who presses for marriage. In the second act, Leo also suggests it. The morality of the characters' actions is consistently a troubling question. Although the play comes to no conclusions and even unites the three at the end, the suggestion is made that it is Gilda's predatory, confused, untidy female nature that causes the problems. If she really had self-control, it is implied, the problem would be resolved. Both in moral terms and in reference to human nature, therefore, the play presents the various sexual couplings as less than positive. They are erotic, but derive some of the their eroticism from their sinfulness.

In the film, however, sex is a positive natural development. Gilda may be less than a gentleman for allowing their agreement to be discarded, but it is only the agreement and not the laws of social rectitude that are cast aside. Marriage is never introduced as a possibility and so the actions of the three are never held up as morally suspect. Gilda's marriage to Max is more an escape into his socially stifling world, a negative move, than a morally cleansing, or positive decision. Although Gilda says, "It feels nice to be legal for a change," she has no desire to be forgiven for her past and sees nothing for which to be ashamed.

There is no sense in the film of Gilda as a sexual predator, upsetting a balanced equilibrium. All three succumb to the lures of sex and Gilda's failure is shown only in the confusion that leads her to run off with Max. Or, as George puts it: "The Mother of the arts wants to be a nice girl."

In the film the focus is much more clearly on romance than it is in the play, which digresses at length into both the burlesques of unrelated characters and the discussions of success and its meaning. The verbal sexual innuendo of the play is in large measure replaced by visual touches in the film, where, through Lubitsch's control of the film medium, information is conveyed by cutting and editing.

While the film lacks the patina of social grace and the earnest wit of the drawing room comedy, it is no less sophisticated. The play achieves its sophistication through the assumption of elitism. Coward's bright, glib characters belong to an artistic aristocracy, which, while it disdains the boring rich, is also far removed from the mob below and is responsible only to itself. As Nathan noted about the play, its elitism is defined in part by its knowledge of the right names to drop and, as Brooks Atkinson observed, "Mr. Coward needs a few dull persons to victimise."[21] The central characters demonstrate their superiority by outwitting newspaper reporters, maids, butlers, and telephones.

Coward's attitude towards the wealthy is ambivalent. The rich of London may be a little silly but Leo enjoys their company. The wealthy of New York are not attacked for their wealth, but for their lack of taste. (They do not like Wagner or understand modern art.) Even so, Otto and Leo seem to pick them out as targets simply because they are convenient. Ernest is neither silly nor tasteless.

Since George and Tom define themselves as Bohemians, and therefore place themselves outside the traditional elite, they do not hold this group in reverence, as Leo and Otto do, and they do not attempt to imitate it, either in their conversation or in their attachments. Their chief enemy is stodginess, as well as tastelessness, and for them these attributes reside mainly in the wealthy, especially since the wealthy have power based on the element Tom, George and Gilda chiefly lack, money.

Although they are not often seen in the film, the common people when glimpsed are sharp and sympathetic. Frankfurter sellers, cloak room attendants, maids, and housekeepers are friendly and are clever enough to blackmail Tom and George. In general, the film derives its humor from character interplay rather than from attacks on other groups, but when a group is attacked it is usually the wealthy. Max is the chief target, and he is identified with Strump and Eaglebauer, Kaplan and McGuire. With them, he represents the stodginess and closed-mindedness of the well entrenched. They have time for social pretension. The rich are tasteless (Max's reaction to art), silly (Twenty Questions) and juvenile about sex (Max's disinterest and the risqué game of Post Office). Beyond this, their code of behavior has more to do with appearances than with morality. Strump and Eaglebauer can not be invited to the party together because of an intra-office affair. This does not diminish them in Max's eyes because it is private, but he would like to be able to judge and magnanimously forgive Gilda for her more public transgressions.

Coward must be careful that his satrical cuts do not reflect on his artists. The lower classes are safer targets. In the film, the reverse is true. Since Tom and George are outsiders and the wealthy possess the power, the wealthy are the logical targets, although a Bohemian rather than a strictly class bias shapes the attack.

The targets in the film are also American. The wealthy may be silly, stodgy, childlike in their sexuality and insincere in their morality, but these attributes are not theirs necessarily because they are wealthy as much as because they are American wealthy. While in the play the English of whatever class may be just as easily attacked, the film carefully identifies all the characters as American from Gilda, Tom, and George, to Max, Strump and Eaglebauer, and Kaplan and McGuire.

This American frame of reference is crucial to an understanding of the film's goals and achievements. The film does not identify with Coward's sophistication and continually denies its importance. In this area, Hecht's work on the film becomes most apparent. The film differs from Lubitsch's work in that it is wholly American in its concerns and judgments. Since this represents a basic change from the original and yet is atypical of Lubitsch, it probably can be attributed to Hecht's skills.

This personal reshaping of material and viewpoint is not always perceived as an improvement. Richard Corliss believes that Hecht dominated the project but that in the process he ruined the film. Hecht reduced the sophistication of the original to the "snappy patter of his own bourgeois bohemia, the energetic pressrooms of Jazz Age Chicago." Tom and George, he contends, are "really old time newspaper men pretending to be continentals."[22] The dialogue is simply not funny.

Molly Haskell, on the other hand, likes the film often for the same elements that Corliss so dislikes. She suggests that casting such unsuave American actors made the film a success by "disinfecting" it from its original tone and transforming it into something "iconoclastic and moving."[23] While she likes the film, however, Haskell does not believe that the positive work on it could have been Hecht's. Lubitsch must have been responsible for saving the film from Hecht's "backroom juvenilism" that would have forced the men to dominate the story.

Using other Lubitsch films, Haskell identifies a number of elements as characteristic of the director's approach. Working in a European setting to distance the morality of the material was his common practice. Many of his films involve a triangular relationship which is explored throughout the film. Lubitsch, therefore, changed the Otto-Leo focus of the play and used his master touch to create "the perfect balance of the triangle, three people in a state of permanent, breathless, suspension."[24] While Lubitsch was firmly heterosexual in his creations, he was also firmly against male groups. He, therefore, kept Tom and George in check. It is only Gilda's presence that allows the men to live together in peace.

Both critics at least agree that the characters are American, and typical of the fast talking Bohemians Hecht had created in *The Front Page* and continued to write about throughout the decade. While these critics' individual perspectives may have their base in an irreconcilable difference of taste, they are also biased by a preconceived attack that may prevent lucidity. Corliss ignores the possibility that George and Tom were not intended to imitate Coward's drawing room sophistication but represented a different comic attitude, one that perceived Otto and Leo's elitist pose as just another empty facade.

In her enthusiasm for Lubitsch and in her desire to see him possess a positive attitude towards women, Haskell does not always analyze with her usual perspicacity. She comments, for instance, that in Lubitsch's films women often dominate the relationships. While this is true, it is also true that in a number of films there is a reversal at the end of the story which puts the man in the dominant position. (This is particularly true in *The Smiling Lieutenant, The Love Parade,* and *Design for Living.*)

While it is true that Lubitsch placed his films in European settings, he also distanced them with European characters. An American character appeared at times but only as a contrast to the Europeans. Unlike any other of Lubitsch's films, *Design for Living* is totally American in its characters, choice of cast, and frame of reference. The film is a hybrid of Lubitsch's continental fairy tales and Hecht's American Bohemia.

The strength and importance of the male relationship is one of the most distinctive elements in the film. In contrast to the play, Gilda's importance is reduced to a balance with the men where it formerly had been a dominant one. If in the play she was on stage most of the time, dealing with her three males, in the film, Tom and George share the screen with her. She is as often with both of them as with any single individual, and they are often alone without her. The male relationship, established early in the film and developed throughout, is used as the basic situation into which Gilda comes as an outsider. Although she comes to dominate them as she becomes a focus of tension, when the men pull themselves together a tighter bond is formed that allows them as a unit to deal with Gilda where earlier in the film they were willing to put love before friendship. It is the strength and balance of the men's relationship that allows the triangle to endure through the end of the film where the normal pattern in Lubitsch's films, as Haskell notes, is for the triangle to devolve into a couple.

The thesis that the men are dependent on Gilda and that "far from indicating any inclination for a kind of closed and infantile buddy system found in so many American films, March and Cooper suggest two individuals who, without Hopkins, would probably get on each other's nerves after a while,"[25] is belied by the fact that they lived together for eleven years before they met her, that they reunite in the drinking scene, have since traveled around the world together, and that they present a united front in the final scene just as they had in the first scene on the train.

The male relationship thus forms the basic norm from which action evolves. At the end of the film the relationship has been expanded to include another member, but the basic relationship remains intact. Gilda, the new member, always seen as a comrade, has come to accept their point of view. It is the balance and resilience of Tom and George's friendship, which can exist without Gilda, that allows the triangle to exist and not shrink to a pairing. If Haskell is correct in her judgment of Lubitsch as being opposed to male groups, then the evolution of the film into this form (from its original Gilda-dominated, couple-oriented source) must have been achieved with the help of Hecht rather than against his sensibilities.

The changes from Coward's play to Hecht's film: the Bohemian Americans in place of Coward's cosmopolitan artists and predatory female, and the substitution of a heightened slang diction that is both mocking and exuberant for Coward's studied wit, result in a film that possesses a healthy democratic zaniness essential to screwball comedy. Although more exotic in its locales and story and more erotic and unusual in its sexual design, the world view and social attitudes of the Hecht film are similar to subsequent examples of the genre such as *It Happened One Night* made a year later under stricter censorship.

As the Production Code increased its hold over film content the amoral sexuality of films such as *Design for Living* would be bowdlerized into the safer conduct of oddball romance. Although his characters would have no greater sense of social responsibility than Tom, George, and Gilda, Hecht would limit himself in future films to more mundane couples rather than trios. But the movement from the all male solution of *The Front Page* to the male-female menage of *Design for Living* would remain part of his writing attitude. The image of woman as an accessory to freedom rather than as a suppressive force of social entrapment would help establish a sense of liberation inherent to screwball comedy and separate the form from more conventional romance.

5

The Screwball Comedy Vogue: *The Twentieth Century, Nothing Sacred, His Girl Friday*

Screwball comedy had its greatest period of popular success between 1934 and 1938. The vogue was reinforced by the imposition of the Production Code in 1934 and waned with the intrusion of world events which forced America out of its isolationist mood. The Code necessitated a transformation of the open sexual attitudes of the early thirties into a battle of wit and personality between hero and heroine, suggestive but not risque. The increased awareness of world affairs, a gradual process culminating in the Second World War, made the sophisticated pairings of two lovers to the exclusion of outside events seem frivolous and even irresponsible. Films would eventually take as themes the idea that romantic entanglements were inconsequential compared to one's obligations to society as, for instance, in *Casablanca* (1942) where Humphrey Bogart sends Ingrid Bergman back to Paul Henreid and goes off with Claude Rains to fight the Nazis.

In his summary of the qualities of thirty's films, Donald McCaffrey in *The Golden Age of Sound Comedy* chose what he felt were the most representative and his personal favorite films of each genre. For sophisticated or screwball comedy he chose *The Twentieth Century* (1934) and *Nothing Sacred* (1937), both written by Ben Hecht, the former in collaboration with Charles MacArthur. To McCaffrey, these films represent the culmination of the spirit of wit and license in the thirties. They also show Hecht's ideas and styles at their most integrated. In these films, as in *His Girl Friday* (1940), there is little gap in either world view or energy between writer, production, and audience. Hecht was in rhythm with his surroundings and, consequently, these scripts were among his most vital films and some of those that have dated the least.

The Twentieth Century and *Nothing Sacred* are constructed on the familiar patterns of Hecht's view of group relationships and human calumny. Although both films manifest attributes of the screwball comedy, they are tougher and less sentimental than most examples of the genre. While both are romances, the romances are excuses for burlesques of larger targets, such as the theatre, journalism, and public displays of emotion. The inevitable lovers generate only enough sympathy to keep the audience's good will. There is less sympathy for the protagonists in *The Twentieth Century*, where the satire is realized in the central characters, than in *Nothing Sacred*, where society at large is the object of ridicule. As is often true in Hecht's work, his affection for his subjects keeps the comedy from taking on a black tone.

The Twentieth Century was adapted for the screen in much the same way Hecht had rewritten Noel Coward's *Design for Living,* with the advantage that Hecht and MacArthur were adapting their own play so that more of the original was retained. Some antecedent action was supplied; the remaining scenes were trimmed considerably; and the material was refocused for a broader audience and, in this case, in response to different censorship requirements. The difference between film and play, unlike *Design for Living,* clearly shows the effect of stiff censorship codes on material. Even so, *The Twentieth Century* displays a degree of license, verbally and sexually, that is absent in later movies.

As a play directed by George Abbot, *The Twentieth Century* had been very successfully produced in New York in 1932. Hecht and MacArthur's play, in turn, was based on *The Napoleon of Broadway,* a script by Charles Milholland. The entire action of the play takes place on "The Twentieth Century," a train going from Chicago to New York. Oscar Jaffe, theatrical producer and director, is returning from another flop, the fifth he has had since Lily Garland, his star and lover, left him after catching him in bed with another woman. She has since been starring in the movies, but Jaffe has learned she will be travelling on this train. Her name on a contract would save his theatre from bankruptcy. After contriving to get rid of her boyfriend, Jaffe attempts a reconciliation with Lily. It fails. His attempt to lure her with money also fails when his benefactor is revealed to be a lunatic. But Jaffe is finally saved when he is shot. Although he receives only a flesh wound, he bamboozles Lily into signing the contract as the last wish of a dying man. In the final scene Lily and Jaffe leave the train for the theatre—Lily sitting on the arm of Jaffe's wheel chair.

Oscar Jaffe was patterned in part after David Belasco with whom MacArthur had worked when Belasco directed MacArthur and Edward Sheldon's play *Lulu Belle*. MacArthur was delighted by the "Guvnor" (Belasco). Hecht wrote: "Belasco was the Land of the Theatre. He had a voice borrowed from a thousand actors, mystic and foolish with sham importance that was not sham in the theatre."[1] He was an engaging scoundrel who got his way through superbly highhanded tricks. MacArthur relates that at one point Belasco wanted to make a cut in *Lulu Belle*. He told Lenore Ulric, the actress in the part, that "I'm making the cut so that you won't have to talk so fast on the stage, darling, it will enable you to get some sense and a little emotion into what you are trying to do, darling," and responded to MacArthur's protests with,

"Quiet you rat. I am going to make you rich and famous with my genius."[2] He silenced the outraged cast by spending ten minutes pacing in the back of the stage and returning to say that he had been speaking with the ghost of Charles Frohman and that Frohman had said he was right to make the cut. "How could you argue with such a goddamn wonderful ham?" concluded MacArthur.[3] Hecht said they used Belasco's ornate speech and sibilant diction, produced by his antique dental plates, when they came to write the play.

The play revels in the make-believe of the theatre. The Broadway it creates is not one of serious drama but of grandiose romantic entertainment. The theatre people in this world perform both on stage and off. As Brooks Atkinson said in his review of the play: "If you are familiar with the flatulent hokum of Broadway characters you will enjoy the dizziness and malice of these people. You will recognize them as show folk: there is not an honest man among them."[4]

Essentially, the play is *The Front Page* rewritten from Walter Burns's point of view. *The Front Page* carefully prepares for Burns's arrival and does not explode until Burns enters half way through the play. In *The Twentieth Century* by contrast, Jaffe arrives in the second scene and dominates the rest of the play with his ego. Like Belasco, but even more like Burns, Jaffe is energy embodied in a mock heroic pose; he is "the little Colonel returning from another Moscow. His head bloodied—but still unbowed."[5] The theatre is his personal empire cut off from the concerns of lower mortals just as the newspaper pressroom is for Burns. He runs it autocratically, surrounded by his faithful underlings, in this case his press agent and his manager, drinking and swearing but completely faithful to his banner. Together they make another set of Hechtian musketeers.

As in *The Front Page,* the main action is textured by a number of minor characters: Lockwood, a businessman, and Anita, his secretary, running off to New York for a little fling; Dr. Johnson, a woman who has a lesbian version of the Joan of Arc story for Jaffe to read; Matthew Craig, who roams the train putting up stickers which say "Repent for the end is at hand" and passing out bad checks; and two German actors from the *Passion Play* (Christ and Judas) who have been deserted by their manager and are in need of funds. Each of these characters and their subplot is carefully woven into the main action.

Lily Garland is the Hildy Johnson of the play. Like Hildy she was the protegee of her boss who has changed her name from Mildred Plotka and taught her how to act. But unlike Hildy, Lily has actually managed to leave her boss and has been working in the movies, the theatrical equivalent of a newsman working in advertising. She is just as full of sham and playacting as Jaffe. At one point, for instance, they compete simultaneously for attention by shamming fainting spells. Like Hildy, Lily has a lover who pulls her away from her boss, in this case her agent George Smith. MacArthur said that Burns's order to have Hildy arrested at the end of *The Front Page* "was not a double-cross so much as the desperate act of Damon refusing to part with Pythias."[6] In *The Twentieth Century* Pythias is a woman; she is a woman who shares the hermetic life of the theatre, a former member of Jaffe's musketeers, a member of the professional group. The switch from male to female in the character combines the love attraction and the work and friendship into a single conflict which allows for a decisive ending by bringing the two lovers/workers together where the male friendship versus female love conflict in *The Front Page* would have made a total victory by Burns unpalatable. Lily can have love and the theatre, whereas Hildy has to choose between love and newspapers.

Although friendship and love are the real issues, compulsive professionalism is the lure. Just as the Earl Williams story is used by Burns to keep Hildy working, so Jaffe attempts to dazzle Lily with the part of the Magdalene in an opulently staged version of the *Passion Play*. For both it is the indignities suffered at the hands of their boss that infuriates them. Hildy hates being "treated like a hired girl,"[7] or having the copy ripped out of his typewriter. Lily says:

> The man belittled me and tortured me for six years. Ran around telling everybody "Where would Lily Garland be without the great Jaffe." Well, I think I showed him. Right on top of the ladder, kid—and going up. The lies he told about me—and my name. Called himself my Svengali.[8]

For all her complaints, Lily treats George with the same high handedness that she learned from Jaffe. She plays extravagant scenes of sorrow, anger, and hurt that she can start and stop at will.

Lil: I want people to stop hammering and hammering at me.
Geo: You're hysterical.
Lil: It happens I am as calm as a fish.
Geo: Lying to me, swearing on your love and honor.
Lil: I haven't any.
Geo: What a fake you are!
Lil: *I'M* a fake (She stops suddenly, looks at him and bursts into unexpected laughter.)
Geo: What are you laughing at?
Lil: Do you want to know something? I never told you the truth in my life.
Geo: (Screaming) What?
Lil: All my lovers—opera tenors and acrobats, and that Italian Count. All lies. I never had any lovers in six years, let me see, seven years except that broken down Romeo, Mr. Jaffe. He was the only one.
Geo: What are you trying to tell me?
Lil: I was faithful to him.
Geo: Faithful?
Lil: (Innocently) Of course, he watched me like a hawk.
Geo: My God and you wanted my respect!

Lil:	Who cares for your respect. I'm too big to be respected. The men I've known have understood that.
Geo:	(Shouting) Men you've known! Jaffe you mean!
Lil:	Yes—Jaffe. He'll tell you what I am—a first class passenger entitled to privileges.
Geo:	Oh—(very sarcastically)—You're an artist.
Lil:	You're God damn right I am.⁹

While Lily has fake hysteria, Jaffe threatens suicide whenever he is in need of sympathy. They deserve each other. Their matched temperaments and histrionics are used in place of sentiment to show their mutual need. Even the act of sending Lily flowers is a theatrical device for Jaffe rather than a show of true affection. As O'Malley, his press agent, says in the film, "In some humpty dumpty kind of way, that was true love."

Jaf:	I want those gardenias to contain a message... "To the little lady of the snows—" No. We won't use that this time. Just a minute.... Yes. Get out your pencil, Owen. I want the message to read, "From the Grave of Someone you loved yesterday." (He sighs, shakes his head.) How's that?
Web:	(sourly) That's fine.
O'M:	A little on the sad side, isn't it?
Jaf:	It's perfect. Why can't I get a few playwrights to write like that?¹⁰

For Jaffe even a moment of confession calls for melodrama:

(Hoarsely; HE clutches the seat to support himself, then puts his hand across his stomach and bends over as if in terrific pain. O'MALLEY watchs with solicitude and concern. JAFFE clutches O'MALLEY's sleeve.) Owen—she's getting on here—Lily—Lily Garland. I've tried for a year to tear her out of my brain, but I've failed. Owen. She's in here, eating at my heart like some grey rat. I've hidden it from the world, from you boys especially, because... I didn't want you to know... how hard I've been hit. Owen, you're Irish, you'll never understand—when I love a woman I'm an oriental. It never dies. The only way I'll ever get hold of myself again is to get her back. (With something like hatred.) Make her pay for what she's done to me.¹¹

When he does see Lily, Jaffe is by far the more consummate actor of the two. He sees everything that goes on in life as a theatrical event having only a tenuous connection with reality. When George stalks out on Lily, Jaffe remarks, "What an exit! Not a word! That's what we should have had in 'Gypsy Heart.'"¹² Believing he has softened up Lily, he tells Owen that he has played a scene that Sardou might have written.

When he attacks again he readily accepts blame for all the hurt she feels he has done her. Even though Lily is more aware of the real world than Oscar and does not want to get involved in his schemes or snared again by his magnetism, he disarms her by calling himself despicable and soon has her lost in the dream of her new part as the Magdalene, imagining even more grandiose and melodramatic moments than he. Suddenly, remembering that he has no money, she turns and laughs at him. They argue, fight, kick, and scream. She calls him a swindler and a fake and he storms out—but only after getting the last word: "As there is a God in heaven, Mildred Plotka, you'll end up where you belong—in the burlesque houses."[13]

While it is firmly in the tradition of American low comedy that Atkinson, in a discussion of the play called the "sort of thing the American stage does with the greatest skill,"[14] the play is a stage version of film's screwball comedy. It contains all the ingredients of that form: low farce, fighting lovers, a world with urban characters, strong minor personalities, brassiness in the dialogue, and gentle satire. In its transition from stage to screen the play was rewritten to follow the conventions of the screen comedy even more closely. Because the adaptation was made by the original authors, the changes have more to do with the media than with personalities and are therefore instructive in a study of the genre. Following *Design for Living* by a year, the film shows the effects of a harsher but not completely unrestrained censorship. References to sex and religion were excised but the basic structure of the play was undisturbed. The play was stripped of its insular Broadway references, but these were replaced by effective satire on the theatre in general. The structure was reshaped in much the same way that Hecht and Lubitsch had reworked *Design for Living,* by starting the story from the beginning of Jaffe and Garland's affair rather than from the late point of attack used to compress the action in the play.

The romantic content of the film was also enhanced. There are clearer indications that Jaffe and Garland are still in love, and the one or two moments of tenderness between them were underlined. These changes, however, did not change the basic outlook and cynicism of the original script. Jaffe and Garland may have more sentiment for one another, but they still fight incessantly, not merely in the middle of the film but at the end as well. It is a battle of egos that draws them together. Their love will not dissolve their early conflicts as it does in *It Happened One Night* (1934) or *Bringing Up Baby* (1938). Characters do not change, they are merely forced back into their old circumstances where they were secretly happy.

The Hecht-MacArthur film version was directed by Howard Hawks and released in May 1934, with John Barrymore as Jaffe, Carole Lombard as Garland, Walter Connolly as Oliver Webb and Roscoe Karns as Owen O'Malley. In the process of adaptation the central design of the play was strengthened. Where the play opened with a long scene between Lockwood and Anita surreptitiously making themselves comfortable, and a long fight as O'Malley and Webb get them out of the compartment that Jaffe wants, the film opens years earlier when Mildred Plotka is working on her first role. Jaffe's minions want to dump the former lingerie model but Jaffe wrings a performance out of her, chalking out her blocking on the floor and sticking her

7. *Twentieth Century* (1934). Oscar Jaffe (John Barrymore) attempts to turn lingerie model Mildred Plotka into the actress Lily Garland (Carole Lombard), assisted by Oliver Webb (Walter Connolly). In this background scene written for the film Jaffe attempts to teach Plotka her moves by marking them on the stage floor in chalk. (Photo: Museum of Modern Art/Film Stills Archive courtesy Columbia.)

with a pin to get her to scream. The show is a hit and Jaffe, underplaying his role in her success, choreographs her seduction by wooing her with stardom rather than sex.

A few years later Lily wants to go out for the evening rather than sit around listening to Oscar talk about his genius. With the support of his men, he feigns suicide but when she tries to walk out on his big death scene he is enraged. They fight but are eventually reconciled. The next day he pledges to be less jealous, but the moment she leaves he has a detective follow her and tap her telephone. When Lily discovers the tap she leaves Oscar for Hollywood.

In Chicago, Oscar must hide from the Sheriff for lack of funds. He hides out in a hotel under the name of Ernest Hemingway. Posing as a Southern gentleman, he bluffs his way onto the train. He is just settling in when he discovers that Lily is getting on at the first stop. At this point the action of the play is picked up and proceeds with more deletions than changes until the end of the film where there is a repetition of the first scene, with Jaffe leading rehearsal. Even though Lily is now well dressed and has her maid with her, Jaffe begins to chalk out her blocking, and they fight as the picture ends.

The added early scenes establish the events on which the later scenes are based. In doing so, they clarify characters by indicating which of their contradictory stories are true. Lily and Jaffe often argue about who did what to whom before they separated. It is useful, therefore, to see that, contrary to what she remembers, he did manufacture one of her performances and that his egoism was so grandiose that a marquee reads "Open September 25. Mr. Oscar Jaffe announces a new play/ Personally supervised by Mr. Jaffe/ with a typical Jaffe cast/ to be presented at the Jaffe Theatre/ the play 'The Heart of Kentucky' by E. A. Burns/ 'An Oscar Jaffe Production is a guarantee of wit and genius in the theatre.' Percey Winters.[15] New York Times." Seeing a little bit of *The Heart of Kentucky* (a typical Jaffe production) also underlines O'Malley's comment about Jaffe's recent failure—*Joan of Arc*:

> He's going to end up on the breadlines unless he realizes pretty soon that all those dithering horse operas with everybody staggering around in those foul iron suits, ain't entertainment. A lot of Gadzooks by my halidome.[16]

In the latter half of the film, the subplots, such as those with Dr. Johnson and Lockwood, are jettisonned, exposition made unnecessary by the earlier scenes is excised, and lines are discarded for greater speed. Even so, much of the original script survives, although many of the lines are approximations of the wording in the script. As a result of these deletions the film moves at an even faster pace than the play.

The relationship between Jaffe and Garland changes slightly. In the original there is a greater sexuality in both characters. In the play, Lily left Jaffe when she caught him with another woman; in the film she leaves him because he is jealous and overbearing. In the film, she brings out the pin that Jaffe jabbed her with in the first scene. She keeps it in a special box, and her moment with it shows her affection for Jaffe. She handles her agent (in the film a society swell in a much condensed role) with such ease and with such disdain that it is clear she misses a good fight. During one fight with Jaffe she has a moment of honesty. When he tells her that he suffers so much he could cut his throat, she responds: "If you did grease paint would run out of it," and continues, "That's the trouble with you Oscar, with both of us. We're not people. We're lithographs. We don't know anything about love unless its written and rehearsed. We're only real in between curtains." She and Jaffe belong to the same fraternity and, while she hates to admit it, she is proud to be a member with "first class privileges."

Lily's attraction to Jaffe excuses some of his highhanded tricks, just as Hildy's secret desire to stay excused Burns's actions. In both play and film Oscar wants Lily back, but in the film the romantic motivation is stressed slightly more than the monetary one. We see Oscar jealous as well as egocentric in the early scenes. In the previous year he has spent $1,800 on phone calls to her and each time she hung up, and although he pretends to be aloof his need is apparent.

> I wouldn't take that woman back if she and I were the last people in the world and the future of the human race depended on it. Besides, she's two thousand miles away.

If romance has been increased slightly, the satire has lost a bit of its edge in transition. Part of this is merely due to censorship. The character of Matthew Clark, who not only wants to finance Jaffe's production but play the Christ as well, suffers the most. The religious satire embodied in Clark and in the subject of the *Passion Play* shrinks in transition just as O'Malley's complaint that the stickers are "foul Protestant propaganda"[17] is reduced to "foul propaganda" lest someone be offended.

The language of the play has also been affected. Although Atkinson said that "in many respects, '20th Century' is a clean play, which marks a new trend in the works of this collaboration,"[18] the play is peppered with Hells, damns, and goddamns, and the characters—particularly O'Malley—use a wide range of ethnic epithets: "inadequate Navajo," "unfortunate Aztec," "double-crossing Filipino" and well as "mick" and "kike." In obedience to the Hollywood censorship code, all are deleted, as is any mention of a supreme being other than Oscar Jaffe.

What is surprising about the sexual content of the film is how much is left intact. At the core of the plot is Lily's long affair with Jaffe and this remains unchanged. When Jaffe first "seduces" Lily after her first triumphant

8. *Twentieth Century* (1934). Jaffe, faking suicide, tricks Garland into signing a contract. He is abetted by his assistants Owen O'Malley and Webb. (Photo: Museum of Modern Art/Film Stills Archive courtesy Columbia.)

performance, he kisses her as he cuts off the camera's view by suggestively closing her dressing room door with his foot. The next scene takes place months later. Lily, who has an ornate bed shaped like a ship, explains to O'Malley that when she received an invitation Jaffe was right next to her. "Rowing?" he asks. Later Webb and O'Malley wait below while Jaffe and Garland fight. The lights go out, they leave, and the next shot is of Jaffe and Garland together in her apartment the next morning. On the other hand, Dr. Johnson and the lesbian *Joan of Arc* disappear entirely, as do Lockwood and Anita and a reference to "soul kissing."

Another area of satire, at the expense of the theatre, has also been broadened for a more general audience. The discussion of the *Passion Play* is simplified, as are veiled references to habits of Belasco. A scene where a new Somerset Maugham play is read by Lily is deleted, as is a reference to *Dinner at Eight*.

The addition of the early scenes in the theatre make up for these small losses. For instance, early in the play Jaffe takes his first rehearsal with the cast. He is formal, soft spoken and polite.

> I have been looking forward to this little occasion for some time. There is no thrill in the world like launching a play, watching it come to life little by little, seeing the living characters emerge like genii from the bottle. Now, before we begin, I want you all to remember one thing. No matter what I may say, no matter what I may do on this stage during our work, I love you all. And the people who have been through my battles with me will bear me out in testifying that above everything in the world, I love the theatre and the charming people in it.

This speech, repeated in part at the end of the film as the new rehearsals begin (not for the promised *Passion Play* but for another Southern Epic), is in humorous contrast with Jaffe's comment as he pulls and stretches off the putty nose he has worn to sneak past the policeman at the entrance to the train in Chicago: "I never thought I should sink so low as to become an actor. It was humiliating."

It is regrettable that the small amount of satire on the movies in the play has also been diminished. At one point in the play, for instance, Lily shows Oscar the Oscar she has won. He reads the inscription: "'The Academy of Motion Picture Arts and Sciences.' Good God! It's pathetic. Don't fall for this sort of thing, Lily."[19] In general the movie is kinder to the film industry and focuses more on the theatre as its source of humor.

What is impressive about both adaptation and play is how well tuned they are to their specific medium. The stage play creates action in a single space layering plots and characters to create a sense of movement, shifting quickly from railroad drawing room to railroad drawing room. The film stretches out the story but narrows the focus. It brings on the lovers in the first scenes and never strays far from their concerns. While it undergoes changes due to censorship, it makes up for this loss by moving in a different direction, such as the rehearsal scene between Jaffe and Garland.

Reviewers disagreed on which part of the film they preferred. Mordaunt Hall felt that the addition of the early scenes was well advised "for although there is no gainsaying that the happenings on the train are frequently hilarious, the earlier glimpses have the virtue of being more effective through their relative restraint."[20] Thornton Delehanty, writing in the *New York Post* expressed a different point of view: "It is overdetailed in the opening sequences and it misses the frenzied tempo of the stage play."[21] In general, however, the new pieces meshed smoothly with the older sections from the play. The new sequences take up half the length of the film and do not have the feeling of scenes tacked on merely for variety.

The transition is helped by the acting and directing. Barrymore had a romp with the part. The audience needed to have some idea when the characters were performing and when they were as close to being real as they ever were, and Barrymore exaggerates and plays acts with delight. In his hands, Jaffe belongs to the theatre of Belasco, an earlier time when bravura performances were expected to be slightly larger than life. He relishes each syllable, as, for instance, when he calls Max Jacobs, his former lackey and now his rival for the signature of Lily, by his real name—Mandelbaum—MMan dell bawwn, turning each sound into an insult. This was an important success for Carole Lombard who was to appear in many screwball comedies before her death in 1942. In her skintight satin costumes, she plays with more energy than finesse, but she has a conviction in her actions and speech that connect her to the real world and lends credence to her character. This naturalism coupled with enhanced comic skills, also characterizes her performance as Hazel Flagg in *Nothing Sacred*. The character actors in *The Twentieth Century* establish the same kind of hectic and plausibly comic environment that the newsmen do for *The Front Page*.

The director of *The Twentieth Century* was Howard Hawks in his third collaboration with Hecht—*Scarface* (1933) and Hawks's unfinished work on *Viva Villa* (1934). Hawks's direction is clean, unpretentious, and fast-paced. He handled the dialogue well and the film allows the actors and the dialogue room to work effectively. Since Hawks's view of a world of male groups and his personal cynicism about sex, wealth and fame were in tune with the script and with Hecht's views, theirs was a comfortable and productive collaboration. The same compatability of attitude and style also contributed to the second film version of *The Front Page, His Girl Friday* (1940).

Somehow in the transition, *His Girl Friday* became the creation of the *auteur* Hawks while its authors were forgotten. The overlapping dialogue, for instance, even though present in both play and the 1931 film, has been attributed to Hawks. The decision to change Hildy into a girl, the defining element in the film, is also generally regarded as his tremendously imaginative stroke. Hawks has related:

> I was going to prove to somebody that *The Front Page* had the finest modern dialogue that had been written and I asked a girl to read Hildy's part and I read the editor, and I stopped and I said, "Hell, it's better between a girl and a man than between two men."[22]

As Pauline Kael points out: "Now, a charming story is not nothing. Still this is nothing but a charming and superficial story."[23] Even if it was an accident, it perfectly conformed to the box office successes of the period. The screwball comedy vogue had popularized the witty fast-talking working girl, especially the girl reporter.

> By the mid-thirties—after the surprise success of *It Happened One Night*—the new independent, wisecracking girl was very popular, especially in a whole cycle of newspaper pictures with rival boy and girl reporters. Newspaper pictures were now "romantic comedies,"... the movies about girl reporters were almost all based on the highly publicized girl reporter—Hearst's Adela Rogers St. Johns.[24]

The Front Page had become the source for many films, and different versions included *Wedding Present* (1936) with Cary Grant as the hardbitten editor, Joan Bennett as the tough reporter and Conrad Nagel as the square fiancé. Ralph Bellamy had already been typed as a square in *The Awful Truth* (1937) in which Cary Grant prevents him from marrying his former wife. Rosalind Russell had played a reporter-sob sister in *Four's a Crowd* (1938). These were the already well established roles from which *His Girl Friday* was devised, with each actor playing a type of character he had portrayed before and with Russell costumed in the type of striped suit that Adela Rogers St. Johns often wore.

If these types were not suggestive enough, Hawks could look to *The Twentieth Century*, since Hecht and MacArthur had already made the switch from male to female, transforming Hildy into Lily Garland. Andrew Sarris describes Bellamy's character as,

> consistent with Hawks's conception of Bellamy as the "square" outsider who attempts to rescue the heroine from the insane world of journalism, an attempt doomed to failure by the very structure of Hawksian comedy as the defeat of intelligence and dignity by the gratuitous elements of modern life.[25]

This description is as consistent with the Hechtian world as it is with the Hawksian one. The outsider trying to save the protagonist from journalism, or from Jaffe's theatre and the burlesque of outsider's dignity by the faster and tougher insider are defining elements of both *The Front Page* and *The Twentieth Century* in their original form. Rather than argue for a single

9. *The Front Page* (1931). A jaunty Hildy and Walter in handcuffs just before the reversal. The mayor (James Gordon) is at the left. (Photo: Museum of Modern Art/Film Stills Archive courtesy United Artists.)

10. *His Girl Friday* (1940). The same scene as in *The Front Page* with Hildy (Rosalind Russell) and Walter (Cary Grant) still jaunty in handcuffs with Sheriff Hartwell (Gene Lockhart) and the Mayor (Clarence Kolb). (Photo: Museum of Modern Art/Film Stills Archive courtesy Columbia.)

visionary creativity that completely overshadows all others involved in these projects, it would be more productive to point out that just as Hecht's writing collaboration with those who shared his sense of relationships, humor, and world view, such as MacArthur and Charles Lederer, were some of his most fruitful, when Hecht worked with a director whose ideas and abilities complemented his own, superior work emerged as well.

Hawks was not a writer. Usually he would read a script and point out what he liked or did not like about it, and then it would be rewritten. He worked with Hecht and MacArthur a little more closely. According to one newspaper account the only way Hawks could get them to work on *Barbary Coast* (1935) was by promising to teach them a marble game he knew. "They worked on the script for forty-five minutes of each hour and then played with marbles for the other fifteen minutes."[26] Hawks describes a somewhat similar situation and a process that resembles the way Hecht had written plays with Bodenheim. He, Hecht and MacArthur would:

> ... sit in a room and we'd work for two hours and then we'd play backgammon for an hour. Then we'd start again and one of us would be one character and one would be another character. We'd read out lines of dialogue and the whole idea was to try and stump the other people, to see if they could think of something crazier than you could. And that is the kind of dialogue we used, and the kind that was fun.[27]

Hawks only worked with both Hecht and MacArthur on *Barbary Coast* and *The Twentieth Century*, so the collaboration he describes was probably one of these, most likely the comedy.

Hawks brought the skills of a director rather than a writer to his collaboration, and *His Girl Friday* is a successful picture because it combines the dialogue and script with sharp performances and elegant production. Manny Farber says the film

> ... is a tour de force of choreographed action: bravado posturings with body, lucid Cubistic composing with natty lapels and hat brims, as well as a very stylized discourse of short replies based on the idea of topping, out maneuvering the other person with wit, cynicism and bravado.[28]

Although Farber attributes all of these elements to Hawks, a more balanced interpretation would perceive a successful collaboration with the script fully realized in production. Visually the film is clean edged. Each shot is pictorially well composed, yet the camera rarely calls attention to itself even though the editing underscores the different tempos in each scene. Technique is subservient to action and meaning. By comparison, the 1931 version is pictorially very showy; visual artistry and impressive cutting and camera angles, important because the movie was made at a time when the camera was trying to reclaim the freedom it had lost to the early static microphones, are technically proficient but at times distract from the action rather than augment it.

The adaptation for *His Girl Friday* was written by Charles Lederer with an uncredited assist from Hecht. There are a number of substantial changes from the original play. The adaptation shows the same kind of changes Hecht made on *Design for Living* and *The Twentieth Century*: new early scenes added while the later scenes remain substantially the same, though trimmed considerably. The focus of the film shifts in much the same way that *The Twentieth Century* shifts from *The Front Page* as the romance pulls the protagonists together rather than draws them apart. *His Girl Friday* is also much more mellow in its tone, more romantic in its characters and shows the effects of even greater censorship than *The Twentieth Century* or *The Front Page*.

In the early scenes Russell (as Hildy) returns from divorcing Grant (as Walter) to say goodbye to him on her way through to Albany with Bellamy (as Peggy) and his mother. Walter delays their departure by taking them to lunch (a replacement of Burns drinking with Hildy in Pollack Mike's in the 1931 film). To further delay Hildy's departure he agrees to buy an insurance policy from Bellamy if Hildy will do an interview with Williams. Once Hildy reaches the press room the play takes over. Even in the earlier scenes individual lines from the original are inserted at every possible moment. At the end of the film the watch device, which was in an early draft of the film script, is dropped so that Hildy can simply remain with Walter. He pretends to want her to go and her femininity and hitherto concealed love for Walter is fully revealed as she cries because she thinks he does not love her. They are reconciled and will go to Niagara Falls for a honeymoon, a locale which is conveniently close to a local strike which Walter can cover.

Just as Jaffe uses Lily's stardom to seduce her or the role of the Magdalene to woo her back, so Walter uses the Williams story to excite Hildy. He gets rid of the reporter covering the story by saying that the man's wife is having a baby. Some of Hildy's faults in the original are shifted to Walter to justify their divorce. It is Grant who has run off after stories when he was needed by Russell. The basic dynamic of the conflict (love versus work) thus shifts characters but remains basically the same. But where in the original it is the male that has to change by reforming and leaving the business, in *His Girl Friday* it is the female who must compromise. Grant does not change; Russell comes to realize that she loves her job and she loves him. Since she is a fellow worker and his lover, their differences are not insurmountable.

In the process of adaptation, everyone has become nicer. Since Grant wants his wife back he is automatically nicer. Bellamy is in a weaker position than was Peggy. He has a romantic as well as an occupational rival. He is stripped of Peggy's determination in the same way that George in *The*

Twentieth Century changes from Lily's agent and a man of toughness and strength to the weaker society boy of the film (although in both Oscar accuses her of "mousing around with boys"). Russell adds Peggy's determination to Hildy's.

Not only has the Williams story been reduced in importance, but Grant and Russell's journalistic position has also become more humanitarian. The story for its own sake is no longer the most important factor. They want Williams to get a reprieve because he is a little crazy. For this reason Russell pushes him to say something bizarre such as that he used the gun because it was built to be used, and, therefore, he believed in "production for use." Williams is no longer an anarchist; he is merely befuddled. Grant hopes that when they get rid of the present administration they can get a good mayor like Laguardia in New York. Burns and Hildy in the original have no politics but the disdain of politicians and the lust for their own power.

In the same way that the social attitudes of the characters have become more benign, the last vestiges of ethnic or sexual humor have also disappeared. Molly is no longer quite a whore, her leap from the window is underplayed, and although the policeman killed by Williams is still "colored," Pincus, the Jewish messenger with the Governor's reprieve has become a nondescript American, Joe Pettibone.

All the changes mentioned above bring the film more in line with the then current conventions of romantic comedy. The increased romance, the harmlessness of the social philosophy and characters, the increased homogenization of character types and humor, the disappearance of politics and sex make the final product smoother but also slightly less interesting and anarchistic in the same way that the Marx Brothers films lost their humor as they became increasingly sane.

The protagonists in thirties comedies slowly began to change as romance took a greater hold of the genre. According to Ted Sennet in *Lunatics and Lovers*, a study of comedy in the period:

> By the mid-thirties, the evolving optimism began to affect the comedies that flowed from Hollywood.... Attitudes were changing, and the comedies began to center ... on identifiable people, foolish, scatterbrained, and laughably fallible, but also good-natured, honest and likeable.[29]

One of the triumphs of *The Twentieth Century* is that the audience retains interest and allegiance to Jaffe even though he is a master scoundrel and not really a young romantic lead. Garland, although she projects a greater sense of humanity, matches Jaffe in highhanded manipulation both in their confrontations and in her dealings with her own lover and maid. *Nothing Sacred* holds a middle ground between the cynicism of *The Twentieth Century* and the more cordial comedy of *His Girl Friday*. In *Nothing Sacred* Hecht

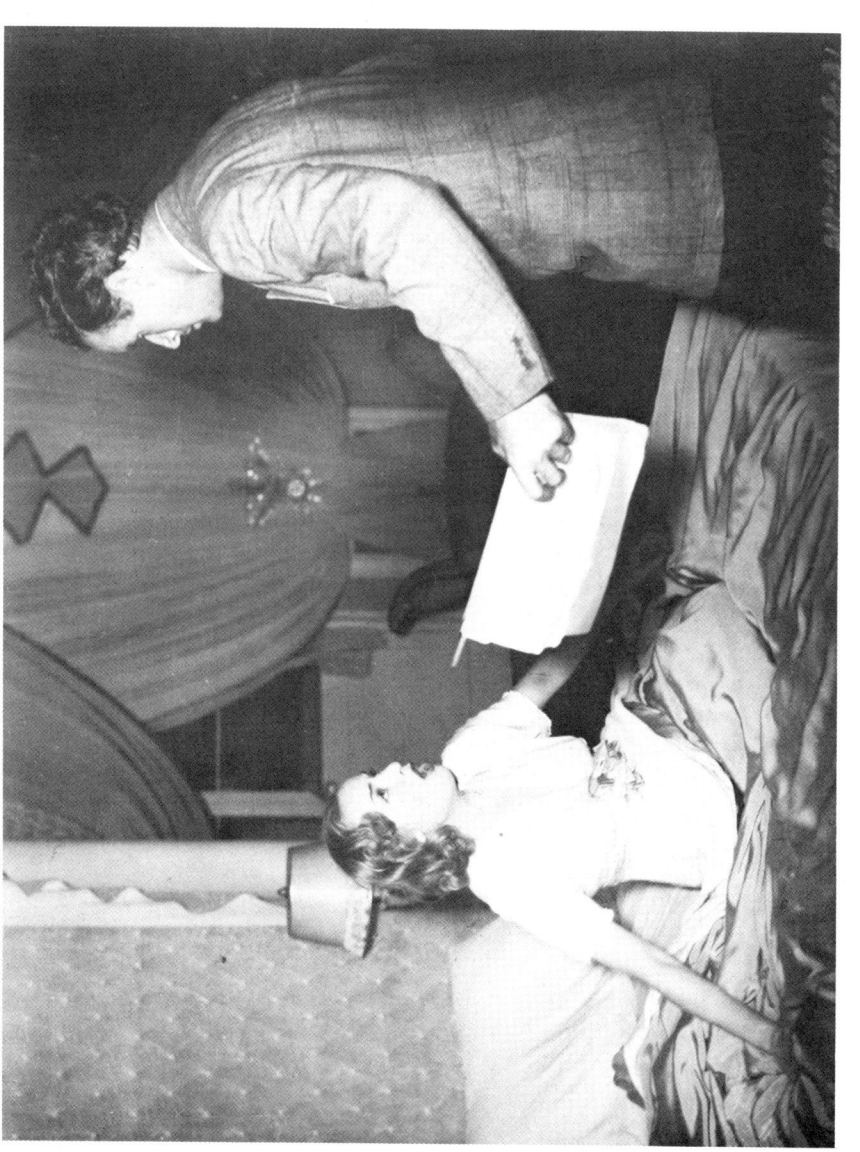

11. *Nothing Sacred* (1937). William Wellman directs Carole Lombard in fake illness scene. In typical Hecht fashion, the two lovers show their affection in a knockdown fight. (Photo: Museum of Modern Art/Film Stills Archive courtesy United Artists.)

turned his satirical focus away from the central characters and aimed outward at the world at large. Even though the protagonists, Hazel Flagg and the reporter Wally Cook, are in one sense the biggest swindlers in the story, they become sympathetic lovers, striking a balance between Hecht's hard-boiled approach and the greater romance that was becoming part of the form. As McCaffrey comments, "the comic attack, while awkwardly and crudely stated in the opening title of *Nothing Sacred*, has more sting than most of the lampoons that can be termed madcap comedies."[30]

In *The Front Page* and *The Twentieth Century*, specific professions and bureaucracies had been burlesqued, while the general public, although gullible enough to accept the pretense and lies spread by these groups, were not major targets. In *Nothing Sacred* Hecht starts with the professional groups, newspapers, doctors, governments, but aims his satire at the general populace, rural and urban. He makes his intentions clear in the opening titles superimposed on cityscapes:

Title #1 This is New York
Skyscraper Champion
Of the World...

Title #2 Where the Slickers and
Know-It-Alls peddle gold
bricks to each other...

Title #3 ...And where Truth,
Crushed to earth, rises
again more phony
than a glass eye...

Nothing Sacred opens with fraud and develops from there. Wally Cook (Fredric March), star reporter, has been bamboozled into thinking a shoeshine boy is a maharajah. The film begins with the *Morning Star*'s editor, Oliver Stone (Walter Connolly) introducing the Maharajah who has promised to donate a vast sum of money for a building program. When the Maharajah's wife comes and drags the man home, Wally is reduced to working on obituaries. He convinces Stone to give him another chance and go to Warsaw, Vermont, to investigate the story of a girl dying of radium poisoning, which he thinks will make a great sob story.

The residents of Warsaw are closemouthed and tightfisted. Wally is insulted, ignored, and finally bitten by a child before he finds the office of Dr. Downer (Charles Winninger), who bears a lifelong grudge against the *Morning Star* because of the contest he lost many years before. "I think you're a

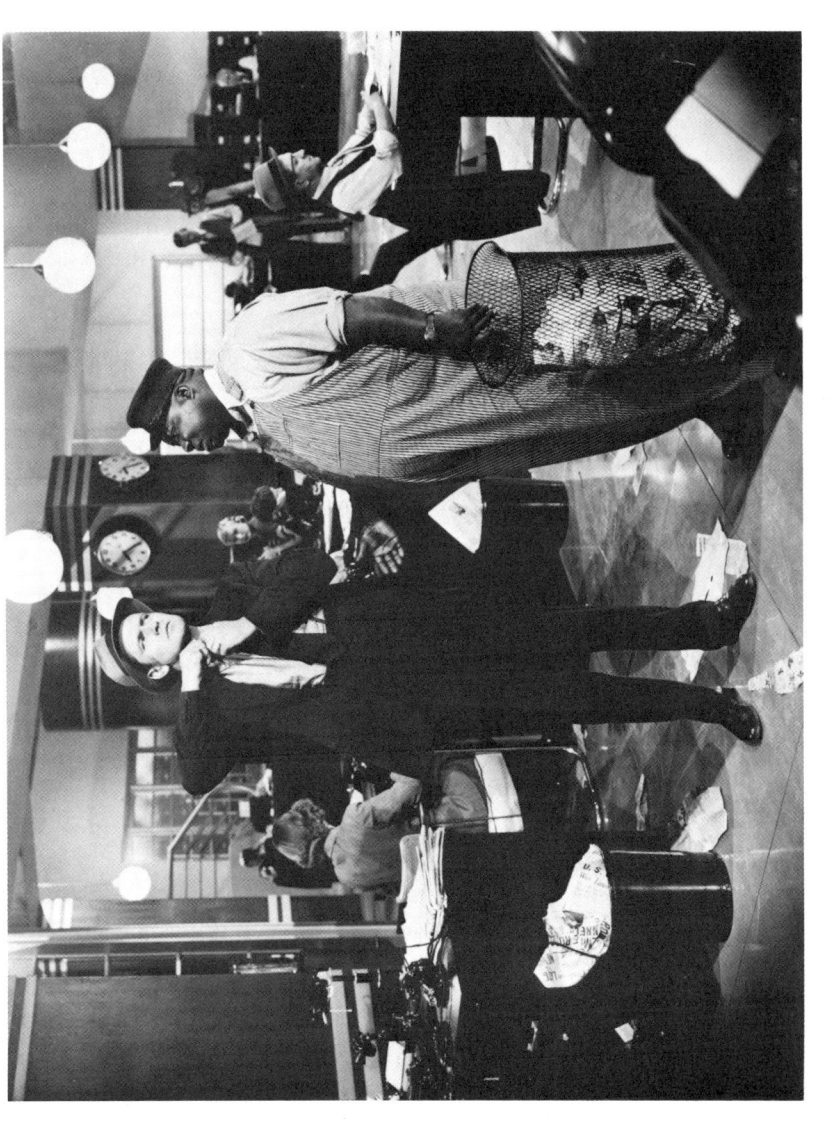

12. *Nothing Sacred* (1937). Wally Cook (Fredric March) in the newsroom with Ernest Walker (Tony Brown), the man who convinced him he was a sultan. Although a tough reporter, Hecht's Cook is gullible as well as soft-hearted. (Photo: Museum of Modern Art/Film Stills Archive courtesy United Artists.)

newspaper man," he says. "I can smell them. The hand of God reaching down into the mire couldn't elevate one of them to the depths of degradation." Although Downer will not help him, Cook finds the girl, Hazel Flagg (Carole Lombard). It turns out she too has just seen the doctor who has told her he made a mistake in the diagnosis and that she's not going to die. She is a bit disappointed because she had planned to spend the money the company gave her for dying to go to New York for a last fling. "It's kind of startling to be brought to life twice and each time in Warsaw," she says. Before she can tell Cook that she's not going to die, he offers her the trip to New York and she accepts.

Wally flies Hazel to New York where she is greeted by skywriters and the mayor who gives her a key to the city. A bit self-conscious at first, she soon begins to enjoy herself, although the crying and mournful expressions of everyone around her does marr her good time. Wally, impressed by what he thinks is Hazel's courage ("I'm not going to bed until I have convulsions and my teeth start falling out.") becomes disillusioned with the falsity of the whole affair and falls in love with Hazel. Hazel in turn falls in love with Wally and begins to worry about what will happen to him if she is exposed. The town meanwhile has gone crazy over Hazel. Wrestling matches are stopped and the round bell is tolled for her; nightclubs hold Hazel Flagg Nights; and troops of children compose songs in her honor.

> For you Hazel we are cheering.
> Now the End is finally nearing.
> Like an angel your appearing
> Hooray for Hazel Flagg.
>
> Hazel Flagg is going fast.
> She's ebbing with the tide.
> She's riding waves of glory
> to that Alien other side.
>
> (To the "Battle Hymn of the Republic")

Hazel passes out with drink and the city goes wild. Stone is very concerned. "Doctor I want to know the worst. I don't want you to spare our feelings. We go to press in fifteen minutes." Unfortunately an expert on radium poisoning, Emil Eggelhoffer (who may be a relative of Max Eggelhoffer, the alienist from *The Front Page*) examines and exposes Hazel to Stone. Wally who has asked Hazel to marry him (her reply: "There's no future in it.") is overjoyed, but Stone is outraged. When Hazel pretends to have developed pneumonia and the doctors are going to re-examine her, Wally gets her involved in a knockdown fight to exhaust her and then slugs her in the jaw to knock her out. When Wally discovers that Stone, undeceived, has watched the whole affair, he is outraged.

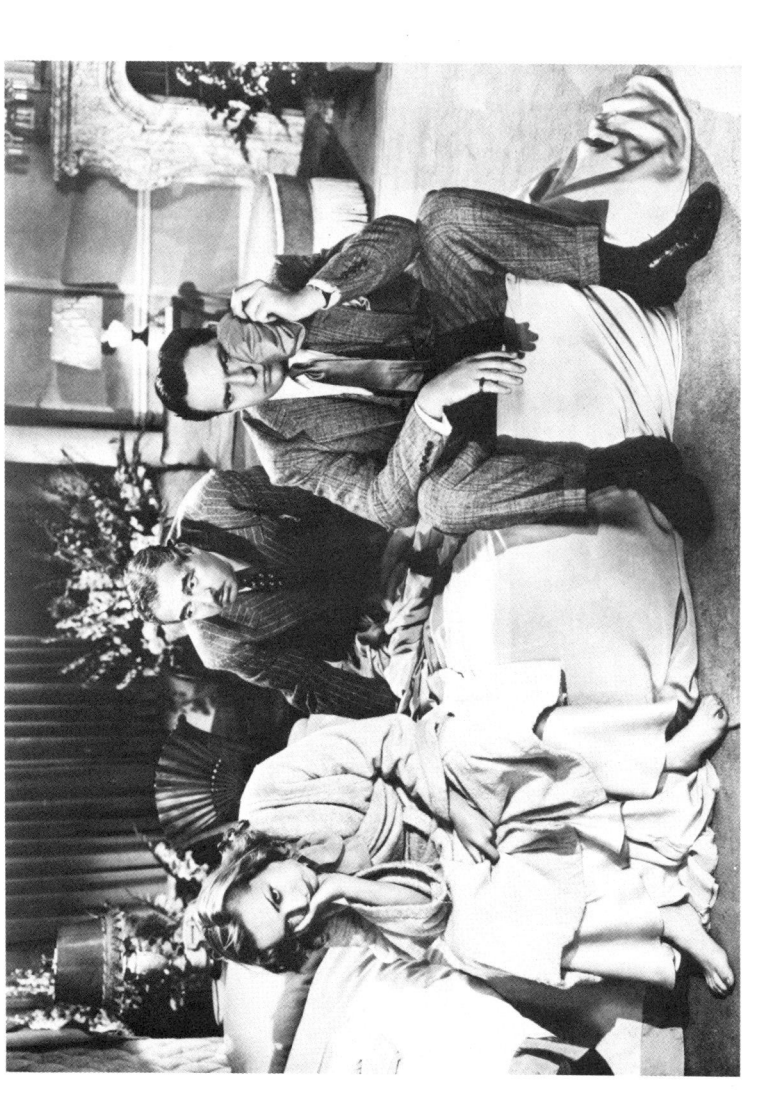

13. *Nothing Sacred* (1937). Hazel Flagg (Carole Lombard) and Wally Cook (Fredric March) in love—a passion they display by socking each other on the jaw. The couple may be romantic but Cook's editor Stone (Walter Connolly), in the tradition of Walter Burns or Oscar Jaffe, has enough nastiness for them both. He is "sort of a cross between a ferris wheel and a werewolf, but with a lovable streak, if you care to blast for it." (Photo: Museum of Modern Art/Film Stills Archive courtesy United Artists.)

Wally:	You mean to say you stood there and let me beat up a defenseless woman?
Stone:	I did, Mr. Cook.
Wally:	Where's your sense of chivalry?
Stone:	My chivalry? Aren't you just a trifle confused, Mr. Cook? You hit her.
Wally:	That's entirely different. I love her.

When Hazel wakes up and discovers the fight has been a waste, she knocks out Wally, rushes into the next room which is filled with dignitaries, and confesses to her deception. The mayor, the scoutleaders, and the other civic potentates will have nothing to do with her confession. They have put their reputations behind their Hazel Flagg campaign and fear they will be hurt if the truth comes out. Hazel must disappear. She leaves a letter to the city:

Dear New York City:
    We've had a lot of good times together, you and I. But even the best of times must end so I've gone to face the end alone like an elephant.

In the final scene Mr. and Mrs. Cook are on a tropical cruise where Wally receives a message that Hazel's funeral has gone beautifully.

With the exception of Wally, there are no innocents in the film. The country people are nasty and the city people, if they are not profiting directly from Hazel's illness, are wallowing in false sentiment over someone else's troubles. Stone and the newspaper are the chief celebrants. Wally is writing stories about Hazel the way Hildy creates death cell interviews for Burns. But where Hildy never questions the sincerity of what he is doing, Wally is much softer. At the wrestling match, he cautions Hazel:

Don't excite yourself too much, it's just a fake, those grapplers. The only square thing about them is the ring. They're a symbol of the whole town, pretending to fight, love, weep and laugh all the time, and they're phonies, all of them. And I head the list.... Using you to get a bonus and a byline on the front page, making good over your poor little pain wracked body. Stop looking so happy and gallant will you, it breaks my heart.

What makes it comic and makes Wally a sap is that it is Wally and the paper that are being exploited. In this sense, the film is much less cynical that *The Front Page* where the real plight of Williams and his impending execution is used for humor. Here the laughs are harmless because Hazel and her drunken doctor are frauds. The excessive sentimentality and exploitation may be a bit morbid but it is not truly callous since the audience is always aware that no one's life is actually at stake.

Because he is duped along with everyone else, Stone is not as formidable a scoundrel as Walter Burns. Wally describes him in Burnsian terms as "sort of a cross between a ferris wheel and a werewolf—but with a lovable streak, if you care to blast for it." Stone himself is capable of flights of misanthropic anger as when he blames Wally for Hazel's deception. He is

> toying with the idea of removing your heart and stuffing it like an olive.... You ruined me. You ruined *The Morning Star*. You blackened the fair name of journalism. You and that foul blotch of nature, Hazel Flagg.... (Pointing to the X-rays) Look at that skeleton, not a bone missing. That's Hazel Flagg, the biggest fake of the century, a lying faking witch with the soul of an eel and the brain of a tarantula.

Richard Corliss believes that, as actors, Walter Connolly as Stone and Fredric March as Cook lack the bite and nastiness of typical Hechtian editors and reporters and that the film is weakened by this inappropriate casting. While it is true that Connolly and March are not "snarling dervishes" in these roles, it is also true that the characters they portray are more victims than predators and are thus deprived of the cavalier ferocity of other Hecht scoundrels. The "unseen hand" that Burns says protects the *Morning Post* does not protect *The Morning Star* from shoeshine boys or country doctors.

Corliss generally dislikes March, who he suggests had "the vegetable magnetism of Hubert Humphrey crossed with Merv Griffin" and lacks *chutzpah* as the reporter.[31] But even in the writing, Wally Cook is a Hecht reporter with his soft belly floating up, and while March's diction may be a bit cleaner than Pat O'Brien's, Wally resembles Peggy more than Hildy. He is capable of invective but because of his love he is far more disillusioned than Hildy. Hildy was upset with Walter and his profession; Wally is soured on the falseness of the whole city:

> I used to love New York when it went gaga over some celebrity. Danced in the streets with a neon light round its heart. I'm getting fed up with its trick tears and phony lamentations.

Hazel is given the bite that Wally lacks, which is proper because while Wally only thinks he is aware on the cynical game being played Hazel is the one in control of the situation. What for Wally in Hazel is courage is merely her desire to forget about her duplicity and have a good time. When Wally, depressed with the show says, "For good clean fun there's nothing like a wake," Hazel is unconcerned: "Oh, please, let's not talk shop."

The basic tension between editor/profession and love has been altered by the sentimentality and disillusionment of the reporter and the cynicism of the lover, but a new obstacle has been thrown in to keep the lovers apart: Hazel's supposed death and her deception. Everything Wally does to help Hazel threatens her exposure. For example, he enlists the aid of Dr. Egglehoffer to examine her. To protect herself, she tries to fake a suicide by leaving a note and jumping into the river. The note:

> Dear New York City:
> Goodbye. Remember me as someone you made very happy. I enjoyed everything. There is only one thing left to enjoy—your river....

elicits an outraged response from Stone:

Stone:	Jumpin' H. Sebastian. She's double-crossed us.
Wally:	She's gone over to another paper?
Stone:	She's gone into the river.

Wally, however, runs off and tries to stop her but ends up dumping them both in the river where, since he cannot swim, she has to save him.

From the first, Hazel is interested in Wally. She asks if newsmen usually marry.

Wally:	Not after they're fourteen or fifteen. That's the dangerous age for the journalist. His ideas are not yet formed, and he falls easy prey to elderly waitresses. Once his finer side is born, he waits.
Hazel:	For what?
Wally:	The sound of the fire alarm, Miss Flagg. Waits to go rushing off to the fire.
Hazel:	What fire is that?
Wally:	Love.
Hazel:	We used to hear about that in Warsaw.
Wally:	It's gotten around.

The obstacle that keeps them apart also keeps the entire courtship away from sentiment. The romance is always undercut by humor or a morbid joke as Wally distances himself from his dying story while Hazel is afraid to tell him the truth. The first kiss comes after they have been in the river and have crawled, drenching wet, into a big crate. He proposes, thinking she will die soon. He is both overjoyed to discover she is not going to die and outraged by her deception. When he confronts her, fighting with her to get her overheated, he is angry as well as in love:

Wally:	(Kicking and slapping her around slightly.) You're going to have plenty of reason to hate me. I'm going to show you cards and spades...for the next fifty years. I'm going to pay you back for every lie you told. I'm gonna flirt, and lie, and cheat, and swindle, right through to our golden wedding.
Hazel:	(exhausted) Yeah, yeah. Let me hit you just once.

Even on the boat as they sail through tropical waters they argue about how important she was and whether or not the city was getting tired of her.

In this ending, the lovers have not repented for their transgressions, nor do they indulge in soothing romance, thus continuing the satire until the conclusion of the film. This consistent viewpoint marks the best but by no means all screwball comedies. Increasingly, as McCaffrey points out:

> Too many of the sophisticated comedies of the forties and quite a few in the thirties tended to compromise the ending of the sentimental drama by having a reformation of sorts in the mating of the romantic leads. At its zenith of quality the screwball madcap, or daffy film comedy avoided the sentimental ending.[32]

Apparently, credit does not go to Hecht for the ending, however. Hecht says he wrote the script in two weeks on a train between New York and Hollywood. This is true, but he had also returned east before David Selznick discovered Hecht had written a facetious ending to the film, an ending that was unusable and had to be reworked by Budd Schulberg and Ring Lardner, Jr.

Despite the lack of sentimentality in the romance, Hecht gives greater weight to the lovers and to Wally's disillusionment than to these elements in his earlier films. Hecht was no longer writing about Chicago but about new York—not merely a change in scenery but a change in society as well. Chicago was a place of innocence, where Ben was not bothered by the implications of the stories he covered. The entertainments were simple and harmless. As a character in *The Twentieth Century* protests to O'Malley, who dislikes Chicago, "It's a good town for a good show. The World's Fair proved that." "Yeah, fan dances and flea circuses." New York seems to touch more on the real world, and Wally is closer in some ways to the maudlin press agent in *Miracle of the Bells* (1948) than to the oblivious Hildy Johnson. Hecht was beginning to feel his age and becoming increasingly nostalgic about his irreverent and noble youth.

The film is caustic, at times, and this shift of emphasis in the reporter's character and his isolation from his own professional group is really only apparent when it is compared with other films. *Nothing Sacred,* directed by William Wellman, still possesses some of the sharpest satire of any screwball comedy. Its dialogue is crisp and sophisticated and its construction well-crafted. Considering that it runs only 75 minutes, it develops its themes and characters exceedingly well. Hecht's screenplay is not mere dialogue, however, it also calls for visual elements to comment on and enhance the material such as the paper with the Hazel Flagg headline being used to wrap a fish. The film was the Scripps-Howard selection for the best film of November of 1937 and had record runs at Radio City Music Hall during its first release.

Wellman's direction is precise and well paced. Hecht may have written another newspaper comedy for Wellman a few years later: *Roxie Hart* (1942), based on the same basic formula and idea of exploiting the public's morbid interest in crime and death.[33] In this film it is a murderess, Roxie Hart and her shady lawyer (Ginger Rogers and Adolph Menjou), who team together with a reporter, Homer Howard (George Montgomery), who falls in love with Roxie and tries to save her.

Roxie Hart is of questionable authorship, but *It's a Wonderful World* (1939) and *Comrade X* (1940) are not. The first was written by Hecht from a story he wrote with Herman Mankiewicz, the second was written with Charles Lederer from a story by Walter Reisch. Both films fit into the screwball comedy mold, but the form was beginning to lose some of its original vivacity.

It's a Wonderful World is about a detective (James Stewart) who escapes from his guards on the way to prison in order to prove that the man he was convicted for helping is innocent. Along the way he gets entangled with a poetess (Claudette Colbert). Stewart is as much after the reward he will get for clearing the man as he is out to right an injustice. He falls in love with Colbert and she with him. His search takes him to a theatre where he acts under the name of Ernest Hemingway. He finds the killer with her help. The film is tightly constructed using detective, romantic, and comic conventions to sustain interest. Frankly commercial, it is also very professionally handled. Otis Ferguson, not one of Hecht's admirers, called the film,

> One of the few genuinely comic pieces in a dog's age. . . . Its virtue is that it does not make you think of plot: suspense holds like a cable, the interest keeps jumping, and there's a pretty good laugh around every corner.[34]

While the film fulfills its own expectations it never takes any risks. It is a good natured comedy rather than a satire, although Hecht has some fun at the expense of poets and the theatre. The character played by Stewart is the familiar sentimental tough guy but Stewart had not yet developed the ornery streak he was to bring to his postwar work, particularly westerns.

Comrade X suffers from an excess of the topical satire that *It's a Wonderful World* lacked. Clark Gable is the mysterious Comrade X, who, posing as an irresponsible drunken journalist from the *Topeka Bugle,* smuggles stories out of Russia, thus bypassing censorship. His servant, Felix Bressart, uncovers his secret and forces Gable to agree to take his daughter, Hedy Lamarr, out of Russia. Lamarr is a staunch Communist and Gable has to pretend that he is too. He convinces her to come to America to help foment the revolution. She wants him to marry her first as a practical gesture, which he does. The nastiness of the regime and a short stay in prison disillusions Lamarr so that finally she is happy to leave with Gable. The couple escape with her father and eventually cross the border driving a tank after a slapstick chase sequence. Eve Arden is present as an old flame and fellow newsman to help the

14. *Comrade X* (1940). Theodore (Hedy Lamarr) gives a lesson in Communist ideology to reporter MacKinley B. Thompson (Clark Gable). Democracy and love prove to be the better systems, and the reporter and his story America's first line of defense. (Photo: Museum of Modern Art/Film Stills Archive courtesy Metro Goldwyn Mayer.)

plot along. The film is not as well integrated in its styling as better Hecht efforts, such as *Nothing Sacred*. Slapstick, political satire and romantic comedy are juxtaposed against each other rather than smoothly meshed. One problem is that the film takes its political satire seriously. Hecht pictures the Communists as no less bumbling but much more dangerous and deadly to individuals and human freedom than the local corrupt governments in his childhood Chicago. Herman Weinberg, in discussing the nonideological brightness of Lubitsch's *Ninotchka* (1939), in comparson to *Comrade X* says:

> One realizes what an innately unhumorous thing *Comrade X* was—the mercurial raffishness of the former versus the flatfooted orthodoxy of the latter, the sardonic energy of one as against the pallid banality of the other.[35]

In *Ninotchka*, Greta Garbo, a Communist official, is converted by her love of a Parisian. *Comrade X* takes a different ideological stance. Communism is inherently dangerous and this political fact as much as her attraction to Gable is the cause of Lamarr's conversion. Capitalism, ignored by *Ninotchka*, is held up as a model in *Comrade X*—as exemplified by the Brooklyn Dodgers.

The film shows a slightly different Hecht than the one usually seen in his comedies. Here he is defending institutions as well as attacking them. Although the film was well received critically, it ran afoul of the changes in the international climate as Russia shifted from ally to adversary in the opening days of the Second World War, and audiences rejected the film. According to Fred Guiles, one audience in Long Beach was so upset by the recent Russian invasion of Finland that they ripped up their theatre seats and threw them at the screen.[36]

Screwball comedy was a uniquely American invention. It drew its humor and originality from the urban slang and an indigenous tradition of self-criticism. As the decade passed, however, the unstable atmosphere of the Depression that had permitted and fostered the irreverence of such films as *The Twentieth Century* or *Nothing Sacred* evaporated, and satire came to seem frivolous or even unpatriotic in the face of world events. Screwball comedy lost its bite and was replaced by wholesome joshing. Films such as *Comrade X* or *It's a Wonderful World* lack the originality and exuberance of earlier comedies. Even *His Girl Friday*, in comparison with the freshness and bite of *The Front Page*, is a smooth, sentimental, inoffensive remake. The attention of the writers who had created the form also began to stray. MacArthur and Lederer would soon be in uniform, and, as will be discussed in Chapter Seven, Hecht was engrossed in political activities from 1939. Whatever force was left to the genre would vanish when America entered the war.

6

Writer-Directors:
The Scoundrel and *Crime Without Passion*

In 1934 Hecht and Charles MacArthur embarked on a new enterprise as movie moguls. Instead of writing scripts to be produced by someone else they agreed to produce four films for Paramount Studios. Hecht and MacArthur were to write, produce, and direct the films under the nominal control of Walter Wanger, Paramount's East Coast production chief.

Early in the summer, Hecht and MacArthur's agent, Leland Hayward called Hecht in Nyack with the offer. Hecht returned to the pool and relayed the information to MacArthur:

> "He says there's a fellow who wants to give us a million dollars to make movies in Astoria, Long Island," I told Charlie. "He wants us to have lunch with this fellow tomorrow." "Nothing doing," said Charlie. It seemed a logical answer.[1]

MacArthur's reflexive bias against bearers of extraordinary gifts may have been logical, but the temptation to produce films and reap their financial dividends far from the indignities of Hollywood and the meddling hands of the studios would have been too much for men of more sober judgment. Hecht and MacArthur grabbed at the offer to make independent films in New York and by the end of the summer were shooting their first film.

In Astoria, Hecht and MacArthur wanted to make films that the Hollywood studios would be afraid to make. They would make sophisticated films that dealt with taboo subjects in unusual ways. Their crime story would be a deep psychological study of panic and guilt; their film about the New York literati would have an exceedingly unattractive hero and a sudden shift to the supernatural; their campus comedy would deal with Communism, radicalism, and capitalism; and their whimsical circus film would be set against the Russian revolution.

They produced the four films in eighteen months: *Crime Without Passion* (1934), *Once in a Blue Moon* (made in 1934, released in 1936), *The Scoundrel* (1935), and *Soak the Rich* (made in 1935, released in 1936). All were deemed financial failures, although *Crime Without Passion* and *The Scoundrel* were well received critically and hailed as harbingers of a new, more sophisticated type of film to be produced in America. The films were innovative in their use of literate dialogue, montage, stream of consciousness narration and in the maturity of their wit and insight, but by the time the last film had been released, the team was back in Hollywood writing *Barbary Coast* for Samuel Goldwyn.

Hecht remembered their experiment in Astoria as an adventure without "any glow of success or burn of failure. It is a memory of a two year party that kept going seven days a week."[2]

Hecht and MacArthur did not abandon their usual pranks merely because they were now their own bosses, nor did they seem to take filmmaking very seriously. Most stories and recollections about this period make it appear a time of unrelieved merriment. Hecht and MacArthur intentionally violated most rules of conventional filmmaking in the studio, on the set, and even in the final films themselves. From the accounts, nothing seemed planned, and a polished end product appeared to be low on a list of their priorities.

But as with many of their other endeavors which were clothed in a mantle of carelessness and frivolity, Hecht and MacArthur had a seriousness about their work which is clearly manifested in the films. There is an intentionality in *Crime Without Passion* and *The Scoundrel* that belies the charge of haphazard irresponsibility. In fact, they may have been overly ambitious, trying to upset too many traditions at once. They wanted to reestablish the East Coast as a center for the filmmaking. They wanted to make films that would appeal to a more literate audience than did the usual Hollywood offering, but they felt that such films could still be financial successes. They wanted these films to reflect their own interests and tastes rather than commercial formulas. They wanted to raise the writer to a place of prominence and control in the filmmaking process by proving that the script was so important to the success of a film that most other production values could be largely ignored. While doing these things, they wanted to produce their own full-time burlesque of the studio system which might have used *Night at the Opera* as a life-imitating-art scenario.

The atmosphere in Astoria had as much in common with the Hollywood studios as Ben Hecht's *Chicago Literary Times* resembled a normal newspaper newsroom. The project was largely a Hecht enterprise. While MacArthur was an active partner, Hecht's influence appears to have dominated. It was Hecht's messianic zeal that carried MacArthur into Astoria. The films they produced were based on material by Ben or his wife Rose Caylor and the films had more in common with Hecht's novels and his subsequent independently made films than with MacArthur's work, or even their collaborations. As often seems to have been the case in their collaboration, however, the tastes and judgment of one sharpened the talents of the other, or at least kept his excesses to a minimum.

At Astoria personal excess often held sway. Helen Hayes described her husband this way:

> My Charlie died a little boy. Throughout his life, he clung along with Ben Hecht and other cronies, to a dream of eternal boyhood where villains and heroes are easily distinguishable, where fun is always to be had and responsibilities are to be shrugged away.[3]

With their own movie studio as a playground, Hecht and MacArthur could indulge themselves at the expense of those that underwrote their enterprise. The playground was visited daily by notables from the social and artistic world of New York such as George Jean Nathan or Harpo Marx. Lunch for the crew was catered by the 21 Club, the food and waiters arriving each day in a fleet of taxis. Huge banners were placed around the studio with such slogans as "Better than Metro Isn't Good Enough," "Cut to the Chase," and "Let the Audience in on Your Secret." Girls were hired from a local bordello as secretaries, and five life-size nude photographs were pasted on office doors to confuse visitors. Incoming mail was ceremoniously burned each afternoon.

Hecht had never thought very highly of most of the producers for whom he had worked. He said he discovered early in his movie career that:

> A movie is never any better than the stupidest man connected with it. There are times when this distinction may be given to the writer or director. Most often it belongs to the producer.[4]

Still, Hecht felt that a producer was needed to handle salesmen and other undesirables. A perfect candidate for the position was found on a visit to a Coney Island side show. According to Helen Hayes he had a

> tall pointed pear-shaped head. He was a weird creature. And they hired him.... They put him in a gray flannel suit and tie and everything and they took him and put him in the office and called a press conference and had him announced as their executive producer.[5]

Charles Lederer, sent into exile by David Selznick, was brought east to "supervise" the work; the janitor was made the Supervisor in Charge of Sanitation; and Oscar Levant was given the title of Assistant President of the Music Department after he complained that the $15 a week he was being paid to keep Hecht's violin playing well tuned would not cover his taxi fares. Hecht sent out memos raising Levant's salary to $350, then to $500, and finally to $1,200 but still paid him only $15 a week.

Once they had the studio running properly, the producers turned their attention to the problems of directing. While Hecht and MacArthur had spent a great deal of time working for producers and were thus well prepared for the jobs as studio moguls they had less knowledge of actual production though probably more than Hecht protested they had:

> Neither Charlie nor I had ever spent an hour on a movie set. We knew nothing of casts, budgets, schedules, booms, gobos, unions, scenery, cutting, lighting. Worse we had barely seen a dozen movies in our lives.... We were, however, not for a moment abashed.[6]

They thought their ignorance of technical matters would be a protection against the excesses of "creative directors," men described by Hecht as a combination of "amateur actors" and "amateur playwrights." Producers rather than directors were thought to wield the creative power as a result of their financial control of films. Thalberg, Selznick, Zanuck and others virtually birthed their films rather than merely managed their productions. Writers, such as Hecht and MacArthur, worked with the producer and rarely saw the directors working on the set. Consequently, they absorbed the producers' view of filmmaking and undervalued the importance of directing. They considered the director to be more likely an obstacle than an asset in realizing their scripts. This attitude is reflected in the great secret that Hecht and MacArthur felt they had discovered about making movies:

> This secret was the fact that 90 percent of the success of a movie (or its failure) lay in the writing of its script. Producer, director and stars could add less to a movie script than they could to a stage play.... We knew that any improvement at all to the writer's script by director and producer was an unlikely matter.[7]

The alteration of the script on its way through production by three to nine people was "certain to distort it and bleed it to death,"[8] as Hecht felt most of his scripts had been mangled. Mediocrity rather than incompetence was usually the cause of the blandness of production by committee, although ineptness also figured in the leveling process.

Hecht honored directors who approached their jobs as craftsmen and who tried to realize the movie contained in the script. (Interestingly, he included in this group directors now thought of as creative geniuses who triumphed over their material, such as Hitchcock, Lubitsch, and Hawks.) Hecht had few kind words for the directors who aspired to "greatness" by distorting

> ...a script so that it would seem a director and not a playwright was telling a tale. To this end, a small, straightforward drama often gets lengthened into a three-hour epic by the addition of fist fights, moody walks, extensive facemaking in close-ups (without any authors' words to deflect from directorial genius), and by explosive mob scenes, panoramas showing the littleness of man and the bigness of the director.[9]

Instead, Hecht and MacArthur set out to transfer their scripts to the screen in the simplest manner possible. They agreed on two basic groundrules: never change a script in production, and never make a pass at girls in their employ (although hiring girls you had made passes at was acceptable).

> With emergency conferences and studio romances, the two greatest handicaps to moviemaking, out of the way, we had plenty of time for honest merriment.[10]

Hecht believed that many directors wasted time on scenes by changing the angle of the shot every few lines and by needlessly reshooting scenes in an attempt to mark the film with their personality.

> These fellows go in for their fifty takes on a scene in the hope of stumbling on some contortion or posture that will take the scene away from actor and playwright and make it "a director's scene."[11]

In Astoria, time was saved by cutting the number of setups in half, and they did so few retakes that *Crime Without Passion* and *The Scoundrel* used only 80,000 feet of film each rather than the one-half million feet Hecht says were normally used for a studio production.

According to the great secret, directing the performances of the actors was also a simple task and

> ...consisted of putting our script on the screen as we had written them. The actors did what the written stage directions said they should do, and recited our lines with a minimum of coaching. They were people of intelligence and knew the meaning of their speeches as well as we did.[12]

In order to demonstrate how easy it actually was and to assure intelligence in their actors, actors with screen experience were avoided in the casting. The casts were comprised of stage actors, such as Noel Coward; vaudevillians such as Jimmy Savo; attractive socialites such as Whitney Bourne; and great personalities such as Alexander Woolcott who were asked to play themselves. As Hecht summed up the entire affair;

> None of the actors we hired for *Crime Without Passion* had ever played in a movie.... Add to this the fact that Charlie and I had never directed anybody or produced anything (except scripts) and you have the full picture of Astoria as an Amateur hour.[13]

Hecht and MacArthur were not totally oblivious to the need for technical resources and they found them in their cameraman Lee Garmes. Garmes, who had won an Academy Award in 1932 for his work on *Shanghai Express* for Josef von Sternberg, provided the visual skills that the directors lacked. Although it

15. (1934). Charles MacArthur and Ben Hecht direct in Astoria, Long Island studios. Cinematographer Lee Garmes (right) consults. On the wall is one of the signs the directors put up to encourage their company. This one says, "Let the Public in on Our Secret." (Photo: Academy of Motion Pictures.)

was not widely known at the time, Garmes "directed" considerable portions of the films he worked on with Hecht. He received screen credit for *Once in a Blue Moon* (associate director), *Angels Over Broadway* (co-director, 1940), *Specter of the Rose* (associate producer, 1946), and *Actors and Sin* (co-director, 1952). He also photographed *China Girls,* a film Hecht wrote and produced in 1942.

Garmes, whom Hecht called his "favorite collaborator," devised the setups, compositions, lighting, worked with the actors, and even called the sacred "cut" at the end of a take. Hecht said that Garmes was not only the finest cameraman but one of the most learned men on the subject of filmmaking that he knew in Hollywood.

> While ridding the set of its wrong nuances of light and shade, Lee also watched the grouping of figures and carried the cutting of the picture in his head.... As director of the movie being shot, I was the final word on all matters. But I would sit by silent and full of admiration as Lee and his overalled magicians prepared the set for my "direction." My job seemed to me little more than putting a frame on a finished canvas.[14]

While Garmas may have been responsible for the technical competence and much of the look of the films, it is clear that the style for each film was rooted in the demands of the script and the tastes of Hecht and MacArthur. Commenting on *Crime Without Passion,* Garmes defines his working relationship with the directors this way:

> [I] directed 60-70 percent of the picture; we'd start at nine a.m. and some days Hecht was there, some days MacArthur; they'd start working on the picture at eleven a.m.! So they relied on me. They set the style of how they wanted the dialogue done, and I would direct the whole physical side of it.[15]

Hecht and MacArthur's attitude toward production, as towards casting, was designed to show how easy filmmaking was. Theatre actors would do just as well or better on the screen; they could make stars out of vaudeville clowns; even personalities could play themselves. Production was so simple that a good technician could realize the script once the style had been set, and all the studio hocus pocus was unnecessary if the script was good.

In their Astoria scripts Hecht and MacArthur felt they had to balance a number of demands. They wanted to write for themselves and for that "intelligent minority" who shared their tastes. As a result, the scripts often resemble Hecht's more personal fiction than his commercial screenwriting. In their desire to show the silliness of contemporary films, however, the authors felt that merely writing intelligent scripts would not be enough, and as a result, the scripts also play off of standard Hollywood conventions. At the same time they wanted to insert enough "commercial" material in the films to assure box office success. Finally, anything they wrote had to conform to the Motion

Picture Production Code. As Fred Guiles comments: "After Walter Wanger, who ran the east coast Paramount Studio, the man most interested in what Hecht and MacArthur were doing was Will H. Hays [author of the Code]."[16] No matter how they planned to confound, titillate or surprise their audience, Good had to triumph over Evil by the end of the last reel in the best Hollywood and American tradition.

For their first film they used a short story written by Hecht for the *Saturday Evening Post* as "Cabellero of the Law," and reprinted in collections of Hecht's work under the title of the film, *Crime Without Passion*. It is a psychological crime story concerning a lawyer who, after killing his lover, constructs an elaborate alibi which is destroyed by a casual observer, the former boyfriend of the girl he has killed. Drunk and under pressure, he shoots the man only to discover that the girl was only stunned not killed and has since recovered.

The story was told as a third person narrative which entered into the mind of the lawyer. In the film the lawyer's thoughts are voiced as a first person narrative with the lawyer's increased hysteria mirrored in his soliloques. In love with a new woman he accidently shoots his mistress. In his narration he crows over the stupidity of the average fool and rehearses what he will say to the police or the court. When he is betrayed by his own cleverness he is destroyed spiritually. The use of a narrator, particularly to enhance character development and tension, was unusual for films at this time. In the adaptation the basic story is elaborated by the addition of the girl for whom the lawyer is leaving his lover. A second plot showing the lawyer falsify evidence in another murder case is also added. Both add tension to the basic story and dimension to the character of the lawyer.

The lawyer, Lou Hendrix in the story and Lee Gentry in the film, is a spectacular trial lawyer of the sort Hecht knew in Chicago (such as Charles Erbstein). The character is the familiar Hechtian man with a New York gloss. Hecht describes him as a distinctly Broadway phenomenon, "one of those popinjays of the flesh pots with the face of a tired and sarcastic boy."[17] This film and *The Scoundrel* draw heavily on the attitudes and ideas expressed in *A Jew in Love* (1931) and demonstrate the social and psychological attitudes which preoccupied Hecht during this period.

Hecht had always been aware of a difference between Chicago and New York. Where Chicago had had a rawness, an industrial vibrancy and an unselfconsciousness about itself, New York was a society of celebrities and surfaces. In Chicago Hecht had been a newspaperman and Bohemian. In New York he was a playwright, wit, and a celebrity. For a time, he was enthralled by the whirl and glitter of the world around him.

> A room full of braggarts, wits and poseurs, of literary kings and stage queens, all bursting with talent and press notices delighted me. I made few friends among them, for I was not looking for friendship. They were like troupes of actors among whom, I, too, could perform.[18]

Hecht continued to enjoy his New York contemporaries even while he became disenchanted with them. He gradually began to sneer at the glamorous parties and the company of the famous. *A Jew in Love* reflects this attitude as early as 1931 and both *Crime Without Passion* and *The Scoundrel* are cynical about different levels of the Manhattan culture. Simultaneously, however, Hecht and MacArthur made the Astoria studios a popular watering hole for the same society they caustically depicted in their scripts. MacArthur, in particular, never ceased to be the beloved "Prince Charming" of the Algonquin group. "What a perfect world this would be if it were full of MacArthurs," Alexander Woolcott once said.[19]

Psychology was a lifelong interest of Hecht's and in the new world of New York he encountered curious and unfamiliar personality types:

> One of these was a new type of male fornicator whom I had met nowhere before. They were men who made seduction their chief activity.... In Chicago bawdiness, in fact, had been a natural atmosphere since boyhood. But in Chicago I had come on no Don Juans. In New York they appeared to be blocking traffic.
> As a psychologist I was pleased, for these were the first men I had known who were eager to relate the ins and outs of amour to me.[20]

Hecht used traits of the New York Don Juan for the characters of his lawyer Gentry in *Crime Without Passion,* Anthony Mallare in *The Scoundrel,* and Jo Boshere of *A Jew in Love.* As with most of his protagonists, however, Hecht also brought some of his own personality to these portraits. Apparently Hecht was often involved in love affairs of his own. According to Fred Guiles:

> Few surviving friends of Ben's fail to mention his need for young ladies (and some not so young), usually actresses and not always in need of money, who could respond to his Edwardian ardor. His wife, Rose Caylor Hecht, as attractive as any of Ben's amours and more perceptive than most (she was a novelist twice published), rarely was heard to complain of Ben's "midinettes." And it is certain that she rarely nagged, for that was something Ben could not abide. She had the good sense to see that these side affairs kept her man's life in some kind of balance.[21]

These affairs usually occurred serially and seemed to satisfy a romantic streak in Hecht, but he was also very domestic and family oriented. Despite his tough guy image and appearance, he was devoted to his parents, wife, and children, and supported many of his needy friends. Hecht took his domesticity with him into his affairs, thus aggravating his involvement. His decription of the hurt

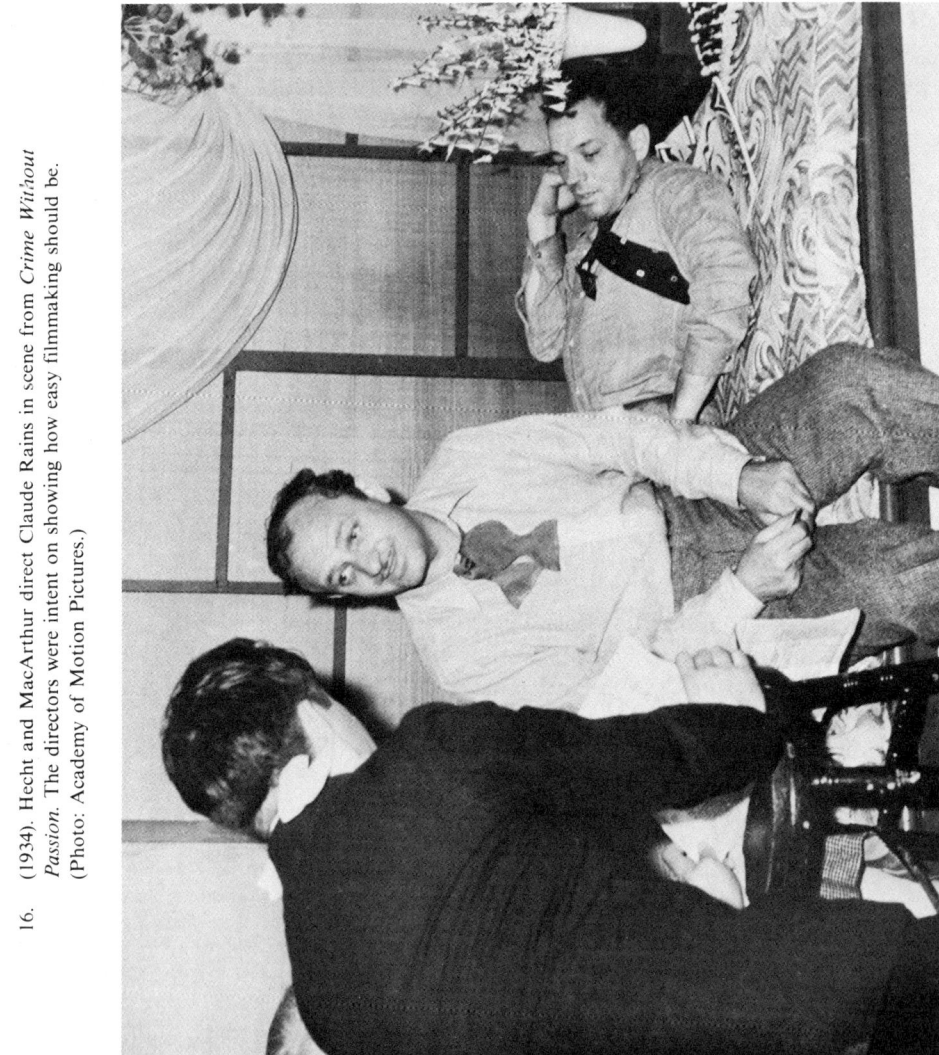

16. (1934). Hecht and MacArthur direct Claude Rains in scene from *Crime Without Passion*. The directors were intent on showing how easy filmmaking should be. (Photo: Academy of Motion Pictures.)

that men and women inflict on one another in their demands for love, affection, and betrayal are probably based on personal knowledge as much as observation of the Duan Juans of New York or any other metropolis. But where personal experience ends and the understanding gained through observation begins as a source for his characters is difficult to say.

Gentry has the ego of the Nietzchian superman, a malignant version of the Hechtian man, torturing himself over his love affairs and too cynical to be part of society. But rather than merely feeling apart from the world, a detached observer like Hecht's newspaperman, Gentry and later Mallare, deem themselves superior to humanity around them. In the first scene of *Crime Without Passion* Gentry, speaking to his secretary, denigrates the crowds passing below his high office window:

Gentry: Fascinating, those insects. The so-called human race. They don't look like porch climbers, murderers, and wife beaters from here. To think those harmless bugs are filled with greed, and lust and all the seven deadly sins. I often wonder, Miss Keeley, why people, intelligent people I mean, go on living.

Keeley: Shall I send out for some bicarbonate of soda. You haven't much time for moods this morning....

Gentry: I wish, Miss Keeley, that you'd stop referring to my philosophical flights as stomach aches.

Although Gentry is a lawyer, he does not represent law or society. His work provides him with an opportunity to show his superiority by outwitting the law and he exalts when his actions allow another murderer to walk the streets. "The only crime punishable by death is stupidity. Somebody ought to be glad that isn't a law," he says.

Hecht's characters often tour with a visitor through their bookshelves voicing their favorable and unfavorable opinions about different authors and works. Usually the list resembles Hecht's own reading choices. Gentry is no exception. His library is full of law and criminology texts; rather than a source of moral or judicial logic, however, he says they contain all the ways a smart lawyer can circumvent the law.

Gentry carries his deceptions into his love affairs. Just as Oscar Jaffe constantly thinks of himself as an actor or even a playwright ("I've just played a scene. Sardou might have written it."), Gentry constantly orchestrates his confrontations and seductions. The dancer Carmen Browne, played in the film by a dancer (Margo), is no match for Gentry's intrigues and is manipulated into playing scenes of passion and betrayal.

As a character, Gentry is much more sympathetic than Hendrix who functions primarily as the pivot for an intricate plot exercise and who becomes secondary to the alibis and reversals in which he snares himself. Both men have an overweening and ultimately destructive cleverness. Rather than hitting

Carmen with an object in a rage, as Hendrix does, Gentry shoots Carmen and then only by accident in a struggle. An attempt is made to explain, if not to justify, Gentry's actions. Miss Keeley tells both Gentry and the audience what a good person he is despite his actions. And Gentry's intrigues are designed to extricate him from his love affair. That is his explanation, but he seems to revel in their execution as well.

> Gentry: Leaving a woman, Miss Keeley, is a long and desperate process like wrestling with a piece of flypaper.
> Keeley: The trouble is you're too nice.
> Gentry: Thank you, Miss Keeley. Fortunately for you I've never been in love with you so you've only seen my best side. In love I am a monster.... I begin where sensible men leave off. Hand holding and what goes with it doesn't seem to be enough. I have to pull them apart and see what makes them tick. Overwhelm them with attention... and the result, that when I show signs of leaving some little thing, she acts like sixty-five wives. Why can't I find something... other than women, like poker or running for Congress.

Gentry pursues a kind of consecutive monogamy. Each new lover becomes his sole interest and source of life. Gentry is moving from Carmen to Katy Costello (Whitney Bourne). There is something honorable in Gentry's intention to be true to each woman, despite his methods. Even so, his needs are vampire-like and obsessive. They have a dangerous quality of megalomania as he expresses them to Katy:

> Have you ever loved anybody. Did you ever feel anything with your heart. Has there ever been anybody in your life that you've loved, that could make you happy, that could make you cry. Well, I want you to love me that way; I'm going to make you love me that way, because I need it. That's my soul—to be loved—without it I'm just part of these books, words, tricks, schemes, a walking breathing machine for outwitting the law. I'm a little bit like Dracula—no life in me, so I need someone else's soul.

Gentry is destroyed by a combination of his own arrogant cleverness and the weakness his obsession for love suggests. The film follows him as he talks and reasons with himself constructing his alibi and losing his grip on reality. Arrested, he finds he does not have the inner discipline to commit suicide with the gun nearby.

As a psychological study, the film resembles Hecht's novels. As a crime melodrama, it ignores normal convention. The big courtroom scene is used to establish situation and character rather than as a climax. As *Variety* noted;

> Always up to now, it has been customary to get the mouthpiece into a jam of his own early and then let him wiggle out of it. To do otherwise apparently seemed to be treason or something to the scripters.[22]

The ending was perceived as either an attempt to satisfy the censors or as a deliberate attempt to confound audiences. Although these considerations may have affected the plotting, the conclusion of the film was consistent with both the original story and its own internal logic depicting the unravelling of a clever mind. The ultimate downfall of Gentry is carefully prepared for, and the reappearance of Carmen is an appropriate ironic twist, but the film was faulted for an ending that was felt to be both melodramatic and self-consciously unconventional.

> To the extent that the cold ironic detachment of this stream of consciousness study of a mental sadist results in a film of style and personality, it deserves admiration and attention. But when the method ends more as a self-conscious stunt, without feeling and dramatic warmth, then I fear that even those of us who admire their methods and hope for their success must accuse the Messrs. Hecht and MacArthur of letting us down a little.[23]

In this review Richard Watts also found Gentry unsympathetic. Despite Gentry's motivation and his comparative warmth when placed beside Hecht's original popinjay, he remains more an interior case study than a romantic lead. The difficulty of audience identification with the protagonist was mentioned by some as the principal problem in an otherwise admirable work:

> Like all Hecht-MacArthur plays, "Crime Without Passion" is a skillful, workmanlike job with an original flavor of its own. It is not emotional nor, because of the deliberate unpleasantness of the principal character, is it very stirring.[24]

In a conventional Hollywood film Gentry would have been more sympathetic and either acquitted of his crime (as occurs in *Upperworld* (1934), written by Hecht) or the revelation that Carmen was alive would cause some sort of repentence and change in Gentry. Here, because the emphasis is placed on the mental deterioration of a brilliant mind, the natural conclusion is the second murder. Carmen's resurrection is an ultimate irony rather than a contrived plot turn.

The dialogue in the film had a filigreed irony that was reminiscent of Hecht's Chicago newspaper work. It ranged from the ornate observations of Gentry, such as his comments on the insect-like movement of humanity, which resembles Hecht's mood pieces, to the sharp urban dialogue of some of the minor characters, particularly Carmen's friend Buster (Paula Trueman) who asks her, "I mean, have you been absent minded once or twice with somebody else?" The stream of consciousness quality of the film, with Rains's voice imposed over the action when Gentry talks to himself, allowed for more dialogue than in most pictures. This innovation did not always find favor, however. The reaction of the reviewer from the *London Times* was not atypical:

> When the climax is reached, indeed, the film becomes quite exciting, but Mr. Rains has to get through a terrible amount of talking before anything happens at all.[25]

In general, the reviews followed the patterns of the ones already cited; the film was interesting, ingenious, even remarkable, but most critics found something in the production with which to quarrel. The visual elements of the production added to its offbeat and innovative character. The film was introduced by a montage sequence depicting the murder of Carmen and a drop of blood from which Furies rise to avenge the crime. Slavko Vorkapich, the Yugoslavian writer and montage maker, devised this and later montages in the film. According to Hecht, Vorkapich had been hired by accident:

> We had thought he was a movie cutter. It developed he was a montage expert. Not wanting to waste Vorky's talents and paychecks, Charlie and I wrote a montage prologue for our movie. Vorky put together four handsome minutes of Furies flying through the canyons of New York.[26]

Titles in the film indicate that the Furies are the three sisters of evil. They lurk behind the dreams of men and destroy them when they can. They reappear to heighten both the murder and Gentry's downfall. The use of mythic figures or supernatural figures was not unusual in Hecht's short stories. He would use them again in other films such as *The Scoundrel*. At times what is taken to be a miracle occurs through the agency of men, as in *Angels Over Broadway* (1940), at other times there is a direct intervention of some sort of divine power. In *Crime Without Passion,* the Furies help embody the dissipation of Gentry's mind.

Garmes added his own touches in a technically proficient film, some for style, others from necessity. While the directors were never seeking a pictorial realism, their first attempts at settings were not always feasible and led to a more abstract visual quality. According to Garmes:

> They brought in a stage designer who built everything to the proscenium, with bedrooms forty feet wide and twenty feet high; so I said, it won't work, let's thank him and say goodbye. I redid the sets myself with a construction man, to bring the bedroom to ten by twelve, and make all the other sets the proper size.[27]

The night club scene was built for twelve dollars with a few drapes, cellophane, a couple of chairs, table, and a tiny stage. The effect of a stage show was achieved by photographing the silhouettes of the legs of chorus girls cast on an opaque screen. The courtroom scene was filmed without a long shot which would have revealed that there was no actual set. All the pieces were on wheels for easier movement. (The exclusion of long shots also allowed Rains, who was having trouble with his feet, to keep them soaking in medicated water while playing his scenes.) A split screen was used when Gentry talked to himself, directing his alibi.

Many of these shortcuts kept the cost of production down. They were only possible, however, because the preplanning that went into production eliminated unnecessary shots and angles. Regardless of how haphazardly the sets may have been arrived at, the simplified theatrical look of the film also lent it an expressionistic tone that was consistent with other production elements. The script has the kind of exaggerated language and urban poetry that characterized the expressionistic influences apparent in Hecht's Chicago writing. The subject matter, a subjective portrait of the breakdown of a brilliant mind is similar to the monodramatic material usually associated with expressionist literature, as is the attempt to connect the subject matter with large symbolic forces, such as the Furies. The stylization is augmented additionally by painted scenery in the film, such as the buildings outside the windows that slanted together. In some ways the visual look of the film can also be connected to the early sound horror films such as *Dracula* (1931) which utilized German stage and cinematic expressionistic scenic devices.

While some of the acting had an extreme quality about it, this does not seem to have been planned. Hecht and MacArthur relied on the intelligence of the actors to realize their script and by and large they read with intelligence but not always with skill. The film centers on Rains who was a skilled professional character actor. He holds the ensemble together and brings his own natural sympathy to the role of Gentry. The other performances range from the brashness of Paula Trueman's Buster to the sultry quiet of Margo's Carmen. Margo's lack of volume may have been used to achieve a more natural tone but as the reviewer in *Variety* commented: "When dialogue is so vital to the motivation of the plot, besides being so beautifully written as it is in this picture, it's wise to let 'em hear it."[28]

Crime Without Passion, despite the critical reservations, received good reviews, although few showed the enthusiasm of Herman Weinberg's evaluation:

> Thirty years ago when I first saw the Hecht-MacArthur *Crime Without Passion,* I thought it ten or fifteen years ahead of its time. I was optimistic. Seeing it recently again I feel we haven't caught up with it.[29]

The film did not do well in the theatres, however, although it may not have done as poorly as the studio claimed, since it cost only $172,000 to make. Even

17. *Crime Without Passion* (1934). MacArthur (left) and Hecht (right) appear in the film as reporters questioning lawyer Lee Gentry (Claude Rains) outside the courtroom. (Photo: Museum of Modern Art/Film Stills Archive courtesy Paramount.)

so, the public was not jubilant about the film as this letter to the Film Editor of the *New York Times* indicates:

> "Crime Without Passion" opened here for a run (one week is the usual time) and it played one day. When I asked the cashier at the ticket box why it was taken off she, clucking and gum-chewing, chirped: "Ah, it was a punk; nobody knew what it was all about. We got Janet Gaynor now, though, and say—it's swell. How many?"
> I finally saw "Crime Without Passion" in one of the neighborhood theatres. It was on a special Saturday double bill—with a Tim McCoy Western.[30]

If *Crime Without Passion* confused its few viewers, *The Scoundrel* was even more outlandish. The authors abandoned the easy crime story formula and produced a sophisticated morality tale which combined biting satire aimed at the literary circles of New York with a sentimental mysticism. The film tells the story of Anthony Mallare (Noel Coward), a satyric publisher who is as nasty to his lovers as he is to his clients. He moves from his current lovers to Cora Moore, an innocent poetess, who had been engaged to Paul Decker, an aviator. He later leaves her for a pianist who is as calculating and amused by him as he has been in his former affairs. Unexpectedly he dies in a plane crash but miraculously returns, trailing seaweed, to achieve redemption by finding someone to cry for him. He only has a month to do this and on the last day he finds Cora and her now broken fiancé. Decker shoots Mallare and himself but Mallare's plea for divine intervention brings Decker back to life. Cora cries for Mallare and he dies a happy soul. Even many of the friends of the film found an inconsistency in the mixture of cynicism and mysticism in the approach to the story. Drama critics like John Mason Brown reviewed the film calling it "courageous." Brown was delighted by the dialogue:

> ...one not only stops and looks but also listens. And listening—the kind of intent word-by-word and phrase-by-phrase listening to which one is accustomed in the theatre—you must admit is rare in the presence of the motion pictures, even now when they have long since ceased to be silent.[31]

Brown felt that the fantasy marred the film but that this was excusable because of the daring eccentricity of the project:

> ...what it attempts to do—and often what it actually gets done—is such an interesting departure from the ordinary run of movies that it succeeds in holding the attention relentlessly even when it fails to live up to the expectations it raised for itself.[32]

Percy Hammond, drama reviewer for the *New York Herald Tribune,* liked the film so much he also felt compelled to write about it and suggested that it was easily of sufficient caliber to be considered for the Pulitzer Prize. *Variety,* however, was not impressed by these theatrical judgments and with its usual practicality noted: "The film is something of an audible novel. Beaucoup dialog and much palaver, with a minimum of action."[33]

Hecht and MacArthur had set out to impress the town and with *The Scoundrel* they maintained their position as golden boys and champions of movie literacy. They had also pleased themselves, and if the film varies widely from predictable Hollywood constructs it is in part because Hecht used the opportunity to write into the film the characters and attitudes that he had usually reserved for his novels. Even more than Gentry, Mallare was the latest development of the Hechtian hero in the tradition of Erik Dorn and Kent Savaron. *The Scoundrel* was based immediately on an unpublished play by Hecht and his wife entitled "All He Ever Loved," but the roots of the character are clearly to be found in Jo Boshere the central character of *A Jew in Love* who also contributed to the development of Lee Gentry. Mallare is also related to the title figure of Hecht's banned novel *Fatanzius Mallare* (1922).

Boshere is a New York publisher who, like his literary predecessors, has difficulty relating with feeling to other people. Love is his single most important preoccupation. He moves from affair to affair in a vain attempt to keep the ecstacy of passion going. Although alienated from the world around him and disdainful of everyone, including his lovers, like Gentry, he is himself lifeless except when being loved by another person. "He desired to create a love in a woman she herself found impossible to evolve."[34] Surrounded by lovers (wife, mistress, friend's wife), Boshere pursues a cold woman about whom he does not really care. He is obsessed first with making her love him and then making her betray him.

Mallare also moves restlessly from woman to woman. Marriage is a trap that his thoughtful girlfriend would not even consider: "She knows it would only increase my indifference, double by deceit, and ruin my character." He has no belief in the ability of love to endure. Mallare is accustomed to lovers who are experienced enough to protect themselves, make few demands on him, and accept his departure with a reasonable and malicious grace. He is unthreatened by women like Carlotta (Rosita Moreno) who can cover their wounds with pointed humor.

Carlotta: Oh forgive me Tony, I have to run away....
Mallare: Darling, I am surprised. You promised never to speak to me again.
Carlotta: I know I did, I have nothing to say anymore, which alters matters, don't you think.
Mallare: The earrings are something new aren't they?
Carlotta: My psychoanalyst advised them, to give me confidence.
Mallare: You never needed confidence.
Carlotta: That was before Mallare—
Mallare: —wrecked your life?
Carlotta: No, decorated it.
Mallare: Ah, if only women were as charming during a love affair as they are after it's over.

18. (1935). A duet during a break from the shooting of *The Scoundrel* in Astoria with Hecht on violin, Noel Coward at the piano and Julie Haydon in attendance. (Photo: Museum of Modern Art/Film Stills Archive courtesy Paramount.)

Mallare is amazed by Cora Moore (Julie Haydon) his principal victim in the film. Cora is a young poet with a firm belief that life is good and people are nice. Unlike Mallare and his circle, she believes that love can be eternal rather then ephemeral.

> Cora: Must love always die?
> Mallare: Always.
> Cora: Shakespeare says it doesn't....
> Mallare: He was lying.... They [poets] lie out of ignorance and keep it up for royalties.

Mallare becomes infatuated with Cora and cares enough about her to try to scare her away from him warning her that "Before I tell a woman I love her, I rattle six times like a snake." Before he does take her from her solid, honorable fiancé Paul Decker (Stanley Ridges), he not only rattles at least a half dozen times but even tries to send her away. But Cora believes Mallare has a redeemable heart and a good soul just as Miss Keeley admired Gentry, and she pursues him until she is no longer innocent nor virginal. Mallare declares that he is trying to take "My first steps in sincerity," but he proves incapable of maintaining a relationship even with a woman of genuine devotion.

Gradually the feeling of entrapment envelops Mallare. When love dies for him, he feels himself victimized by the love he has inspired in the other person but which has not disappeared as his has. Just as Gentry fabricates evidence to accuse Carmen of betraying him, Mallare tries to make Cora feel guilty for his own lack of ardor.

> Mallare: Do you think it's easy for me to stand here watching you sob your heart out. You like our present relations. The victim and the criminal. The victim howling. The criminal cringing. All the typical aftermath of love known as married bliss. Oh, no thank you, no.
> Cora: Dont' you want my love.
> Mallare: Not when it's handed to me on a platter, like the head of John the Baptist; not when it's lying in the middle of the road, run over.

Hecht believed that the Don Juan was often more interested in the passion of the love affair than in love itself, that he "is apt to prefer the hullaballoo of spurious passion to the simpler noises of honest sex. His own love racket is also more windy than seminal."[35] Because of his desire for dramatics, the Don Juan is often attracted to unresponsive women. Hecht quotes Fanny Brice on the subject, "Men always fall for frigid women because they put on the best show."[36] Boshere and Gentry fall into this pattern as does Mallare. He is soon infatuated with Maggie (Hope Williams) a pianist and composer, vivacious, but cold enough to be called a Valkyrie by her friends. Her indifference excites him, and even drives him to contemplate marriage. "It'll be a perfect match," he says, "two empty paper bags belaboring each other." Ironically, he dies chasing a phantom; flying to Bermuda in the mistaken belief that she has gone there, his plane crashes into the sea.

Mallare is Hecht's film portrait of the New York Don Juan, but the picture would not be complete if he did not fill in the social and professional background. Boshere and Mallare were principly but not exclusively patterned after producer Jed Harris (see Chapter 7) and after Horace Liveright, publisher, friend of Hecht's and one of the new species of lovers he encountered in New York. In his work, Mallare exhibits a disdain for moral issues, an unconcern for political questions, and a firm belief in the low taste of the public. When his assistant Jimmy Clay (Ernest Cossart) asks: "Are we interested in the workingman's woes," Mallare's committed reply is, "Only vaguely." Mallare disapproves of the ad campaign planned to publicize Vanderveer Veyden's (Alexander Woollcott, not really playing anything) new book:

Mallare: Too glittering. Professor Veyden's vogue is based on the fact that his readers mistake the boredom he inspires for mental improvement. We mustn't tamper with this delusion. We must never suggest in our ads that he has anything remotely entertaining to say. The intellectuals would shy to another windbag.
Clay: Then you want us to cut out all this about the modern libido and paganism etcetera.
Mallare: Right. Just "A Book for Thinkers." The boobs will gobble it up.

He also disapproves of the Masses as a hero in a novel. Mallare shares with Gentry and Boshere a superior attitude towards the world but does not feel it his duty to elevate their taste and says he will not publish books he likes for fear of corrupting the republic. His only true belief is in his ego and its need for stimulation.

In the inevitable tour through his library, Mallare reveals his preoccupations. Just as Gentry was most interested in law books, using them as a resource for outwitting the criminal codes, Mallare is appropriately a collector, a man without taste except for rarity. His shelves are filled with first editions of authors in whom he has only a passing interest, such as Shelley ("He sighed well.") or Proust ("I am very polite to him.").

Mallare's friends spend most of their time trading epithets. The group includes Veyden, Mallare's former lovers, and Rothstein (Lionel Stander). Rothstein is this film's version of Maxwell Bodenheim, poet and Hecht's old friend who becomes an almost indispensible figure in his films. Rothstein is purposely obnoxious and flowery in his speech (everything is "exquisite" to him) and delivers every remark (from his comment that he is "Just studying insect life," used to describe the people in Mallare's anteroom, to calling a girl "A maid with hair like a tortured midnight" in a vain attempt at seduction) as if it were carefully scored for a coffee grinder. The group is bonded together by a mutual interest in literate insult, drinking, and very bored seduction.

Even in this group, Mallare is the serpent's serpent, a position he seems intent on protecting against any rumors of possible humanity on his part. When Slezak, an author refused an advance by Mallare, commits suicide by hanging himself in an empty closet, even Mallare's friends think his judgment, "A foolish effort to call attention to his bad writing," somewhat callous. Until his death the lack of warmth he instills in others does not seem to bother Mallare. Nor does it seem to bother his creators, which is part of the triumph of the film. Hecht and MacArthur were as enthralled with Mallare as they were with Walter Burns or Oscar Jaffe and they probably chortled every time they thought of a nasty epithet for him to drop into conversation. Andre Sennwald in his *New York Times* review thought this was the secret of the film, that "although presented as the most odious man on earth, Mallare really has the admiration of the Frankensteins who made him."[37]

The problem comes when he turns repentant. The epitaphs of his friends: "Poor Tony, I'd be quite sad if he'd been a little more real," and "When a man dies people weep; when an attitude dies, people shrug," seem much more appropriate than his being kept from rest by his sins and, worse, his caring about it. As Sennwald commented: "This column, sharing the authors' admiration for their fascinating gargoyle thought it very ungracious of them to have Mallare become a repentant sinner like an ordinary mortal."[38]

Over shots of waves and clouds, Coward's voice passes his own judgment:

> Poor Mallare. Poor Traveler. You died and no one cried for you. Your body is tossing. There is no rest for those who die unloved, unmourned. Go back before your doom is written for all eternity. You have one month. Go back and find one heart that loved you. One out of all the thousands among whom you lived. Let one heart cry for you and you will rest . . . rest.

Mallare returns with a vengeance, trailing seaweed behind him (a device borrowed from an Alexander Woollcott ghost story). He tries to find Cora to make amends, but he really is no nicer than before, simply a little more self-righteous in his condemnations, as when he dismisses a group of his friends:

> You comfortable little fools sitting snug and dry in your taxidermists' window. So satisfied with your crackling egos, looking at life with beady eyes. You're sick all of you, little scribblers, sick with your greedy pursuit of trifles, sick with making life small. Quite right, I was one of you. I wore that same smirk that's on all your faces that same cheap sneer at God and man.

Mallare pursues Cora who has found Decker in a flop house (two of whose inhabitants are the directors in cameo appearances) and is trying to reinterest him in the goodness of life. The miracle of Mallare's resurrection and regeneration is doubled when, after Decker shoots both Mallare and himself, Mallare prays to heaven to undo his sins and Decker too is resurrected (actually

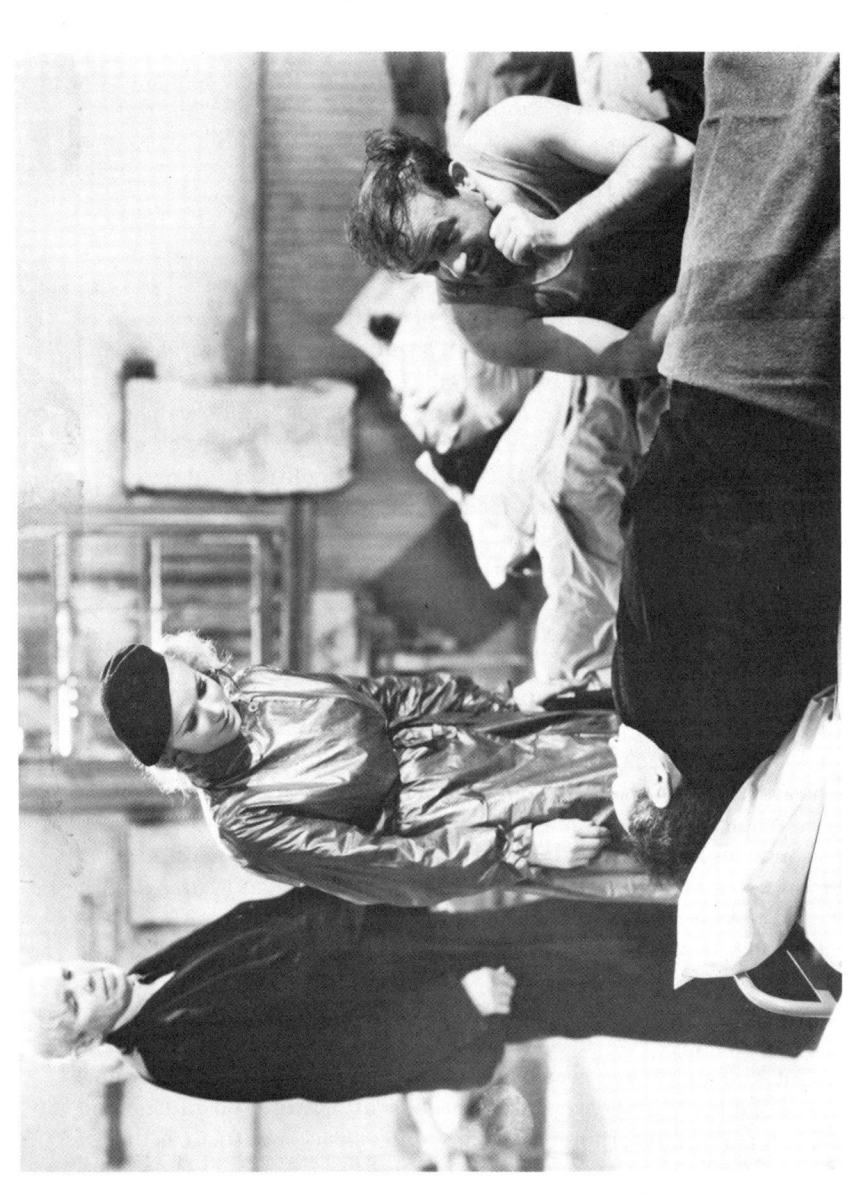

19. *The Scoundrel* (1935). In another piece of whimsy MacArthur and Hecht appear as derelicts in a flop house where Cora Moore (Julie Haydon) has gone to look for her fiance. (Photo: Museum of Modern Art/Film Stills Archive.)

the fourth such incident in the film). Cora cries for Mallare, who can now rest peacefully.

Few were sure why the film took a turn to fantasy. Some thought it another example of the perverseness of the directors in their quest for the exotic. Others saw it as an attempt to placate the censors and appeal to the more conventional members of the audience whose taste resembled the public's enthusiasm for one of Mallare's more popular authors, whose ads he examines:

> The moviegoers in their painful moments of intellectuality turn to Mr. Calhoun's idiotic wares. Make these ads an insult to my taste and intelligence and we'll sell a hundred thousand copies.

While these factors may have affected the shaping of the film, just as they probably affected the writing of *Crime Without Passion,* the moralism and fantasy of the film appears quite frequently in Hecht's stories and later films. In 1939 he published *A Book of Miracles,* comprised of seven stories dealing with aspects of the supernatural. They range in their approach. "The Little Candle" deals with an old Jew's suicide, which is mistaken for a miracle, but the others all deal with some form of divine intervention, from the burlesque of ad agencies and radios in "The Heavenly Choir" to the more serious "Death of Eleazer" where a Rabbi in routing out the soul of a *gilgul* (a spirit) is killed only to rise again to finish his task. All display Hecht's fascination for the supernatural and the grotesque, which also manifested itself in his support of Charles Fort (author of *The Book of the Damned*) who during this period wrote, at length and with imagination, his own explanations of unexplained natural phenomenon. Like *The Scoundrel* (whose working title was *Miracle on 49th Street),* most of Hecht's stories maintain a witty, urbane tone and use the supernatural elements to ridicule familiar Hecht targets ranging from the film industry to religious beliefs. It may have been that fantasy was a safer form in which to couch his attacks, since it has an underlying playfulness and appealing sentimentality while it still makes its earnest point. Two things occur in the last quarter of *The Scoundrel* which should be differentiated: Mallare is resurrected, and Mallare repents for his sins. The resurrection undercuts the impact of Mallare's regeneration. It is forceful but also a bit unbelievable because it is inorganic to the character and always borders on the facetious. Although Hecht may have been serious in his desire to demonstrate the emptiness of Mallare's life, it is evident from the film that he also admired his superior scoundrel. Morality acquired through an act of God rather than through personal trial incorporates Hecht's ambivalence into the structure of the film. The fantasy allows him to be a moralist while remaining true to Mallare after a fashion. While there is still a change in tone as the film moves from the artificiality of the *School for Scandal*-like repartee to the fairy tale redemption, it is not as drastic or jarring a change as would be the shift from repartee to gross sincerity. The solution may be more clever than profound or moving but it is consistent with the level of reality and didacticism of the early portion of the film.

Although some, such as John Reddington writing in the Brooklyn *Daily Eagle,* thought the mysticism of the film "at once unimpressive and insincere; and certainly so tenuous a philosophic attitude, lacking both impressiveness and sincerity, can be condoned on no basis,"[39] most agreed with *Time*'s judgment that "The remarkable thing about the picture is that its treatment, cast and direction are sufficiently expert to make this weakness seem almost negligible."[40]

The production contributes to the success of the script. Although the cast was filled with actors inexperienced in film, the principal characters were well played. This was Coward's first film role (although he hated Hecht's *Design for Living* he admired *Crime Without Passion* and so agreed to do the film), and he is the quintessence of bored nastiness, a drink in one hand and smoke wafting out of his mouth, each line well turned but not overplayed.

The part of Cora was originally written for Helen Hayes and some of Cora's attributes, especially her inability to fit easily into Mallare's backbiting circle may reflect some of the problems the quiet Hayes had in being accepted by MacArthur's protective friends. Hayes was unable to play the role, which disappointed Coward who had been lured into the project in part by the promise of working with her. Julie Haydon is effective as Cora, although possibly not as brilliant as Percy Hammond suggested in his review:

> If Miss Cornell, our First Actress, were to give half as penetrating an interpretation as that of Miss Haydon's in "The Scoundrel," we drama-reviewers would hammer our cymbals deafeningly in celebration and triumph.[41]

Haydon was a protegee of George Jean Nathan. This led to some tension when the reviewer visited the set the morning after panning Coward's play *Point Valaine.* Hecht and MacArthur worried whether Coward would even appear, but he was there and with Nathan grinning at him, did one of his brightest pieces of acting.

Actors such as Stanley Ridges and Ernest Cossart would go on to movie careers as character actors. Lionel Stander would reappear in other Hecht projects *(Soak the Rich* and *Specter of the Rose)* in his Bodenheim role. Woollcott returned to his literary activities.

Visually the film was efficiently handled. The storm and water scenes were impressive and Garmes won praise for his rich halftone photography. Even so, much of the acting and the shot for shot handling and cutting of the film was often no better than servicable. But the film had an immediate cult following.

Teenagers like Betty Comden and Adolph Green could perform the entire script at parties and later used the restaurant where Coward and Haydon had been filmed in a love scene for their own wedding luncheon. The writer and critic Penelope Gilliatt said in 1972 that she had gone around mumbling lines from it since the age of ten or twelve, and Hollis Alpert explains that:

> At the time of *The Scoundrel*'s release, a good many who were surfeited by typical Hollywood products were pleasantly surprised by a film that dared to treat and satirize the publishing-intellectual milieu of New York.... The touch of the supernatural, as represented by the seaweed, gave us a chuckling kind of chill—again quite daring for the time and for the film's context. In fact, in my circle it became a sort of parlor joke—"Seaweed!"[42]

When The American Film Institute was polling its members for the ten best American Films of all time, Alpert said that *The Scoundrel* would be on his personal list.

Reviewers wanted to like the film, fearing that if the film failed there would be less chance for independent projects in the future. They were therefore ready to excuse the film's faults. As Regina Crewes stated the problem in the *New York American:*

> Well, that's the story. Take it or leave it. But remember that upon your thumbs up or down depends whether the screen goes ahead or is relegated yet further to "Tillie's Punctured Romance!"[43]

Despite its reception and its triumphant opening at Radio City, the film did not find a sufficient audience. Fred Guiles says the film failed in Dubuque because Coward looked effete and everyone in the film except "Julie Haydon was absolutely morally 'rotten.' They had produced an oddity; a fascinating portrait of a man with whom not more than 5 percent of the audience could make contact."[44]

Although *Crime Without Passion* and *The Scoundrel* had, at least, found a cult of adherents, *Once in a Blue Moon* and *Soak the Rich* did not even have a vocal minority in their favor. Made at the end of the summer of 1934 after *Crime Without Passion* was finished, *Once in a Blue Moon* was a lavish affair. The film, based on a story by Rose Caylor and falling back on Hecht's experience in the circus, concerns a group of Russian nobility who disguise themselves as side show artists and conceal themselves in a traveling company in order to escape Russia after the Revolution in 1917. Political satire and a large measure of whimsy were the intention, but a leaden production was the result.

It was a grandiose attempt. Hecht and MacArthur were going to turn Jimmy Savo, a vaudeville clown popular among the literati but with few others, into a new Chaplin. The cast was filled with vaudeville and circus personalities

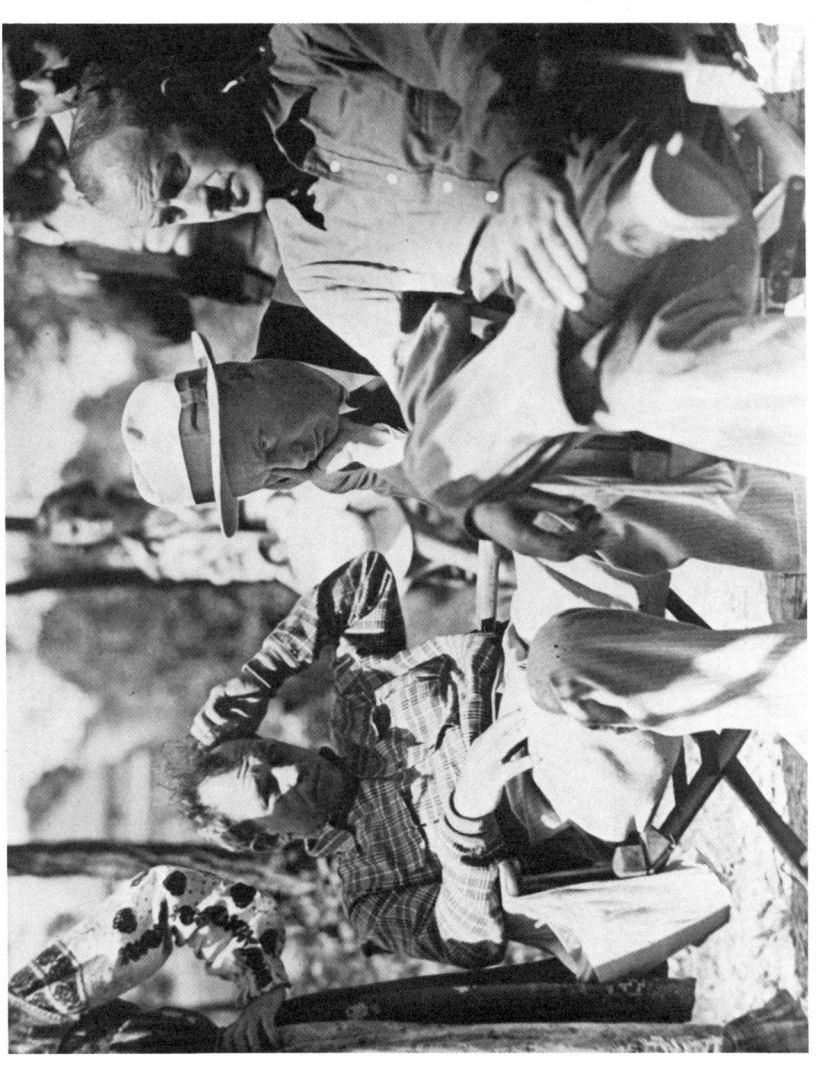

20. (1934). On location shooting *Once in a Blue Moon*, the directors seem to have lost some of the joy of movie making. Tuxedo, New York stands in for revolutionary Russia. According to the reviews even the photography was bad. (Photo: Academy of Motion Pictures.)

21. Rose Caylor, Hecht's wife, at work in Astoria, Long Island studio. A story by Caylor formed the basis for *Once in a Blue Moon*. (Photo: Academy of Motion Pictures.)

such as Sandor Szabo the wrestler. Whitney Bourne was one of the few with film experience and she had acquired hers in *Crime Without Passion.* Hecht's daughter by his first marriage, Edwina Armstrong, also appeared in the film, along with 400 children and a Cossack choir. The film was shot on location in the Catskills, in Tuxedo, New York, and the set resembled a summer camp more than a working film company.

What had been intended as a fairytale and satire on Russian life with Savo as the clown whom children love but who never gets the princess (the kind of character Harpo Marx became in his later films, including the one to which Hecht contributed, *Love Happy,* 1949) was neither amusing nor charming. As *Variety* put it: "There's no sense kidding about 'Once in a Blue Moon,' or mincing language, or being cute about it. It's a bad picture."[45] George Antheil had provided an interesting score for the film but the sound recording was so bad that it was difficult to hear many of the lines much less the music. Lee Garmes was promoted on the project to Associate Director.

Hecht summed up the problem this way:

> The truth was that Charlie and I had "gone Hollywood" in making *Blue Moon.* We had forgotten the Secret. Our script for *Once in a Blue Moon* was a dud.[46]

Soak the Rich, their final film, had a different problem. The script, a satire on college radicals, was a well written comedy but the production failed to support the writing. The film was unamusing. As Frank Nugent said in his review of the film in the *New York Times,* the

> spoofing of youth in revolt is frequently amusing and the quality of the dialogue proves that the premier filmmakers of Astoria have lost none of their wit. The same alas, cannot be said of their sense of direction.[47]

The script has no ideological base except an iconoclasm that attacks all established positions, the die-hard capitalists, campus radicals, and communism ("What is communism? Communism is the growing pains of the young.") Belinda Craig (Mary Taylor, a good looking woman who reportedly had a close association with Hecht) attends the college her father (Walter Connolly) heavily endows. She gets embroiled in a dispute over the firing of a professor, and because her boyfriend is a radical she becomes a communist too. Joe Muglia (Lionel Stander), the self-appointed president of the Society for the Abolition of Monstrosities, kidnaps her, which confuses Belinda:

Belinda: I thought you said you were a radical.
Muglia: Who do I sound like—Herbert Hoover?
Belinda: You're not behaving like a radical.
Muglia: Of the eagle who disappears beyond the clouds, who shall say whether he behaves right or wrong? I am beyond good and evil. [Muglia has more than a bit of Bodenheim in him.]

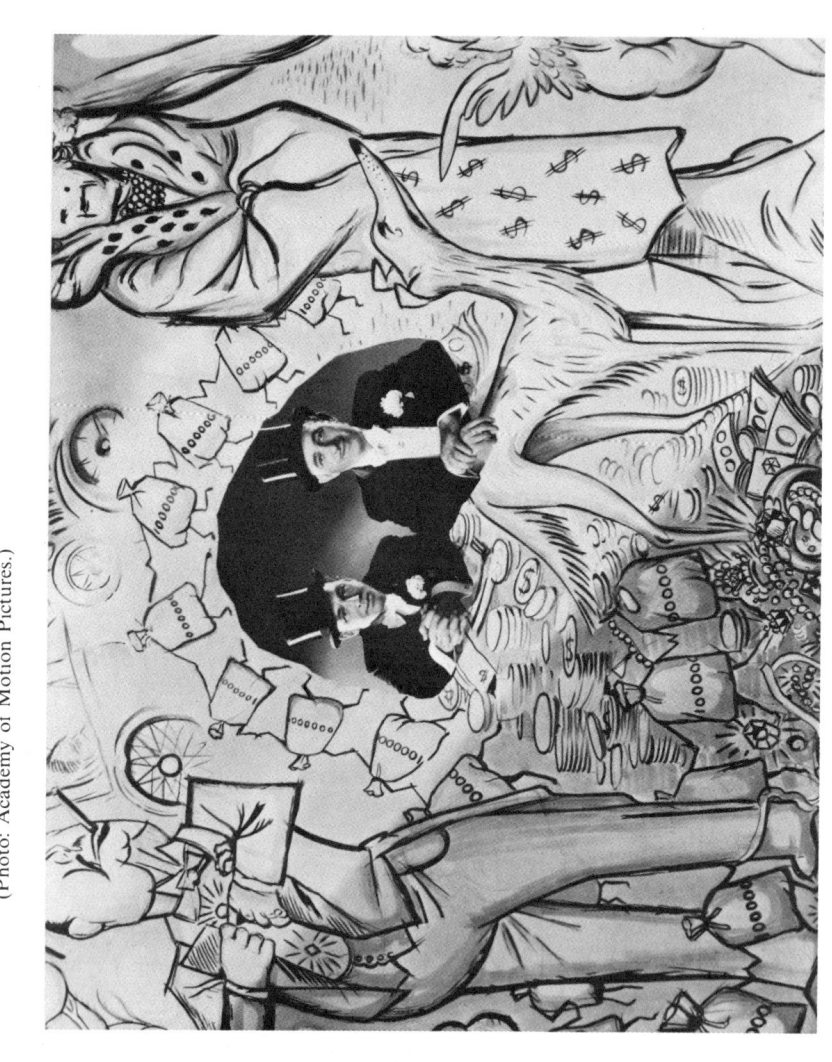

22. *Soak the Rich* (1935). Hecht and MacArthur in one of the title shots for their last film in Astoria. The cartoon was designed by their friend George Grosz. The atmosphere in the studio had grown more serious according to Frank Nugent in the *New York Times*. "The Puck and Pan of North Astoria," as he called them, "have reformed." (Photo: Academy of Motion Pictures.)

Although her boyfriend Buzz Jones (John Hayward) says he can not marry her because communists do not believe in marriage (in *Comrade X* they believe in convenient and easy marriages), Belinda's father arranges for a shotgun ceremony, happy in the assurance that:

> Theirs is not radicalism, sir. They will grow up to be quite conventional gentlemen. While they are young they sing, struggle, and dream of something else. A few years ago it was the fashion to be Don Juans. Today ideas have taken the place of drink and revolt is the latest form of necking.

More than any other genre, comedy demands the hand of a director with craft who can keep the pace fast and clean and the dialogue sharp, especially with inexperienced actors who are in need of a sense of ensemble. The film fails because it lacks this necessary precision. The directing at Astoria was never very disciplined but there were other factors that contributed to this particular deficiency. The most important may have been the absence of Lee Garmes from the project. Leon Shamroy shot the film and contributed to the direction. "I co-directed it; they wanted to give me 250 bucks less a week in return for billing as co-director."[48] Visually the stripped down sets of the Garmes-Hecht projects were replaced by studio realism, with sets designed by Walter Keller. Realism was demanded to the extent that it took two hours to spray rubber cobwebs on the sets. Possibly because he was unfamiliar with his producers and their style of work, Shamroy does not seem to have exerted the modifying influence over production that is evident in Garmes's work.

Hecht and MacArthur were also distracted during the period of the filming by the staging of their play *Jumbo* by Billy Rose at the Hippodrome. At nights they were at rehearsals with Jimmy Durante and the elephants and during the day they worked in Astoria. Their divided attention may have affected the film. Hecht and MacArthur lacked the energy to continue to make parties and films, and the atmosphere on the set become quite serious. The games at the studio were reduced to innocuous activities like stud poker, and although Hecht and MacArthur could still spend an hour on the set arguing whether anchovy paste was proper for serving in a drawing room (Hecht who was against the paste is reported to have walked away with the argument), the atmosphere in the studio was much more earnest than for the earlier films, either because of pressing deadlines or because of pressure from Paramount to produce a more commercially successful movie. It may even be that Hecht and MacArthur were tiring of their roles as studio executives.

The fate of *Soak the Rich* only emphasized the importance of directing to the realization of even a good script. *The Scoundrel* and *Crime Without Passion*, despite their occasional flaccidness and awkwardness coalesced into admired films because of a combination of the uniqueness of the project, interesting performances by Rains and Coward, and the helpful hand of Garmes. In the more exacting field of comedy and without Garmes, the defects in the acting and the literary quality of the script had little support. Directed by Hawks, Wellman, Milestone, or Lubitsch the script might have been made into a much more acceptable film.

In any case, box office failure doomed the Astoria experiment, and Hecht and MacArthur went back to being high paid employees churning out film scripts and ideas. Their failure to achieve financial independence made it much more difficult for other writers to produce their own films. *Crime Without Passion* and *The Scoundrel* would be kindly remembered, but, although he would make three more of his own films, Hecht was disillusioned. While he had not feared failure, he had not imagined that his tastes would find so little sympathy and it confirmed his estimation of the low intelligence of the American public.

7

"My Tribe is Israel": World War II and the Irgun

Well into the 1930s, Hecht managed to maintain the belief that he was still young and the world a beneficent playground. His artistic qualms were manageable, since his rewards, in coin and often in respect and praise, seemed to insulate him from the need for tremendous introspection. Hecht was a cynic long before he suffered any real personal disillusionment. His cynicism was an attitude, much the same as wearing a slouching hat or flicking ashes on the boss's carpet. His cynicism was often touched with an admiration for the objects of his abuse either because he was making fun of his friends or because the inequities he attacked were exterior to his experience.

As the 1930s progressed, world events insinuated themselves into the dream factory, and the security of Hecht's cynicism was challenged and eroded by the harsh realities of a world intent on displaying its dark side. Anti-Semitism was the enemy that surprised and angered him most deeply because it forced him to confront his own identity and re-evaluate his social responsibilities. For the first time in his life, he joined political organizations. He attempted to salvage part of his Jewish integrity by trying to force America into the war, trying to put a Jewish army into the field against the Nazis in the Middle East, trying to save Jews in Europe, and, with his support of a Jewish underground organization, trying to force the establishment of a Jewish state. Although his political activities were part time affairs, they interfered with his career. In 1948 his films were banned in England and, in consequence, the studios, when they would hire him, used his troubles as an excuse for acquiring his talents cheaply.

His youth seemed to evaporate over these years, beginning approximately in 1941. It had all but disappeared by the time Hecht abandoned his political activity in 1948. Many of his friends were by then dissipated, dead, or aging visibly and in 1946 Hecht himself was seriously ill. Hecht became a father for the second time in 1944. As he fought for the establishment of the state of Israel he simultaneously entered a period of reflection and personal contentment even while he continued to rage with an anger born of Nazi genocide and American and British inaction. He turned from a character of spirited hijinks and irreverent iconoclasm to a cantankerous and often sentimental late middle-aged man.

The optimism and buoyancy that marked his earlier films, regardless of their measure of cynicism, becomes progressively less evident in his films. His disenchantment is more real, and increasingly there is an attempt by his characters (some of the actors, too, are now aging) to come to terms with themselves, their pasts, and the people around them in a search for personal peace rather than for a principled independence. When there is good will, it is much more sentimental than that allowed by the tough guy code of his earlier films which had kept "schmaltz" to a minimum even where love and devotion existed.

Despite some of Hecht's own protestations and the neat convenience it would provide, there is no single date or event when his ideas and attitudes shifted. The change seems to have been gradual. His concern for his Jewishness, for instance, is often evident long before the political crisis in Europe. His awareness of a need for personal commitment and identitiy can be felt in much of his narrative fiction in the late thirties. His play, *To Quito and Back,* which deals with a writer accepting the need for social-political commitment, was produced by the Theatre Guild in 1937. It displays his new awareness of the crisis developing in the larger world and his partial acceptance of the challenge with which these events had confronted him. Since Hecht used his fiction and plays for personal statement and tended to consider his film work as skilled piecework, his movies of this period tend to be less overtly political, although here, too, the awareness of impending crisis is apparent. In 1940, for instance, Hecht worked on *His Girl Friday, The Shop Around the Corner, Comrade X, Foreign Correspondent, Let Freedom Ring,* and *Angels Over Broadway.* As a group they demonstrate the tension between the familiar film patterns, particularly screwball comedy, and the pressure of changing concerns for Hecht, as well as for the studios and the audience.

His Girl Friday, as discussed earlier, was one of the final polished examples of screwball comedy. With the exception of a few topical references, it is hermetically sealed from concerns beyond the personal rivalry of Hildy and Walter; no real events intrude upon its innocence. *Comrade X,* however, attempts to combine political satire against the Soviets, allies of the Nazis at the time, with the screwball comedy mode. At its heart, however, it is still centrally concerned with Gable and Lamarr, although the film does take a serious turn when it deals with the mass execution of dissidents.

Let Freedom Ring is the Hechtian version of *The Mark of Zorro.* Instead of the finest swordsman in Southern California returning home and pretending to be a fop while he rids the country of its tyrannous rulers, Hecht's hero returns from Harvard and pretends political indifference while he uses his printing press and secret identity as the "Hornet" to urge the immigrant "hunkies" into open revolt and to combat the railroad owners who are terrorizing the local landowners. Hecht never wrote a film that directly applied to the Jewish situation, but in this film, as in *Comrade X* and later in *China Girl* (1942) where he attacks Japanese treatment of the Chinese, he presents the case for persecuted minorities whenever the story allows. In both *Comrade X* and *Let Freedom Ring,* he particularly focuses on the suppression of free speech as well as human rights, and it is clear that Hecht believes in the power of propaganda and ideas to sow rebellion. Hecht's major contribution to the war effort was as a propagandist—writing plays, books, pamphlets, articles, and films in an attempt to mobilize support for his cause.

The degree of Hecht's contribution to *Foreign Correspondent,* directed by Alfred Hitchcock, is open to question. Hitchcock does not mention any Hecht collaboration when he discusses the film, and Hecht received no screen credit (screenplay: Charles Bennett and Joan Harrison; additional dialogue: James Hilton and Robert Benchley). The film is characteristic of Hitchcock's interests and techniques, but it also contains elements common in Hecht's work and Hecht listed the film among his projects. In the movie, an American crime reporter (Joel McCrea) is sent to Europe to cover the political scene—the biggest crime story of the century. His experiences are quite similar to those of the naive Hecht in Germany after World War I—the reporter sees events which no one will believe took place. The plot involves a kidnapped world leader (Van Meer), a secret clause in a treaty, a pacifist (Herbert Marshall) who is actually working for the Nazis, and his daughter who is not (Laraine Day) and who falls in love with McCrea. The use of the reporter, lost in the dignified European setting where his floppy felt hat or bare head is at odds with seas of bowlers, with his ability to find the crime story that eludes his fellows, and his inelegant manners in work and love, are the most identifiable Hechtian elements. At a time when both Hecht and Hitchcock were among those working to overcome America's isolationism, the use of a pacifist as the villain functioned as a clear indictment of those who maintained that the war was no business of the United States. During this period there were a number of films which supported an American involvement in European affairs. These included Chaplin's *The Great Dictator* (1940), *Confessions of a Nazi Spy* (1939) about espionage in America, and *The Mortal Storm* (1940) about German anti-Semitism.

Since Hecht wrote, produced, directed, and even appeared (as a pander in a court scene) in *Angels Over Broadway,* this film may be the most accurate indicator of the shift in Hecht's personal concerns. The film was co-produced by Douglas Fairbanks, Jr. and co-directed by Lee Garmes. It displays an increase in the sentimentality that had been held in check in Hecht's collaborations with MacArthur. It is also more verbally artificial than the Astoria projects, but, in general, the look and sound of the film are quite similar to the Hecht-MacArthur-Garmes projects.

23. Hecht with co-director Lee Garmes working on scene from *Angels Over Broadway* (1940). Hecht tried to break with Hollywood tradition by using small scale sets, making no more than two takes of a scene, editing as he shot, and showing his relaxation by directing in his bedroom slippers.
(Photo: Academy of Motion Pictures.)

The film was produced for Columbia studios and shot in California under its $350,000 budget and seven days ahead of its thirty day shooting schedule. The modest size of the budget is slightly deceptive. If Hecht had been paid for each of his three functions on the project rather than agreeing to receive only a percentage of the profits, the initial cost of the film would have been much higher. This financial arrangement is typical of Hecht's directorial undertakings.

For his story, Hecht turned again to the theatres, clubs, and gutters of Broadway. Three people, a playwright, Gene Gibbons (Thomas Mitchell); a former bellhop and sharpie, Bill O'Brien (Douglas Fairbanks, Jr.); and a chippie, Nina Barona (Rita Hayworth) have their lives redeemed by helping a suicidal loser, Charles Engles (John Qualen), acquire three thousand dollars to replace the funds he embezzled from his partner in the hopes of retaining the affections of his faithless wife. They steer Qualen into a crooked card game where gangsters allow him to win a few hands. Before the gangsters can take their money back, Qualen, with the help of Fairbanks, gets away. Although he is the pivot for the plot, Qualen is the least interesting character. Hecht is far more concerned with the choices the other characters make in deciding to help him. Fairbanks and Hayworth form the love-hate interest. Fairbanks is even too sharp for himself and cannot justify doing anything unless he thinks there is a percentage in it for him, however illusory. Nor will he allow himself to think of Hayworth as anything better than a good-time girl and, therefore, insults her through most of the film, largely to deny his own attraction to her. In opposition to Fairbanks' blustering cynicism, Hayworth insists on the importance of illusion and optimism. The events, which take place over the course of one night and in the rain that always accompanies Hecht's miracles, indicates to Hayworth that: "People aren't really mean. They can be better than they are if they want, if they let themselves, even if it doesn't last." Fairbanks first gives up hope of gaining financial reward and takes a beating to help Qualen, then he also gives up his personal protectiveness and goes off in the bright dawn with Hayworth.

Fairbanks is the familiar Hechtian cynic whose idea of self-interest and image are in conflict with a new awareness of his connection to humanity and a larger world. He is Lee Gentry or Anthony Mallare as a nice guy or Hildy Johnson giving in to his sentimentality. But Hecht is less interested in the love problems of his young characters than in the character played by Thomas Mitchell who, with his personal weight as an actor and with a preponderance of the dialogue, dominates much of the film. Once a Pulitzer Prize winner, Mitchell is now a drunk. As he pontificates in his inebriated state to Qualen:

> Fellow cadaver, I'm being divorced by my wife, whom I love dearly, in my own nasty way. I was disembowled by another woman. I've written three bad plays in a row, and next year I'll write a worse one. I have neither a home, a single hope, nor a shred of curiosity left.... I've destroyed myself, sir, in becoming famous, I'm no longer a man. I'm an epitaph over an ashcan.

24. *Angels Over Broadway* (1940). Playwright Gene Gibbons (Thomas Mitchell) explains and arranges the life of suicidal Charles Engle (John Qualen). Nina Baron (Rita Hayworth) and Bill O'Brien (Douglas Fairbanks, Jr.) are his other two angels. As one reviewer put it, the characters were more loquacious than eloquent. (Photo: Museum of Modern Art/Film Stills Archive courtesy Columbia.)

Bankrupt and broke, Mitchell sees in Qualen an untidy plot which he can rewrite: "I do not approve of your exit, Mr. Engle. Now if you'll be patient and have faith in a dramatist who once was second to none, I'll rewrite your last act." He does not share Hayworth's youthful hope but has his own more cynical, if less demanding, secret of life: "Yesterday's pain is tomorrow's joke, and you'll always end up laughing if you can manage not to cut your throat. That's the message of my last three flops." He enjoys playing God but passes out before the final act (which is also the problem with his plays, according to Fairbanks).

Mitchell is the most fully developed as well as the most verbose character in the film. His success and failure and the loss of his wife leave him rudderless and pathetic despite his bravado. When he wakes up in another hotel room, remembering neither where he is nor the plot he has devised for Qualen and himself, he calls his wife and begs her to take him back:

> I wanna come home. I don't seem to be able to write anywhere else... you're sweet.... The only warm place I've ever been has been in your heart. You're the only light that didn't go out on me. All the others went out, but not you. Thank you. Yes, I can find my way home.

Mitchell exits leaving Fairbanks and Hayworth to extricate Qualen. Whether it is a reflection of the society Hecht saw around him or an echo from his own life is not clear, but the image in Hecht's film of the middle-aged man, faithless and failed, finding his way back to a good woman—finding his way home—gradually replaces the independent professional untied to a woman and disbelieving in the possibility of her goodness. Even Fairbanks, the younger man, still protected by his innocence, eventually accepts the possibility of trust. In the middle of the film, when he finds Mitchell's cigarette case inscribed "To Gene, my first, last, and only. Harriet. June 1924," Fairbanks's comment to Hayworth is "'My first, last, and only,' imagine a dame writin that and meanin it. Naw, I suppose you can't. Wouldn't look so hot on a rain check anyway, would it?" But, by the end of the film, he is ready to believe in such a possibility.

The change in Hechtian attitudes are most clear if Mitchell's comment that without his wife he is no longer a man and Fairbanks's choice of love and trust are juxtaposed against Fairbanks's choice a year before in *Gunga Din*. In that film (story by Hecht and MacArthur based loosely on Kipling), in order to be a man, he must leave his fiancee and go off in perpetual adolescence to fight with his friends.

Hayworth is another of Hecht's hard luck women in the tradition of Carmen Brown from *Crime Without Passion*. In his later films, Hecht uses the prostitute, the loose woman, or the unfaithful wife as an obstacle to trust and faith for the central character who, in order to establish a mature relationship, must overcome social interdiction as well as the threat to his personal freedom.

This is particularly true in *Notorious* (1946), *Gilda* (1946), *Legend of the Lost* (1957), and *Circus World* (1964). By aligning himself with a fallen woman, the man remains unconventional even while he accepts traditional values of love.

Hayworth does not get the best of the dialogue, which is reserved for Mitchell and Fairbanks, and only Mitchell manages to insert a drunken conviction into Hecht's over-articulateness. Fairbanks plays with concentration but without the gritty reality needed to spit out what is intended as an elevated use of urban dialect (what we would today call Runyonesque but actually based on a then common speech pattern). The screenplay resembles those of Hecht's short stories which concentrate on simple characters, complicated but smoothly working plot devices, clear thematic assumptions and morals, and a sureness with language that when handled by an actor who can abosrb it into himself rather than merely play it, is marvelous to hear. Unfortunately, the production techniques on which Hecht insisted mitigated against this kind of characterization. Two takes were enough for Hecht; after that, he felt, attitudes went stale.

The technical schizophrenia that had marked the Astoria project is also apparent in *Angels Over Broadway* (and in Hecht's later two films as well). On some matters Hecht showed a concern for minute detail while in other areas he seemed more intent on showing how easy filmmaking was. He was concerned that all the sets be about the correct size rather than the larger and more lavish standard Hollywood environments, yet the look of the film is as artificial and theatrical as any industry product. He and Garmes carefully planned the shooting in much the same way that Lubitsch planned his productions, saving time on the set and in cutting by producing a screenplay that carefully dictated shooting and editing. He and Garmes used what Hecht called a "roving camera" allowing the camera to move freely during shots to minimize the need for constant cutting. But despite the careful preplanning, the 78 minute film needs editing, and despite the moving camera, two-person shots dominate the film for long periods of time as the camera sits back and lets the scene, which even by theatrical standards is inactive, wind itself down.

For all its drawbacks, however, the film cannot be dismissed as an oddity. A mannered production in an industry that increasingly sought naturalism, produced from a supremely literate script in an age that was turning towards the rambling of "realistic" speech, it clearly belongs to the thirties' tradition of "talkies," and, although not a comedy, it shares with Hecht's comedies an unashamed pleasure in its own cleverness. The realities of the war destroyed the climate necessary for an abstract concern for construction or language, and after the war Hecht wrote few successful films in this mode, turning instead to psychiatry and violent aberration. The shift in emphasis and interest to a middle-aged character and to a belief in romantic and humanitarian commitment, evident in *Angels Over Broadway* and other Hecht films in 1940, were magnified during and after the war as his political activity increased and his personal attitudes continued to shift.

Hecht commented that by becoming a Jew he also became an American, and his new interest in European and American foreign policy was the direct result of his realization that he was a Jew. It was not really that he ever denied his Judaism; it was rather that he ignored it until it was brought to his attention. He had formerly believed that his ethnic difference from others was much the same as his separation by virtue of his talent or his intellect. In this, he identified with many of his "un-Jewish" Jewish friends:

> They have healthy minds and they answer the smile of curiousity that sometimes touches the mouth of the Gentile with a smile of their own—who says a little alienism is a sin?[1]

Raised in New York in a family of Russian Jewish immigrants, Hecht spoke Yiddish as fluently as he did English until the age of ten. When he moved to Racine, however, where there were only two Jews in his school, he largely lost touch with his Jewish identity except through his family, who were always a source of love and security for him. In Chicago it was much the same. He identified himself as a newspaperman or as an artist rather than as a Jew. His background only intruded in minor ways during this period. He convinced his editors, for instance, that he could not work on Jewish holidays; he was amazed and impressed to find that Jewish shops were closed on the twenty-fifth anniversary of the publication of the Yiddish poet Bialik's work "The Eagle;" and when covering a Zionist convention in Chicago during the teens, he met Louis Brandeis and Shmarya Levin who turned him into an ardent Zionist for a two week period after which Zionism dropped from his consciousness for many years.

In New York, Hecht met a world of Jews unlike his relatives. Hecht was convinced that all the artists in New York were Jewish, but as with his own, their Jewishness was neither something to be denied or affirmed. It was merely a part of their background.

> These Jews in New York were not like my aunts and uncles but like myself. Semites far away from Semitism—writers, publishers, theatrical producers, journalists, wits, actors, and mighty drinkers whose only synagogue was Broadway. I imagine that there were also clever and accomplished Gentiles in the city, but I did not meet them.[2]

Despite his disclaimers, Hecht's Judaism was only restlessly hibernating and it slowly awoke in him. Although it was only one of many sources, his work in Chicago included stories and plays about Jewish immigrants. When he first arrived in New York, he and Rose Caylor moved down into the Jewish ghetto and lived on Henry Street near the Jewish settlement. Although they made no contact with the Jewish population around them, Hecht enjoyed living among these unassimilated Jews, and he felt secure in being surrounded by people who reminded him so strongly of his own family. It was not part of his active life and did not fully satisfy him, but he "loved something faraway and had spent a while looking at its ghost."[3]

Hecht's stay on Henry Street was only an interlude. In general, he felt disassociated from the ghetto Judaism of his parents. But although he did not think of his background as anything important, he began to differentiate between his Semitic friends who did not care about their Jewishness from those who were embarrassed by it. For his own part Hecht said he never

> ...sought to hide myself in an artist's smock or in an infatuation for other people's origins. Nor have I ever hurled myself into Jewishness as the only way of hiding from its troubles, as the shrewd way of making the best of a bad bargain.[4]

Among his New York fellows, Hecht found a number of sophisticates who denied their Jewishness, and in his novel *A Jew in Love* (1931) he caricatured these attitudes in the person of Jo Boshere (nee Abe Nussbaum), who was patterned after aspects of both the life of publisher Horace Liveright and the attitudes of producer Jed Harris.[5] Hecht had used Jewish protagonists before, notably in *Erik Dorn* (1921), but in this earlier work, Dorn was a manifestation of Hecht's persona, and, for all his failings, the semiautobiographical character was sympathetic. Boshere, however, is a character of overweening cleverness in the tradition of Lou Hendrix from the story "Crime Without Passion." He is an entrepreneur, a publisher, who contributes little other than his own ego in his manic manipulations of the talent, creativity, and love of others. Hecht gives Boshere an exaggerated Jewish face that Boshere must work to deny. In the first sentence, he describes Boshere as "a dark-skinned little Jew with a vulturous and moody face, a reedy body and a sense of posture."[6] Leslie Fiedler, in his essay, "The Jew in the American Novel," says that Boshere is "portrayed by Hecht as the caricature of the anti-Semite come to life: not merely the Jew, but the nightmare of the Jew (as hawkbeaked and vulpine as Mr. Peixada) as Don Juan."[7] In Anglo-Saxon form, Boshere would reappear as Anthony Mallare in *The Scoundrel* (1935).

Unflattering portraits of Jews by other Jews have often been greeted with suspicion by the Jewish community. The assumption is made that the author is writing about himself out of a great weight of self-hatred. Fiedler, even while he suggests that Boshere is a satiric caricature, also believes that the work is one of "inspired self-hatred: a portrait of the Jewish author as his own worst (Jewish) enemy."[8] Sol Liptzin, in his study *The Jew in American Literature,* dubs Hecht the "Chief of the self-hating Jewish hedonists."[9] Critical evaluation of Hecht since World War II is often further discolored by the violent antipathy to his pro-Irgunist activities. But even noting that Hecht's plays and stories commonly contain a good deal of broad ethnic humor of all sorts, the portrait of Boshere seems excessive even for Hecht's satiric purposes and it may be that Boshere's neuroticism, his desire for the one *shikse* (female gentile) in his orbit, and his emphasis on the titillation of his own ego in place of any artisic or social responsibility reflect some of Hecht's own ambivalence about identity or purpose. It is just as likely, however, that since many of his circle were Jewish, including Harris, Hecht felt that not to report his ethnic background would be to paint an incomplete portrait. Interestingly, four years later when Hecht adapted the novel into the screenplay for *The Scoundrel* the character loses his Jewish identity. In the intervening years Hecht might have become sensitive about his ethnic characterization of Boshere or he might simply have felt that while he wrote his fiction for himself, his friends, and the small sophisticated book buying public, movies were produced for a mass audience who would misunderstand private jokes and personal references.

Whatever the state of Hecht's identity in 1931, it is clear that the rise of anti-Semitism in Europe caused Hecht to acknowledge his Jewish identity. He became aware of what he called the tag around his neck that said, "Jew."

> The history of the Jews is not like the history of any other people. It is more than a tombstone or a fairytale. It is an identity tag and hangs like a tidy bit of haberdashery from the neck of every living Jew....
>
> I discovered late the tag on my neck and the thing written on it. It is written in a deep language and is exceedingly hard to read.[10]

The translation that Hecht evolved was peculiarly his own. The Jew had nothing to do with God, he said, but with the ego. Monotheism was the triumph of the Jewish ego in conceiving of itself as God. He did not perceive this act as one of tribal conformity but as an act of individualism and ego usually found only in the solitary artist.

> There were other egoists in the world of the Prophet Samuel. But they were accidents of circumstance or biology. Or they may have been artists who are happily everywhere and always. They were not a religion of egoism. The Jews were that. They said God was all powerful but they meant something quite otherwise. They meant that the mind that could conceive of Him was all powerful. They meant the human spirit that could dream of its own perfection was a mighty spirit.[11]

Hecht discovered that the Jew was nothing more than the kind of hero he had always favored, an individualist devoted to his own egoism. Egoism for Hecht was not selfishness but rather "the creative force that has urged man to assert and improve himself."[12]

Having found his own comfortable understanding of what his heritage meant, Hecht refused to become a Jewish apologist or to accept what he considered the traditional Jewish manner of self-defense: to announce your distress and to advertise your virtues. The first, he said, would attract three hooligans and sadists to every Samaritan that came in aid. The second he saw as a gesture of futility:

> In a world that admires only victors, the Jews have persisted in advertising themselves as victims only. This the Jews are not. I am not writing of those murdered but those alive. No man alive is a victim. It is not only stupid but dangerous to pronounce himself one.[13]

Hecht had earlier come to the conclusion that some form of dedication to the social good beyond the individual was important. His play *To Quito and Back* showed his willingness to commit himself to a cause—but only if the cause was hopeless and the consequences personal. In this play, which was produced by the Theatre Guild and opened in New York on October 6, 1937, the Hechtian character, Alexander Sterns, arrives in Ecuador, a country convulsed by a proletarian revolution. He is in the company of his lover, on the run from his wife, and suffers from a lack of direction. By the end of the play he decides that personal problems or taking sides in a discussion is not enough. Rather than go back to his wife, he will die on the barricades. Sterns is a restless, epigrammatic, indecisive character in the tradition of Kent Savaron or Erik Dorn. But a distracted pursuit of art or actualization is no longer sufficient. Sterns is a fatalist—happier fighting for a losing cause than having to endure the compromises of a winning one. The play suffers from its emphasis on polemics and dialectic over character and action.

In his writing, Hecht's new interest in the Jewish cause took two forms. His fiction, particularly his stories about Jews, such as *A Book of Miracles* (1939), tended towards a touching sentimentality, a belief in life, in the power of love, and in a degree of mysticism. This sentimentality and his increased belief in the power of love remained with Hecht and would become more important in his films. His political writings, however, were without gentility. Through the arrangements of his wife, Hecht began in 1939 to write a daily column in *P.M.*, the leftist morning newspaper edited by Ralph Ingersoll. The column was entitled *1001 Afternoons in New York,* and while it contained some of the sketches and fiction that had been the subject matter of his *1001 Afternoons in Chicago* pieces for the *Chicago Daily News,* Hecht's main purpose was to compel America and American Jewry to intercede in Europe.

Hecht says his conversion to Judaism finally occurred in 1939. For the first time in his life, he joined an organization, Fight for Freedom, whose intention it was to bring America into the war. He and MacArthur wrote a pageant, *Fun to Be Free,* as propaganda and fundraiser for the cause. It was produced by Billy Rose at Madison Square Garden, and later Hecht wrote other shows for the Red Cross, the War Bond Drive, and the State Department.

Hecht's activities did not always find favor, particularly among the Jewish community. He attacked the Germans with messianic zeal calling them, at best, a race of butchers. But he also attacked the isolationists in America and the American Jews who, through their fear of offending their fellow Americans, remained silent. This was largely the attitude of the film industry. Joseph Kennedy, acting for President Roosevelt, suggested in meeting with the studio heads that for them to cry too loudly about the plight of the Jews might alienate the American public, who would not want to fight a war to save Jews. The studio heads, many of them Jewish in background if not in self-identification, readily agreed.

After Pearl Harbor the studios supported the war effort against the Nazis and Japanese and many persecuted nationalities were depicted in Hollywood's anti-Nazi films, such as *Song of Russia* (1943), *Hangmen Also Die* (Czechoslovakians, 1943), *The Moon is Down* (Norwegians, 1943), and *Paris Underground* (1945), but Jews were invisible on the screen, as though the Nazis had succeeded in wiping out even the memory of them. This was to continue until well after the war, and even then the first films about anti-Semitism, such as *Crossfire* (1947) and *Gentleman's Agreement* (1947), dealt with the subject in an American context.

Hecht defended one such safe minority in his film *China Girl* (1942), which he wrote and produced. It was directed by Henry Hathaway, and Hecht relied on Lee Garmes for the photography. Because he had production control, the film probably manifests Hecht's political attitudes and concerns as far as the Hollywood system would allow. In the film, newsreel journalist Johnny Williams (George Montgomery) is drawn away from his cynical self-interest to a position behind a machine gun through the Japanese murder of Chinese civilians and children and the death of his Chinese girl friend (Gene Tierney).

On a propaganda level, one of the film's intentions is to demonstrate the brutality of the Japanese by depicting graphic scenes of executions, piles of bodies, and the bombing of children. Hecht's most important means of inducing war fervor, however, is basically romantic, as the titles which open the film suggest:

> The American will fight for three things: for a woman; for himself; and for a better world. He was fighting for two of these when this story begins. November 1941. Luchow: the Jap invader brings the new order into China—with bullets.

Williams, not realizing that he is being helped by two Japanese agents Bull Weed (Victor McLaglen) and Fifi (Lynn Bari), escapes from the Japanese and flies to Mandalay. There he joins friends in the Flying Tigers who urge him to enlist. He is not interested.

> I say I ain't joinin' any American volunteers in Burma, China or anywhere else.... How do you like that, you gotta give guys reasons around here for wantin' to stay alive. Listen Lafayette, I ain't dying for China, I'm dying for Johnny Williams, and I ain't even doing that if there's an angle out.

Johnny has all the traits of other Hecht newsmen—a tough professional, with a large ego and ready colloquial wit. He is fired by his boss for going into Japanese territory after phoney scoops, and he distrusts women. He is more at home with the sluttish Bari than with the Vassar-educated, dedicated Tierney who works with her father caring for and teaching refugee children. When his romance with Tierney blooms, it is a poetic affair, but Williams (and the script) is most alive when he retains his belief in original sin as when, disappointed with Tierney, he comes on to Bari:

Williams: (drinking) Here's to when we were young and innocent and had answers to all the questions.
Fifi: That was a nice time.
Williams: Yeah. Ever been up in the Wang-ho country.
Fifi: No.
Williams: They got snakes up there with great big green eyes like yours.
Fifi: I've done most of my crawling in warmer places.
Williams: I like you.
Fifi: Snake fancier, huh?
Williams: No, I like you because you're everything a woman should be—a hundred and fifteen pounds of crookedness and kisses, with a laugh for a finish.
Fifi: You've got a fine sales talk, Mr. Williams.
Williams: Yeah. There's only one thing about a dame that's real.
Fifi: What's that?
Williams: (kissing her) This.

Williams is, of course, redeemed by love, as is Fifi. To reinforce sympathy, Williams is befriended by an adorable native boy, whom he calls Gunga Din, and who follows him around. Williams comes to care for the boy in his own tough way.

The plot is complicated with Williams's unknowing possession of information of the bombing of Pearl Harbor and his desire to shoot and sell footage of the Burma road. Hecht manipulates his attitudes and his love affairs so that, by the end of the film, he is willing to give up his neutral cynicism and join his friends.

Unlike Hecht's own producing-directing efforts, the visual effects are quite dramatic, and the acting and action sequences are taut. Using popular melodrama for propaganda purposes, Hecht focused on romance as the key to awakening Williams's sense of moral outrage, unlike his more personal play, *To Quito and Back,* in which inner malaise was enough to force a new awareness. The play may have been written to help sort out his own emotions, but the film is clearly intended to influence others.

China Girl may have aided the war effort and may have made the public more aware of the plight of conquered peoples, but it did little to address directly his concern for European Jews and America's awareness of their plight. Hecht felt that one reason the Germans believed they could persecute and murder Jews with impunity was that nobody in the world would care enough to interfere. He became one of the first to publicize the Nazi massacres in Europe when in February 1943 he published an article in *The Reader's Digest* entitled "Remember Us." His information about the genocide in Europe was based on material he received from Dr. Hayim Greenberg, editor of *The Jewish Frontier*. Although the Yiddish press had been mourning the slaughter of Jews for some time, the American and British press and governments had been largely silent.[14]

Hecht's other efforts to incite public concern included *A Guide for the Bedeviled* (echoing Maimonides's *A Guide for the Perplexed*), a book length attack on anti-Semitism he published in 1944. In it, Hecht used his considerable verbal skills to denounce not only the Germans but any who believed that the Jews were somehow responsible for the hatred aimed against them. Hecht's work again brought him some friends and many enemies. He was accused of lacking a balanced view of the situation, of being filled with his own hatred. Hecht responded:

> Much has been written to explain the recurrence among the Germans of their old and bloody hobby of exterminating Jews. But it has been an oblique writing. Looking on the blood-drenched massacre hands of the Germans, our writers have continued to discuss the political holes in the Nazi ideology. During the time of the massacre of 1940 onwards, I have read every day vibrant disputations on almost every subject except Germans. Our soldiers are allowed to fight Germans as fiercely as they can. But our writers are not allowed to discuss them. Not allowed! Who dares to stop our writers? Wheel him out for Congress to pillory!
>
> But he is a hydra-faced villain, who stops our writers. He is anti-Semitism and he is Semitism. He is also what the psychiatrists call "ambivalence"—a secret love of the thing one hates. Half of our most rabid anti-Nazi journalists are secretly infatuated with the Germans. That is the way of many writers: there is too much sickness in them to make them of any use in a Cause.
>
> The villain who halts our pens is also called by the name Good Taste. Virtue is to an ugly woman what good taste is to a stupid man—false riches. Writers who are too timorous, too vacuous, too thin-hearted, to set to paper anything but the dullest of matters are usually full of the greatest of pride. They are proud of not writing. This pride in not being able to say anything is flaunted by all the votaries of good taste. They are obviously not people to tackle the Germans.[15]

When *Guide for the Bedeviled* was published in 1944, Hecht had been associated with the Irgun Zvai Leumi for three years. In April 1941 Hecht had drinks at The Twenty-One Club with Irgun members, among them Peter Bergson, who had been impressed with Hecht's *P.M.* articles. The Irgun Zvai Leumi, Hebrew for National Military Organization, also known as Etzel, was composed of a group of Palestinean Jews devoted to more active means of driving the British out of that country than those of the Haganah, the military arm of the official Zionist movement. The Irgun was aligned with the splinter

Revisionist Party headed by Vladimir Jabotinsky and had developed out of the militant Betar of Eastern European Jewish radicalism. Bergson wanted Hecht's aid, his writing skills, his famous name, and his contacts to help the Irgun cause. Hecht was enthralled by Bergson and impressed with the Irgun's attempt to fight the British without the help of the Zionists, whose position was that the British were honor bound by the Balfour declaration to give them a Jewish State. He agreed with the Irgun that no one was going to give the Jews anything they did not first take for themselves. But Palestine was not Hecht's concern. While he admired Bergson and the Irgun, he did not feel it touched his life or his interests. He was concerned with the European situation. This was fine with Bergson, whose short-range goals dealt first with fighting the Germans, and Hecht was soon the co-chairman of a long list of committees seeking in one way or another th help the Jews in Europe. The first was The Committee for a Jewish Army of Stateless and Palestinian Jews, whose aim was to put a Jewish army in the field in the Middle East to help fight in North Africa. The idea found many friends but was undermined by a combination of British hostility and American Jewry's fear of being offensive.

During the next few years, many of Hecht's friends (including Ernst Lubitsch, Kurt Weill, and Billy Rose) came to his aid with financial and creative support, helping with the pageants he put on in New York or the ads the Irgun printed in the newspapers. Other friends thought him a traitor or worse. He and Rose put on *We Will Never Die,* a "Memorial to Two Million Dead in Europe," with the help of Weill and Moss Hart. This pageant was sponsored by The Emergency Committee to Save the Jewish People of Europe. Hecht was, as usual, co-chairman.[16]

The purpose of the pageant was to apprise the public of the situation in Europe and to counteract what he called the germs of spiritual corruption burrowing into the soul of man as a result of the Nazis. He explained its purpose in an article in *P.M.*:

> What good will it do? Will it save Jews from having their four million defenseless heads bashed in, from being burned in piles like the refuse in Riker's Island? I don't know. Maybe we can awaken some of the vacationing hearts in our government. And maybe we can induce a voice to sound somewhere in behalf of human dignity—a voice powerful enough to cause Hans and Fritz to pause and blink and drop their happy extermination torches.
>
> But whether or not such an objective is achieved, one thing we can produce: we can promise that the numbness will be lifted for two hours from all who come to our memorial service. We can promise that the song to the two million Jewish dead will not rise entirely in vain.[17]

The pageant played for two performances on the night of March 9, 1943. Beyond the forty thousand in the audience, thousands listened to it on the street through loudspeakers. Over the objections of more conservative and established elements in the Jewish community, Governor Dewey declared it an official day of mourning of the State of New York. The pageant toured to Washington, Philadelphia, Boston, Chicago, St. Louis, and Los Angeles. It was the catalyst for some of the first American newspaper reports of the Holocaust.

Until the end of the war, Hecht continued to work for the relief of European Jewry. Eventually, he came to realize that he had been wrong about the power of propaganda and the moral outrage it induced. It failed to hinder the Germans, nor did it impel the United States or Great Britain as governments to take any action to help the Jews. Hecht had found his Judaism; he had found that he loved Jews, particularly the kind of immigrant Jew who represented the security and warmth of his own family memories, but his actions during the war had failed to save lives and this added to his sense of loss:

> I looked at the Jews around me still trying to believe themselves intact. But the intactness was gone. However they twisted about to evade the truth, they were members of a race, a tribe, a religion or whatever Jews are, that had been burned alive in a great public bonfire with no friend in the world to cry "shame" or "stop."...
>
> The American in me came to a painful conclusion: "The Jew is not much good as a Jew. But he's fine and brave as anything else. The best thing a Jew can do is forget there is any Jewish cause—and stick to causes that he can back up under a flag—and with a gun."
>
> I nodded to my honest American counselor—myself from Racine and Chicago. It was sensible advice. I would go back to being an American, full of American pride and victory. There would remain a small, private area of defeat in me called Jew.[18]

Although even at the end of the war he had had small interest in the Irgun cause in Palestine, Hecht was soon again a co-chairman, this time of The American League for a Free Palestine. Hecht's involvement was, in part, due to his relationship with Bergson. All through his life, Hecht had what he called Sindbads, men who came into his life excited by a dream or a project who infected him with their excitement. Although, because of his intellectual nimbleness, Hecht often appeared a creature of reason, he was easily swayed by his emotions and his enthusiasm, more impressed by personalities than by persuasian. Even without Bergson, however, if Hecht were to be involved in helping the Jews in Palestine, the Irgun was the logical place for him. His natural distrust for institutions and cynicism towards the benevolence of Britain would have kept him from an alignment with any of the mainstream Zionist organizations headed by Chaim Weizmann and David Ben Gurion, both dedicated to accommodation with Britain as the means to a free state. The Irgun, on the other hand, believed that the British would only leave Palestine when their position there became intolerable.

Hecht supported the Irgun by writing propaganda and by fundraising. One Irgun ship called the *S.S. Ben Hecht*, and another, the *Altalena*, were purchased through American contributions. The importance of both the Irgun and its American committee has been debated for years. When Israel won its independence, the Jewish Agency Zionists became the ruling party. As a result, the official histories of the period tend to minimize the importance of the Irgun. In recent years, and particularly since the reemergence of Menachem Begin, former commander of the Irgun, a more balanced view of the independence period has emerged. A reasonable conclusion, although it is not universally shared, is that it was the military and public pressure put on the British, in part by the Irgun, that forced the British into an untenable position in Palestine and precipitated their departure. With pageants such as *A Flag is Born* and other propaganda efforts, Hecht and the American Committee contributed to the Irgun's success by publicizing their goals and achievements and through fundraising.

Hecht was hardly the only American working for the Irgun, whose many supporters included congressmen and senators, nor did he work for the Irgun full-time. Although co-chairman of their many committees, he functioned more as their chief writer and lightning rod for criticism than as a policy maker. When involved in a project, he could rally the support of his friends in the arts, but he was frequently involved in his own affairs. The same comment might be made about the full range of his political activities, dating from when he joined Fight for Freedom. Hecht was only one of a multitude in the entertainment world who lent their support to the war effort. His uniqueness was in the iconoclastic and often adversary stance he took even as an advocate of the war. He was as strident in support of his cause as he had been in the past in his attack on complacent institutions, only without his former humor, for he was in deadly earnest.

Hecht attacked the British with the same zeal he had used on the Germans, and his position as the most visible and vulnerable supporter of the Irgun gained him notoriety and brought him troubles out of proportion to his actions or importance. His most spectacular splash was not *A Flag is Born*, directed by Luther Adler, which featured a cast of luminaries led by Paul Muni and Celia Adler (and including Marlon Brando), but a piece he dashed off while still in an oxygen tent after an operation. Printed as an ad in fifteen papers, principally in the *New York Herald Tribune,* on May 15, 1947, it was reprinted all over the hemisphere and in Europe as a news story. The ad was a letter addressed to the "Terrorists of Palestine" explaining why the money they needed was coming slowly. In it Hecht said:

> Every time you blow up a British arsenal, or wreck a British Jail, or send a British railroad train sky high, or rob a British bank, or let go with your guns and bombs at the British betrayers and invaders of your homeland, the Jews of America make a little holiday in their hearts.

There was more, including an attack on the timidity of Jews too respectable to do anything but apologize, but the "little holiday in their hearts" was enough to bring the weight of the British Empire down on Hecht. He was denounced in Parliament, and Lord Beaverbrook, the newspaper potentate, turned Hecht into Public Villain No. 1. Hecht was called a "penthouse warrior," and on May 30 the *Evening Standard* devoted its entire correspondence column to letters attacking him. One called him "a Nazi at heart." Other letters suggested his pictures be banned in England, and they were boycotted.

The British Cinematograph Exhibitor's Association did ban Hecht's films. The ban occurred in two stages. In 1948 a ban was imposed for a short time, but there were so many films, up to eighteen, with which Hecht was associated in current release, that it would have been too much of a hardship for the exhibitors to allow political considerations to override financial concerns. Later, when Hecht again made a statement that outraged the British, three more films—*Love Happy, Whirlpool,* and *Where the Sidewalk Ends*—were banned, but the ban actually only delayed their release. His name only appeared on *Whirlpool.* For *Where the Sidewalk Ends* his chauffeur, Lester Barstow, received credit. He got no screen credit for *Love Happy.* The second ban was imposed in 1950 and was lifted in 1952 but during the entire period from late in 1947 until well after 1952 because of the threat of the boycott, Hecht found it difficult to obtain work and then only at drastically reduced wages and often with no credit. (Doug Fetherling states that as late as 1956 Hecht did not receive credit on *The Iron Petticoat* because there was still fear of losing the British market, but, in fact, it was Hecht who withdrew his name from the picture after he argued with the film's star, Bob Hope, over the cutting of the movie.)

Hecht's involvement with Palestine ended for a time after the war for Israeli independence when the Zionists sank the *Altalena* in an attempt to discredit and tame the Irgun,[19] but a decade later he wrote a study of the Kastner Affair in Israel. The work, *Perfidy* (1961), was concerned with the trial of a man accused of libel for writing that Kastner, an Israeli government official, was guilty of complicity in the Nazi massacre. The libel trial turned into an investigation of Kastner and became an embarrassing scandal for the ruling party. Although basically a polemic, it is Hecht's only work with copious and detailed notes. This was the result of the book having been written in collaboration with an Israeli lawyer, a former Irgun member, who insisted on accuracy in the work. Hecht's attitude in the book, beyond his indignation, is that all governments are inherently perfidious and corrupt by their very nature, and a Jewish government is no different, although he defends the right of the Jews to be as corrupt as anyone else.

Despite the publication of *Perfidy,* Hecht's career as a Jewish leader had ended years earlier. He had never been comfortable as a politician, even as representative of such a disreputable group as the Irgun.

> To be a leader a man has to learn to stand still, and be content with repeating himself. I was going nowhere that I knew of, and never again might have anything as interesting to utter as I had uttered about Jews. But having said my say, it was my nature to wander off, hoping for other topics.[20]

His disillusionment with the Zionists, then establishing a government in Israel, was a perfect excuse for leaving his political activities, although he continued to make news as he reacted to events reflexively and publicly and was followed by the spectre of a boycott for a number of years.

Hecht returned to writing movies and raising his daughter. The changes in his attitudes and work could not be abandoned so easily. The bountiful world he had hitherto enjoyed had surprised him, stripping him of his innocence and his youth. During the war his commitment to his new ethnic and patriotic identity kept his spirit in sympathy with a movie industry geared to supporting the fighting effort. Films like *China Girl* reflected his belief in the importance of personal and political commitment. But his uneasy unity of purpose ended in 1945 and by 1948 his Irgun activities had taken him far from the interests of conservative Hollywood. His new understanding of the evil in the world would continue to color his films with both a dark malevolence and a faith in miracles.

8

Gaily, Gaily: 1945–1964

When the war ended, there was no return to normality for the film industry. Even though attendance records were set in 1946, changing audience tastes and a combination of other factors, such as the resurgence of foreign film industries, soon damaged the studio system which had provided Hecht with such an accommodating playground and easy target. Aside from a new audience raised on the brutality of war and the reality of newsreel footage, the structure and atmosphere of the movie colony was drastically altered by a number of factors: the advent of commercial television, antitrust decisions changing the distribution systems, thereby diminishing the need for the studio to turn out a massive number of films to keep their theatres busy, and the investigations of the House Un-American Activities Committee (which precipitated the blacklistings of many artists). By 1950, the large studios, led by MGM in 1949, were selling off their property, releasing their large staffs from contract, and peddling their film libraries to television.

Tastes also changed. By 1942 sophisticated comedy had been replaced by a more harmless approach to humor, and the end of the war brought with it an emphasis on introversion, random violence, and psychology that could not be easily developed by the story construction methods of the studio writing system. Preoccupied by domestic and political concerns and disillusioned with the industry, Hecht was less synchronized with the pulse of his society and the tastes of his audience than he had been in the prewar years. As a professional still respected by the aging men who continued to produce and direct films, even with the British boycott Hecht's film production does not seem to have diminished substantially during these years. (Hecht had always limited the number of films bearing his name and was often paid under the table, possibly to dodge taxes or to keep the money for his lothario activities secret from Rose, who kept the books, or possibly just to insure that his name did not appear too frequently and so lessen in value. With the imposition of the boycott, however, the specific quantity of his work is even more difficult to measure.)

Becoming a father for the second time at the age of fifty, Hecht doted on his daughter Jenny, dedicating both *A Guide for the Bedeviled* and *Child of the*

Century to her. In later years he came to her defense when as an actress she became involved in backstage and legal spats. His new parental duties strengthened Hecht's already pronounced domesticity, as did his gallbladder operations in 1946. Hecht had always lived as if he were still the youthful, carefree reporter. As his age, and that of his friends, became impossible to ignore, he acknowledged his years but mourned the passing of friends and his society in a series of memoirs and complaints. *A Guide for the Bedeviled* contained large sections of reminiscences, but *A Child of the Century*, begun in 1946 and published in 1954, was a sustained autobiography. Interestingly, Hecht wrote little about Hollywood and filmmaking in the book, although he includes many profiles of his friends from that period. Most of the book is taken up with his earlier life, childhood, journalistic career and his early days in New York. A large section is devoted to his Jewish political activities, and, while as a factual account of these years it is more romantic than accurate, it does express his emotions and reactions to the events and changes during this period. There is a mellowness about the work, an acceptance of life, an embracing of the world and humanity which Hecht says grows in part from his changing health and from seeing things through the eyes of his daughter.

Hecht would add to his reminiscences with three more books, *Charlie: The Improbable Life and Times of Charles MacArthur* (1957), *Gaily, Gaily* (1963), and *Letters from Bohemia* (1964). The book on MacArthur is much more a personal eulogy than a biography, as are the profiles of his other deceased friends in *Letters from Bohemia*, although the letters themselves, all to Hecht, are often no more than messages and thank you notes. *Gaily, Gaily* is a rewritten compilation of articles, most published in *Playboy*, relating fanciful recollections of Chicago. They are in the form of much of his early fiction, with the Hecht persona present but often as merely a filter for the story.

Hecht published only two novels after the beginning of World War II. Neither have the literary stature or pretentions of his earlier extended fiction. Both are mysteries. The first *I Hate Actors* (1944) is a comic mystery—a satire based in Hollywood. Its protagonist is the agent Orlando Higgens, central character in Hecht's story and film "Concerning a Woman of Sin." The second, *The Sensualists* (1959), is a crime story which continues the study of sexuality, eroticism, and deviation that had always fascinated Hecht.

Hecht wrote few comedies in this period. For the most part, he worked on thrillers, gangster films and psychological dramas, such as *Ride the Pink Horse, Kiss of Death, Dishonored Lady, The Paradine Case* (all 1947), *Whirlpool* (1949) or *Where the Sidewalk Ends* (1950). Psychology and the psychopath were important in these films, particularly *Kiss of Death* which featured Richard Widmark in his first important screen role as the grinning psychotic killer, Johnny Udo, who terrorizes stool pigeon Victor Mature, an ex-con trying to find domestic happiness.

Hecht no longer found great joy in working in Hollywood, and he was grateful that the vogue of shooting films on location tied him less to the studios. His disaffection began, he says, in 1947. Until that time, despite his carping, Hollywood had been an exhilarating playground. Of Hollywood of that earlier time Hecht comments, "All these things I loved. How can you help doting on a town so daft, so dizzy, so sizzling; a town bubbling with the alarms and delights of a fairytale book?"[1] When, after recuperating from his operation, he needed funds, he returned to work again, as he had done many times before. But, he writes:

> Here my farewell to Hollywood began. It was to continue for several years. During these years all that I remembered of Hollywood kept vanishing. The movie people grew timorous and cynical. There was no elation to be tapped in the studios. From the owner to the smallest of his stooges rose a fog of weariness.
>
> I found myself too bored by the tasks I took on to ponder much on the causes of this collapse of movieland.[2]

Despite his growing disillusionment Hecht could still turn out workable material in less time than other writers. According to Otto Preminger:

> ... [I] learned a great deal from Hecht about writing. He was not only very fast and usually superb but also took criticism without the least sign of stress.... For Hecht nothing was impossible. He considered himself an employee who was delivering a product on order.[3]

In the films, the Hecht character also aged, resembling Thomas Mitchell more than Fairbanks in *Angels Over Broadway*, a little wizened by defeat, still feisty but more in search of solace than independence. At the end of the war, for instance, Hecht wrote two films in collaboration with Alfred Hitchcock, *Spellbound* (1945) and *Notorious* (1946). Together they reflect the changing emphasis of Hecht's concerns. Both films are thrillers rather than straight mysteries focusing more on inward psychological struggle than on external plot manipulations. In *Spellbound*, Ingrid Bergman, the seemingly cold psychoanalyst, helps Gregory Peck regain his memory, find his identity, and clear himself of a murder committed by Leo G. Carroll, the head of the clinic where Bergman works. The film is prefaced by a set of titles extolling the virtues of psychoanalysis:

> Our story deals with psychoanalysis, the method by which modern science treats the emotional problems of the sane. The analyst seeks only to induce the patient to talk about his hidden problems, to open the locked doors of his mind. Once the complexes that have been disturbing the patient are uncovered and interpreted, the illness and confusion disappear,... the devils of unreason are driven from the human soul.

The use of psychiatry as a plot device gained wide usage after the war possibly because the war had revealed the world to be a place of irrational violence where security and trust were difficult to achieve. On the screen, these fears were reflected in the reemergence of the gangster film with an emphasis on the gangster as psychopath, in *film noir*, really more an atmosphere of darkness, danger, and distrust than an actual genre, and in the use of psychiatry as a panacea. According to Richard Griffith:

> The proposed remedy for this sudden spread of madness throughout the world is, of course, psychiatry, a science belatedly endowed by Hollywood with godlike powers. The significance of the flood of psychological films, and of the fact that psychiatry is represented in them as a witch doctor cure, needs no underlining.[4]

Hecht had a lifelong interest in psychology and since his days in Chicago had been thought by his friends to be an authority on the subject. Hitchcock considered himself fortunate to be working with Hecht on the project both because of Hecht's supposed psychiatric expertise and because Hitchcock considered Hecht a skilled professional screenwriter. In the film, the dreams of the amnesiac Peck are used as a plot device, as if they were detective clues, to reveal his identity and actions. The dream sequences were vividly designed by Salvador Dali.

The love story central to the plot is the unprofessional passion Bergman develops for her patient. It is not really their professional relationship that keeps them apart as much as the problem of trust. The doctor loves her patient, but the patient has no name and may be guilty of murder. This tension is heightened by subjective camera work which allows the audience to believe that there is a danger in Peck's actions (justified by Bergman's own fears and uncertainties) when in fact he is quite benign. In order for Bergman to help Peck and save him, she must disregard the conventional patterns she has been taught to accept. The paranoia of the film is further heightened, since the head of the clinic himself is not merely a murderer, but an imbalanced killer as well, wielding violence without rationality. Since institutions and professional codes of conduct are of no use, the lovers can only fall back on personal emotion and trust.

This pattern of uncertain morality, corrupt institutions, and the necessity of commitment made on faith is present in *Notorious* as well. In this film Bergman is the character in need of trust. The guilt-ridden daughter of a condemned Nazi spy, she agrees to go to Rio to work for the F.B.I. Her job is to seduce Claude Rains, the leader of a Nazi underground. The basic complications are two: first, she falls in love with her agent, Cary Grant; and second, Rains wants to marry her. The MacGuffin (Hitchcock's term for objects of tension in a script which have no real meaning beyond the fact that everyone wants them) in the film is a group of bottles filled with uranium ore.

25. *Spellbound* (1945). Hitchcock thought Salvador Dali's surrealism would be an effective way of presenting the subconscious dream state. (Photo: Museum of Modern Art/Film Stills Archive courtesy United Artists.)

Hitchcock described the plot as "simply the story of a man in love with a girl who, in the course of her official duties, had to go to bed with another man and even had to marry him."[5] But the real issue in the film, is, again, whether Cary Grant will overcome his fear of women and professional detachment, and his need for love and desire to trust her. Oddly, it is Rains who nearly evokes the greatest sympathy. Although he is a Nazi and allows assassination to be permitted around him, he loves and marries Bergman with a charming sincerity and vulnerability, unaware that he is being deceived. The constant bickering between Grant and Bergman is juxtaposed against Rains's faith and devotion.

Notorious is considered one of Hitchcock's best films. Truffaut calls it his favorite black-and-white Hitchcock. Hitchcock's emphasis on suspense and simplicity, and his own concern for the dubious nature of authority and the problems of trust, combine well with Hecht's crafting skills and interest in relationships. The result is a collaboration which, according to Donald Spoto in his recent study *The Art of Alfred Hitchcock*, is a scenario which "adds a depth and humanity manifested by few films of that era."[6]

The achievement of *Notorious* is emphasized if it is compared with *Gilda*. Released in 1946, it was directed by Charles Vidor and written by Hecht. *Gilda* is fashioned out of the same material as *Notorious*. George Macready is the head of a Nazi-inspired consortium in South America. He marries Rita Hayworth, unaware that she was formerly the lover of Macready's manager, Glen Ford, a down-at-the-heels gambler he has helped. The terrain is familiar from Hecht films. Ford is a tough guy cynic hiding his hurt. He is caught between, on one side, the man of power and his devotion to his job, and on the other, the girl he loves but distrusts. Macready is the sinister scoundrel, an Anthony Mallare living on hate, an element he says is the only thing that warms him. Hayworth is the girl with an unstated past which must be overcome to permit a true reunion with Ford. It is a busy film with Ford narrating and with two observer-characters, one a philosophic washroom attendant and the other a policeman. Both appear *ex machina* to resolve the plot. By comparison with *Notorious*, it is a heavy handed, convoluted affair, both more bitter and cynical and more romantic and sentimental. The dialogue is clever, perhaps too much so:

Macready: (referring to his cane which conceals a knife) It is a most faithful and obedient friend. It is silent when I wish it to be silent. It talks when I wish to talk.
Ford: That's your idea of a friend?
Macready: That is my idea of a friend.
Ford: You must lead a gay life.
Macready: I lead a life I like to lead.
Ford: You're a lucky man.
Macready: I make my own luck.
Ford: What are you doing in a neighborhood like this?
Macready: I came down to save your life.
Ford: Don't overdo it. He wouldn't have killed me if I'd given him the money.
Macready: But you wouldn't have given him the money.

The dialogue in *Notorious* is stripped down and functional. The plot is simpler. In *Gilda*, Macready's exotic cane is used as the murder weapon, while in *Notorious* the more commonplace poison is used in what Hitchcock calls "an attempt to make the spies behave with reasonable evil."[7] With Rains, the emphasis is on his love and understandable feelings of betrayal when he discovers his wife has been planted. His Nazi sympathies are forceful enough to justify his destruction but are never dwelled on. Macready is a diabolical creature of seemingly supernatural power, lusting after power and delighting in the sight of Ford and Hayworth tearing at each other. *Notorious* follows the simple triangle which *Gilda* doubles back on itself by bringing Macready back from a fake suicide for the finale. As a result, *Notorious* is a film of convincing danger and human emotion whereas *Gilda* merely titillates in a patently artificial world, demonstrating again the kind of work Hecht could do in collaboration with a director of sympathy, vision, and skill. Hecht's script is an effective tool in the hands of Hitchcock who couples it with quietly crafted shooting techniques such as the long tracking shots employed in Rains's home. Both are stories concerned with the conflict between love and duty focusing on the psychologies of the characters, but *Notorious* subsumes the psychology into the character while *Gilda* uses it ostentatiously to precipitate action.

It is commonplace to observe that a script may read better than it plays, a judgement often made about Hecht's work. It is also possible that the writing is perfectly practical for the screen but has not been fully realized by the director. This is often true of the scripts Hecht directed himself, but it can even occur with a director of Hitchcock's skill. There are scenes early in the film (for instance, when Grant attends a party at Bergman's home) in which the action is indifferently directed. The scene is, in a very playable manner, better in the words than as they are spoken. The scene should suggest the loose morality and self-destructiveness of Bergman, the abandon of her companions, and the sharpness of Grant. These goals are achieved but only because the information is conveyed in the dialogue, and not because the actors are using the lines with any effective subtext. It is unfortunate that, because in film a script is rarely used more than once, ineffective results are reflexively attributed to failure by the writers.

While indifferent work with actors mars only one or two scenes in *Notorious*, it is the norm in *Specter of the Rose* (1946) written, produced and directed by Hecht from his own short story based loosely on the madness of Nijinsky and the ballet of the same name. Hecht's films always have a slightly mannered quality, a self-conscious attention to style, which, if the dialogue is sharp enough and the plot has the right touch of ebullient perversion, can be an asset in underlining a suspension of disbelief. But in *Specter of the Rose* the artiness of the enterprise, coupled with a peculiar earnestness, results in a pretention that can only be valued, as it was, for its attempt to produce an "art"

26. *Notorious* (1946). Devlin (Cary Grant) meets the disillusioned Alicia Huberman (Ingrid Bergman) in a scene that is better in Hecht's script than in Hitchcock's final film. François Truffaut calls the film a "model of scenario construction." (Photo: Museum of Modern Art/Film Stills Archive.)

film. The story concerns a ballet dancer whose madness drives him to kill his first wife and then himself rather than harm his second wife. The story is complicated by too many characters: managers, ballet teachers, policemen, poets, union representatives, agents, artists, and dancers. Hecht takes the opportunity to make fun of modern dance as well as his usual New York targets, those who take advantage of the artist without possessing any art themselves. Unfortunately his usual cynicism about the pretentions of artists, the kind he made fun of in *The Twentieth Century*, is sadly absent. What wit there is in the script is dissipated in the playing through tepid acting by some (such as his leading dancer Ivan Kirov), in overacting by others (such as Michael Chekov with a spit curl in the middle of his forehead as Polikoff the producer), and in the artificiality of still others (principally Lionel Stander in his familiar Bodenheim role performing his "minuet over an ashcan"). Stander's character is called Ganz—the name given to the Bodendeim caricature in Hecht's *Count Bruga* (1926).

The film was co-directed by Lee Garmes who photographed most of Hecht's earlier projects, and who helped Hecht achieve a look of an angular, dusty, horror film, and all the actors appear like Hecht's friendly gargoyles. Hecht seems to have taken the ballet world seriously, ignoring his own advice on the subject of ballet: "The lesser the art, the more artistic the admirers."[8] In *Specter of the Rose*, the people are besotted with their artistry. The ballet sequences, which should be a redeeming feature in the film, are only passably effective, adding to the confusion of how seriously the characters can be taken.

In the postwar period Hecht vacillated between the sureness and precision of *Notorious* and the tricky smartness of *Gilda* and *Specter of the Rose*. The dichotomy is evident in Hecht's last directing effort, *Actors and Sin* (1951). The film is really two distinct pieces. The first, based on Hecht's story "Actor's Blood," relates how the father of an actress who commits suicide, kills himself to throw blame on the daughter's many lovers and enemies—husbands, directors, producers, critics—whom he believes were responsible for her death. Edward G. Robinson plays the father with a Victorian zeal, but the plot is a contrivance in the manner of *The Florentine Dagger* and *Count Bruga* and the dialogue is self-consciously pithy. The film ends with the drama critic reviewing Robinson's suicide performance. Years later, the same reviewing device was used at the end of *Theatre of Blood* (1973), a horror film in which Vincent Price revenged himself on the London theatre critics, by killing each with a murder out of Shakespeare, and died himself, playing Lear's death scene. But where Price's death was high camp completely within the tone of the film, Hecht provides no such support and the ending is nasty and flat. In both *Specter of the Rose* and in the "Actor's Blood" portions of *Actors and Sin*, Hecht appears to be venting his frustration at the emptiness and vindictiveness of the New York theatre world where he had had no major critical success since *The Twentieth*

27. *Specter of the Rose* (1946). Sanine (Ivan Kirov, barechested) is the murderous mad dancer protected by his fellow dreamers: La Belle Sylph (Judith Anderson), Polikoff (Michael Chekov), the detective (a nondreamer, Charles Marshall), the poet (Lionel Stander), and Haidi (Viola Essen). Reviewer Neil Rau said the unusual film was "as different as a piece of typical Hecht dialogue." (*L.A. Examiner*, June 15, 1946.) (Photo: Museum of Modern Art/Film Stills Archive.)

Century (1932). It may be that Hecht was not aware of how humorless the films are. The scripts are lighter than the films with a macabre irony which had always been part of Hecht's taste, but was now out of tune with the contemporary scene.

The same comments could be made about the more successful second half of *Actors and Sin*, a short based on another Hecht story, "Concerning a Woman of Sin." Just as *The Front Page* was a valentine to his newspaper days, "Concerning a Woman of Sin" is a loving satire of the days, already gone when this film was made, when the studio boss had more power and less responsibility than a minor deity. The film features Eddie Albert in a parody of agent and friend Leland Hayward, Alan Reed as a studio head, and Hecht's daughter Jenny as a child who writes a torrid love story. Her script somehow gets sent to Reed who seizes on it as the most sophisticated love story ever written, forcing Albert to conceal the identity of the author. The film is a frenetic parody of the studios, but of the studios as they existed before the war, television, slipping attendance and the House Un-American Activities Committee had turned Hollywood into a place of "frowziness and cowardice." The agent hates actors and studio heads and is forever kissing his secretary for long moments and then bouncing immediately back to work. The louder he protests that the script is trash, the more Reed offers for it. The studio boss is the powerful dictator without taste who excises "I love you" from an ad because the line is twenty-five years old. George Antheil scored "Pop Goes the Weasel" as Reed's theme music.

Hecht seems to be having fun with both Jenny and his material in this film. His language is still florid, but it is appropriate to his subject matter. For example, he describes Albert's character, Orlando Higgens, as "A ten percenter, a peddler of genius and beauty, full brother to the Headless Horseman—evasive, double talking, irresponsible as a grasshopper, liason officer between the Mad Hatter and the Three Little Pigs." Hecht cannot resist delivering the diatribe himself as he introduces this portion of the film. Although the satire is harmless, it has the mischievous exhuberance that Hecht had, in earlier times, brought to his comic efforts, especially when he knew his target intimately and loved them as much as he scorned them.

Sophisticated comedy had little place in the domestic postwar world, and the vogue for comedies about the irresponsible but witty had passed. As the critic Raymond Durgnat comments in his analysis of comedy, *The Crazy Mirror*:

> Post-war America remains prosperous, and gracefully carefree sophistication hasn't the appeal it possessed in the 30's.... Comedy tends to be warmer, more thoughtful.... The carefree personal grace ceases to be sufficient, to feel empty rather than liberating, and the comedy of manners is replaced by the comedy of behavior.[9]

28. *Actors and Sin* (1951). In the "Actor's Blood" half of the film, Maurice Tillayou (Edward G. Robinson) is a protective stage father who blames the suicide of his daughter Marcia (Marsha Hunt) on the people around her. (Photo: Museum of Modern Art/Film Stills Archive courtesy United Artists.)

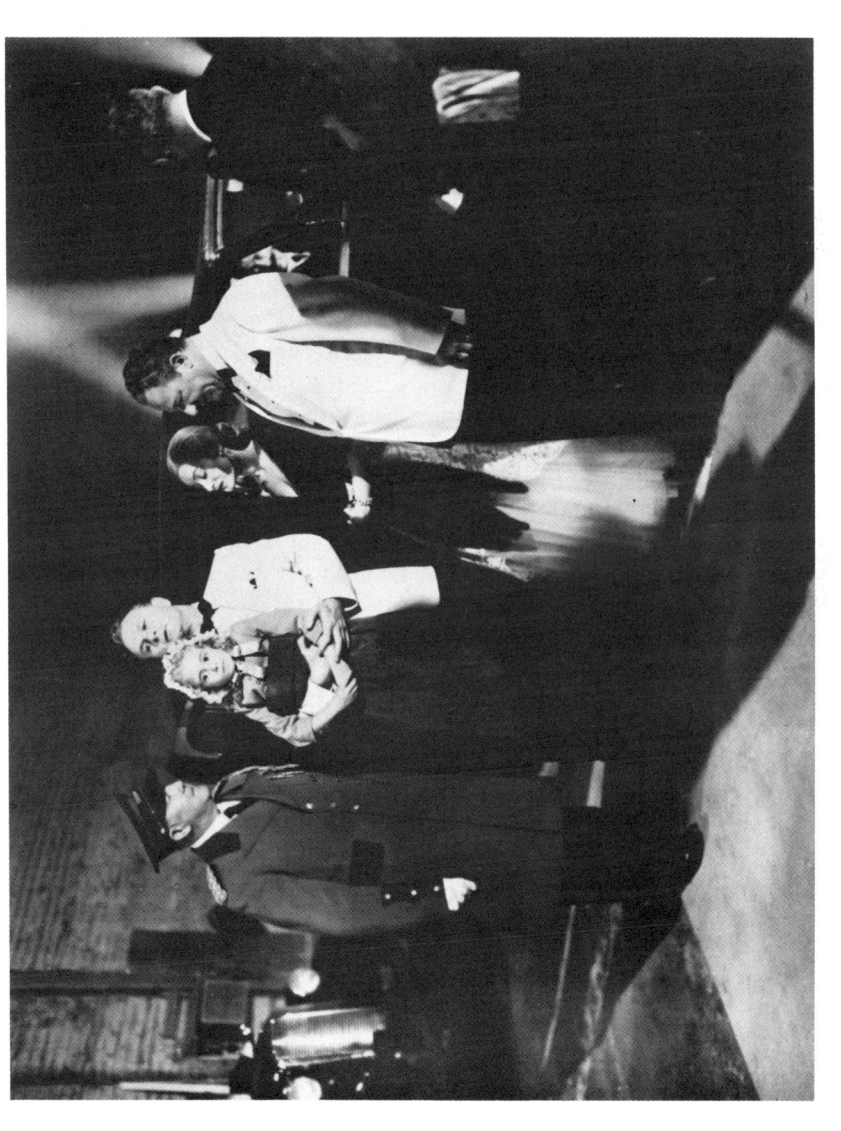

29. *Actors and Sin* (1951). In "Woman of Sin," Daisy Marcher (Hecht's daughter Jenny) is the author of a screenplay which studio head J.B. Cobb (Alan Reed, at right) thinks is sophisticated. Agent Orlando Higgens (Eddie Albert) tries to keep studio chief and authoress apart. (Photo: Museum of Modern Art/Film Stills Archive courtesy United Artists.)

The two most successsful comedies Hecht writes in this period (although not until after 1950) reflect the changes that Durgnat suggests took place in the American sensibility. *Monkey Business* (1952) and *Roman Holiday* (1953) taken together exemplify the contradictions and tensions in Hecht's shifting reaction to himself and his world. *Monkey Business* is a romantic comedy about middle-aged people coping with age in a suburban environment. *Roman Holiday*, resembling the traditional screwball comedy, is much more a fairytale, but it is grounded more firmly in a realistic world where the lovers cannot cut themselves off from society and live happily ever after. Hecht contributed to both scripts. He wrote the second draft for *Roman Holiday*, which is of interest because this version is much closer to the ambience and construction of screwball comedy than is the final film.

In *Monkey Business* the problems of the contemporary world are met frontally. The central figures are no longer the ageless lovers of screwball comedy. Cary Grant, the veteran of many romantic comedies has become a research chemist working on a youth formula. He is a middle-aged man, a bit absent-minded when engrossed in his work, and consequently oblivious of his wife, Ginger Rogers. By mistake a monkey finds the right formula which gets mixed in the drinking water. Grant, Rogers, and others including Charles Coburn, mistakenly take the formula and revert to childish behavior of varying ages for short periods of time. Early in the film Grant complains to Rogers that with age, romance and sex mean less to him. When they were younger he and his wife had stayed home from a party to make love, now they stay home because Grant is too preoccupied to have fun. During the film Grant and Rogers re-experience youth, but they find that their insecurities and immaturity return along with their adolescent energy. Grant begins to wonder

> ... if being young is all it's cracked up to be. The dream of youth. We remember it as a time of nightingales and valentines, and what are the facts. Maladjustment, near idiocy, and a series of low comedy disasters. That's what youth is. I don't see how anyone survives it.

They have never lost their attraction for each other; even in the early scenes they stay home to make love, but now Grant concludes contentedly:

> You're old when you forget you're young.... It's a word you keep in your heart, a light you have in your eye, someone you hold in your arms.

In contrast to Coburn, who wants youth in order to pursue his secretary, Marilyn Monroe, Grant and Rogers have a solid relationship based on mutual knowledge rather than illusion. The film maintains that their shared experience, respect and affection are positive virtues.

30. *Monkey Business* (1952). The characters may be getting older, and the film may be about chemist Dr. Barnaby Fulton (Cary Grant), his wife Edwina (Ginger Rogers), and a youth formula, but reporters still manage to turn up (Harry Carey, Jr. and Jerry Sheldon). (Photo: Museum of Modern Art/Film Stills Archive courtesy Twentieth Century Fox.)

The film was directed by Howard Hawks (with Charles Lederer and I.A.L. Diamond also working on the screenplay) and it has some of the sense of collaborative fun and expertise of Hecht's earlier work with Hawks and Lederer. Their most recent project had been *The Thing (from Another Planet)* (1951). In both films the scientific path is a dangerous one: in *The Thing* it would have led to unleashing the invaders who wanted to use the earth's population as an unwilling source of the blood they feed on. Only mature thinking by nonscientist military leader Kenneth Tobey can prevent disaster. Although the leader of the male group, both his girl friend (Margaret Sheridan) and, strangely, his men, think it is time for him to settle down with her.

In *Monkey Business*, scientists are ridiculed more gently. "That's the problem with being a chemist," Grant says, "you can't actually think." Lederer and Hecht had ganged up on science before in the comedies *Topaze* (1933) and *Her Husband's Affairs* (1947). But in *Monkey Business* much of the humor is derived from Grant and Rogers doing childish things rather than from sophisticated wit. The professionalism of the contributors results in an integration of action and dialogue and the comedy rarely seems to strain, unless as many have, you consider the basic assumption of the film strained. With the exception of Diamond, the major contributors were past forty years old (Hecht was fifty-eight), and there is a cohesiveness in the point of view in the film that helps to establish its comic framework.

In *Roman Holiday*, a young, innocent, princess (Audrey Hepburn), bored with her goodwill tour, sneaks away from her embassy and is found sleeping on a bench by jaded American newsman Joe Bradley (Gregory Peck) who takes her in. Later, realizing who she is, he connives to show her Rome, secretly planning to use the event for an exclusive article. Love intervenes and he decides not to use the story. But princess and commoner are kept apart by the differences in their station, and she returns to her duties. The plot is an obvious variation on *It Happened One Night* (1934), one of the first screwball comedies, which was directed by Frank Capra who originally was to direct *Roman Holiday* with Elizabeth Taylor and Cary Grant playing the leads. By the time Hecht took on the script, however, William Wyler was directing, and the film had not yet been cast. Earlier material had been written by Dalton Trumbo and possibly McClellan Hunter. Hecht wrote a version, a copy of which is dated November 5, 1951 and marked "William Wyler's Production of Roman Holiday, Second Draft Screenplay by Ben Hecht." Wyler shot the film in Rome in the summer of 1952. The final screenplay is credited to Hunter and John Dighton. It is not clear if Hecht contributed to the film beyond the extant draft.

The draft and the final film differ in ways that show Hecht still capable of his earlier styles. The script differs from the film in three substantial areas. First, the tone of Hecht's script offers a story that seems to take place more in

31. *Roman Holiday* (1953). William Wyler directs Gregory Peck and Audrey Hepburn as reporter and princess. (Photo: Museum of Modern Art/Film Stills Archive courtesy Paramount.)

the Italian section of Chicago than in Rome. Hecht's reporter is a graduate of the *Chicago Daily News*, his office is a smaller version of an American city room, his friends are Americans, and the natives resemble comic immigrant types, friendly and amoral, uniting against the police to protect blackmarketers or murderers and standing firmly in favor of young lovers. The film attempts to be more cosmopolitan, more deferential to the local people, and Peck's much more benign than Hecht's journalist, who, his editor believes, is "unfit for European journalism. I am quite fed up with your Chicago police reporter point of view! It's uncouth and juvenile! You regard every assignment as a lynching bee."[10]

The second change is the inclusion in Hecht's draft of a character called Lucky Frankovich, an old Chicago gangster, deported from America and now destitute, whom Peck employs. Peck wants surreptitious pictures of Lucky and the Princess taken so that he can link them romantically in his story. Frankovich, introduced as the poet Maxwell Blauvelt, is also out of thirties (or twenties) Chicago and conveniently disappears when Peck and Hepburn finally come together. In the film Frankovich is deleted, Peck takes her around with Eddie Albert surreptitiously taking pictures of them with a number of cameras. Where Hecht's reporter wants to give the story a love angle by posing Frankovich in suggestive ways, Peck only wants to write about a carefree lark.

Finally, at the close of Hecht's script, Bradley attends a news conference for the Princess and after asking the prepared questions and getting the prepared answers, he asks the Princess to marry him, and she accepts while the other newsmen crowd around. After phoning the story in, they go off together in another of Hecht's rainstorms. In the film, Hepburn is returned to her embassy and the news conference scene is used to convey their mutual affection but also their knowledge that they each have separate duties.

The film's break with the happy ending was seen as a mature step forward in filmmaking. *Saturday Review* called it "poignant," commenting that "By adding a bitter ending to a lighthearted love story [Wyler] unhesitatingly breaks what I had thought was a hard-and-fast Hollywood rule; that comedies of the lighter sort must end with the boy and the girl hard and permanently in each other's arms."[11] Stanley Kauffmann in a reassessment of the film says, "If *Roman Holiday* had been made in 1933 instead of 1953, it might have ended with the princess telling her father (George Barbier or C. Aubrey Smith) that she would return only if she were allowed to marry the commoner."[12] Whether this ending is any more modern or realistic than the ending of the romantic propaganda of *Casablanca* (1942), where Bergman and Bogart separate to their individual destinies, is difficult to say, but it is certainly true that, as Raymond Durgnat observes, "the personal style is slower, quieter and more brooding in sentimentality and bitterness alike"[13] than earlier "high life comedy."

Hecht's reporter is more cynical, conniving, self-protective ("Not mean, baby—realistic," he tells her)[14] than Peck's more laconic, benign reporter. Hecht's Bradley retains some of the familiar linguistic acrobatics, as in a description of a cafe, "artists, poets and all sorts of escaped balloons. They come here every night to remodel the world and steal each other's sweethearts."[15] It is a guiltless romance with a measure of Hecht's cracking-wise wit, and the distance between his second draft script and the final film may be more a measure of the differences between attitudes of two decades than an indication of a greater realism.

In his script, Hecht shows that he can still write about love without getting mawkish, possibly because he keeps his characters young. His Bradley and his friend Sykes are not quite youths, but Hecht is willing to slip them into that category by describing them as "still youngish and casual fellows."[16] When he deals with the character in the throes of middle age, however, as he does in *Monkey Business*, he abandons the make-believe and exuberance he displays in writing *Roman Holiday*.

The middle-aged character making peace with himself, his lovers, and his world is the single most consistent image in Hecht's later films. His protagonists may still have things to learn but their cynicism is grounded in experience rather than in posture. They have followed their sense of honor or their professions. They have tried to remain young, but find it is time to settle. These characters pop up almost any place but they are always outsiders—travelers or expatriots. In *Legend of the Lost* (1957) it is John Wayne coming to accept the reformation of his prostitute girl friend (Sophia Loren) in the Sahara Desert and finding good in the world. In *The Indian Fighter* (1958) it is Kirk Douglas making peace between white and red men then settling down, not with the steady woman on the wagon train, but with the forbidden Indian maiden Elsa Martinelli. In *Circus World* (1964) it is John Wayne again searching Europe and finding Rita Hayworth after fifteen years. The desert, the Indian wars, and the circus all figure prominently in these films, while the grizzled cynic-star always has a little time to ruminate on the moral turpitude of men (and women) while he learns a little about love and trust.

These are only a few of the films Hecht contributed to during this period. The mellowness and acceptness of life noted above found its best expression when tempered with the skill of a director such as Hawks or Wyler. At its worst, Hecht's embrace of mankind could degenerate into mawkish sentimentality as it did in his two miracle films: *Miracle of the Bells* (1948) and *Miracle in the Rain* (1956). The first is the story of a press agent, Fred MacMurray, who uses his considerable talents and the aid of a local priest (Frank Sinatra in his first film role) to force the release of the only picture made by a recently deceased girl—a version of the Joan of Arc story. The second, based on Hecht's own short story, is a romance about a girl and a soldier who mystically reappears to

32. *Miracle in the Rain* (1956). Art (Van Johnson) is the good-hearted soldier with whom Ruth Wood (Jane Wyman) falls in love. His ambition after the war: to write for the *New York Times*, as he is doing in this scene.
(Photo: Museum of Modern Art/Film Stills Archive coutesy Warner Brothers.)

her after he has died overseas. Both films use a hard-boiled character to emphasize the redeeming quality of the miracle, possibly of personal importance to Hecht, who, as he aged and often became more disillusioned, also advocated mystical brotherhood and the redeeming characteristic of love. He was able to integrate in his mind sharp and at times shrill attacks on enemies and governments who, he felt, had betrayed their trust, as in *Perfidy*, with endless valentines in the form of eulogies to his dead friends and his former lives.

In the last two years of his life, Hecht was an unrepentant relic of a gaudy bygone age, or rather, ages. He remained productive, active, feisty, and as indulgent towards his friends as he had always been. But he had outlived the newspapers and renaissance of his youth in Chicago, although he returned in 1958 to write a guest column for the *Daily News*; he had outlived the artistic ferment in New York and an age of playwriting epitomized by *The Front Page*; he had outlived the Hollywood studios and the period when the written word, if not its author, was important to films, just as he had outlived a style of filmwriting of which his screwball comedies remain some of the best examples; he did not quite live to see the historical rehabilitation of the Irgun, but he did see the establishment of the State of Israel; finally, he had outlived many of his friends who had made all of his careers fun. By 1960 he could sit down and write an article for *Playboy* in which he merely counted the corpses of old friends who had died before him.

Up until the day of his death, Saturday, April 18, 1964, Hecht worked on new projects: an interview show for WABC in New York, new films, a new play (*Winkelberg*) about Bodenheim, getting Jenny out of jail where she and other members of the Living Theatre had landed after an aborted performance in New Haven when the Internal Revenue Service seized the sets and arrested the actors. He also adapted the Brecht-Feuchtwanger play *The Visions of Simone Marchand* for Jenny to act in.

Taken one at a time, Hecht's legacy to any individual field fails to measure the stature of the man. Journalists, historians, and students of literature, film, and theatre are all familiar with some portion of his fecundity. To film he brought his diverse talents and skills and applied them to many genres but most joyfully to the screwball comedy of the thirties, where his satire was always a bit self-deprecatory, its hard-boiled edges tinged with affection. It was a time when his peculiar high-sounding journalese had listeners who understood and spoke his dialect. The limitation of this study to Hecht's comedy and directing—to the exclusion of his contributions to other forms and styles (such as gangster films, science fiction, or adaptation)—is more due to the enormous breadth of his accomplishment than to the admitted lack of succinctness on the part of the author.

It may be, therefore, that in order to do any justice to Ben Hecht one must look to the man rather than to the work. In all his work, even those that attack the objects of his disdain or anger most viciously, there resides a man embracing and caring about the world around him. Eventually most people who write about Hecht, whether from first hand knowledge or from the accounts of others and exposure to Hecht's work, mention this love of people and of life. Whether his cynicism was worn loosely or in deep mourning, it clothed a spirit of vitality and curiosity. Henry Justin Smith and Harry Hansen protested that, for all his cynicism, young Ben was too much in love with people and the world to be withering, except for a cause. Fred Guiles says that Hecht, beyond his look of a satyr, was "avuncular." Otto Preminger says that Hecht was the most interesting man he had ever met, a man of uncompromising principle who "had a wonderful original wit which he never turned against anyone with malice."[17]

Hecht was always ambivalent about Hollywood and its easy gifts. It may be that easy money corrupted and seduced him into some inferior work. But he left a body of films important to the evolution and enjoyment of the medium, and he remained intact througout. Hecht always wrote better about earthy, knowing women than about virginity, a state he seemed to have difficulty understanding. His own last imagined conversation with Madam Hollywood may, therefore, be the best summation of his life and work in the movies:

> I rose and said goodbye to this strumpet in her bespangled red gown; goodbye to her lavender-painted cheeks, her coarsened laugh, her straw-dyed hair, her wrinkled fingers bulging with gems. A wench with flaccid tits and a sandpaper skin under her silks; shined up and whistling like a whore in a park; covered with stink like a railroad station pissary and swinging a dead ass in the moonlight.
>
> I said goodbye to her, and she said, "You don't look so good yourself, fella. I remember when you had a feather in your hat and took the steps two at a time." But there was no anger in her eyes. They were weary and kind, for I was as nice a friend as she had ever known.[18]

Appendix A

Filmography

Listings include credits that are both certain and questionable. Where questions exist, the source of information has been indicated. Three other Hecht filmographies have been useful in the present compilation. They may be found in the following:

Stephen Fuller, "Ben Hecht: A Sampler," *Film Comment* (Winter 1970–71).
Fred Guiles, *Hanging On in Paradise* (1975).
Doug Fetherling, *The Five Lives of Ben Hecht* (1977).

The extent of Hecht's contribution to some of the films cited may have been minor, and there are undoubtedly other films on which he worked but where his contribution has never been revealed. A list of projects which never reached fruition follows the list of completed films.

For clarity and brevity the following terms have been shortened:

BH:	Ben Hecht	ST:	Story
unc:	uncredited	Dial:	Dialogue
Pro:	Producer	Adapt:	Adaptation
Dir:	Director	Assoc:	Associate
SP:	Screenplay	Photo:	Photographer
O:	Original		

At the conclusion of each entry the location of copies or versions of the screenplay has been indicated. This list is by no means exhaustive and should be taken to show the presence rather than the conclusive absence of a screenplay from any library mentioned or from other research institutions.

The names of the institutions have been abbreviated in the following manner:

Acad:	Academy of Motion Pictures Arts and Sciences (Los Angeles).
AFI:	American Film Institute (Los Angeles).
BFI:	The British Film Institute (London).
D:	Dartmouth College Library.
Fox:	Twentieth Century Fox Studios.
Ind:	Lilly Library, Indiana University.
LC:	Library of Congress Motion Picture Section.
MOMA:	Museum of Modern Art (New York).
NYPL:	New York Public Library Theatre Collection.
UCLA:	University of California at Los Angeles.
USC:	University of Southern California.

184   Appendix A: Filmography

1915   *Double Trouble* FA/TrI
"Anita Loos in her autobiography stated that BH supplied idea." (Fetherling)

With: Douglas Fairbanks, Sr., Gladys Brockwell, Olga Grey, Tom Kennedy (Judge Blodgett), Monroe Salisbury, Kate Toncray, Margery Wilson.

1927   *Underworld* Paramount
Dir: Josef von Sternberg: Photo: Bert Glennon. 75 min.

With: George Bancroft, Evelyn Brent, Clive Brook, Larry Semon, Fred Kohler, Helen Lynch, Jerry Mandy.

Official credit: Story: BH. Adapt: Charles Furthman, scenarized by R.N. Lee. Academy Library has three versions of script: 1) "*Underworld* original story by Ben Hecht." 21 scenes. 49 pp. double-spaced; 2) "*Underworld* by Ben Hecht." 19 scenes. 78 pp. (legal sized); 3) *Underworld*. March 28, 1927. "Story: Ben Hecht. Scenario: Robert N. Lee." #1 roughly follows Hecht *1001 Afternoons in Chicago* story "The Man Hunt" which embellishes the actual escape of Tommy O'Connor. #2 adds character of Buck Mulligan and the jealousy plot which precipitates Bull Weed's shooting Buck in Buck's flower shop (an actual incident: Dion O'Bannion was murdered in his shop in 1922). Final film varies widely even from changes in #3. Hecht says he went to Hollywood in 1925. 1926 may be more likely but it is questionable if he worked on *Underworld* beyond the first story which is a simple escape story and love triangle. Famous touches, such as "The City is Yours" sign, were added in later versions. Hecht says he wrote the film with Arthur Rossen, that it was eighteen pages long, filled with "moody Sandburgian sentences," and that he received a ten thousand dollar bonus for writing it—his first film. Hecht received an Academy Award for Best Original Story (1927–28). The picture is considered one of the first important gangster films although it really deals with the world of pre-Prohibition thieves rather than with the organized gangs that populated later films.

British Title: *Paying the Penalty*.
SP: Acad.

1928   *The Big Noise* First National
Pro-Dir:Allan Dwan; Adapt-SP: Tom Geraghty. Story: BH.
Titles: George Marion, Jr.

With: Chester Conklin, Alice White, Bodil Rosing.

Photo: Ted Pahle
Newspapers, crime, and romance in New York.

1929   *The Great Gabbo* Sono-Art World Wide
Pro: Henry D. Meyer and Nat Cordish. Dir: James Cruze. Adapt: Ben Hecht of his story "The Rival Dummy." Continuity and dial: Hugh Herbert. Photo: Ira Morgan. One color sequence. 91 min.

With: Erich von Stroheim, Betty Compson, Don Douglas, Margie Kane.

This may be the film Hecht refers to when he says he worked on his first talkie with Stroheim. Original story is about ventriloquist who becomes jealous of his dummy, destroys it, and then thinks himself a fugitive. Film heightens romance, deletes Hecht's newsman narrator and most of story. More psychologically melodramatic, less macabre.

The Unholy Night MGM
Dir: Lionel Barrymore. SP and dial: Edwin Justus Mayer. Continuity: Dorothy Farnum. Story: BH. Photo: Ira Morgan.

With: Ernest Torrence, Roland Young, Boris Karloff, Polly Moran, John Miljan, John Loder, Richard Tucker, Natalie Moorehead, Sydney Jarvis.

Also titled: *The Green Ghost,* and listed by Fuller as 1925. Convoluted mystery complete with a Lord Montague, London fog, Scotland Yard, and a seance. Most of the cast is murdered and resurrected by conclusion.

SP: UCLA, NYPL.

1930 *Roadhouse Nights* Paramount
Pro: Walter Wanger. Dir: Hobart Henley. SP and story: BH. (Fuller: SP: Garrett Fort) 69 min.

With: Helen Morgan, Charles Ruggles, Fred Kohler, Jimmy Durante, Leo Donnelly.

Durante was written into the script by Hecht just before production after Wanger saw his nightclub act. Early sound newspaper film combines comedy with standard crime story. Film includes production numbers by Morgan and Durante.

1931 *The Front Page* UA
Pro: Howard Hughes. Dir: Lewis Milestone. Adapt. and add. dial: Bartlett Cormack. Unc: BH and Charles Lederer. From play by BH and Charles MacArthur. Photo: Glen MacWilliams. 100 min.

With: Adolph Menjou, Pat O'Brien, Mary Brian, Edward Everett Horton, Mae Clark.

Much of the play and film contain theatricalized versions of actual events and personalities. Walter Burns in particular is modeled after MacArthur's former editor, Walter C. Howie, who, if anything, was even more outrageous in his tactics than Hecht and MacArthur thought would be plausible on the stage. O'Brien was cast for the film under the studio's false impression that he had played the role of Hildy in the New York production.

SP: UCLA, AFI.

The Unholy Garden UA
Pro: Samuel Goldwyn. Dir: George Fitzmaurice. SP: BH and Charles MacArthur. 85 min.

Appendix A: Filmography

With: Ronald Colman, Fay Wray, Estelle Taylor, Tully Marshall, Warren Hymer.

Hecht says he dictated this desert adventure story to two secretaries in twelve hours for the eleven thousand dollars Goldwyn had paid the two writers. Hecht says Goldwyn loved it, and the film, faithfully produced from the script, flopped.

1932 *The Scarface—Shame of the Nation* UA/Atlantic
Pro: Howard Hughes. Dir: Howard Hawks. Co-dir: Richard Rossen.
    1931   UA press release: by Ben Hecht from novel by Armitage Trail. Screen story: Seton I. Miller, John Lee Mahin, W.R. Burnett.
    1932   Film print: Screen story by BH. Continuity and dial: Miller, Mahon and Burnett. Photo: Lee Garmes and L.W. O'Connell. 90 min.

With: Paul Muni, Ann Dvorak, Karen Morley, Osgood Perkins, George Raft, Vince Barnett, Boris Karloff.

Film is based on some of the same incidents as *Underworld* plus incidents from life of Al Capone. Scenes calling for martial law and denouncing gangsters added to appease censors. Unlike *Little Caesar* or *Public Enemy,* the film has no sociological bent but is closer to a psychological study of a deviant. The film deals not with morality but with group loyalty and the danger of women to the group. Hecht did not trust Hughes's solvency and was paid at the end of each working day. Al Capone is said to have demanded that the script be shown to him for his approval. The film incorporates many incidents from Capone's life: the murder of "Big Jim" Colisimo in 1920 on the order of Johnny Torrio, the fight against those who resisted Torrio—such as Dion O'Bannion, the pushing aside of Torrio by Capone in 1925, and the St. Valentine's Day Massacre which was organized by Capone.

Stanley Kauffmann: *The Scarface* "has been overrated as are most good American films by rhapsodists eager to create pantheons, but despite Paul Muni's overacting in the title role, it was directed with cinematic imagination; and it was written in Ben Hecht's high style—facile, flashy cynicism. The Hawks film is a relatively serious attempt by the best show biz of the time to examine the criminal world of the time for its greed and blood lust, also as a pressure cooker for sexual aberrance. Tony Camonte, based on Al Capone, burns with animal greed and brutality, and at least part of his fire is sublimated desire for his sister. The last sequence, in which she joins him in the shootout against the police even though he has just murdered her newlywed husband, is true Hawks-Hecht, a quick skim of profundities made impressive by professional skills." (*The New Republic,* Jan. 9 & 16, 1984, p. 24.)

Remade 1983. Universal.
Dir: Brian De Palma. SP: Oliver Stone.

With: Al Pacino, Steven Bauer, Karen Morley, Michelle Pfeiffer.

Remake substitutes Cuban cocaine dealers in Miami for Hecht's Italian bootleggers in Chicago, but the plot outline is roughly the same. "The World is Yours" sign now appears on a blimp. The film is dedicated to Hawks and Hecht.

Stanley Kauffmann: "De Palma and pals are out to pander to new gluttonies, and they have picked the right material, both as excuse and as medium. Hawks's *Scarface* treated a subject; De Palma's *Scarface* hitches a ride on its subject. Characters in the Hawks film are written and acted with some obligation to shatter stereotypes of crime films; with De Palma, characters are stuffed back into their stock shells." (*TNR*, Jan. 9 & 16, 1984, p. 24.)

Pauline Kael: "The original had a core of wit, but Oliver Stone's script just seems to touch the old bases, and after those showy early sequences De Palma tromps through the stock situations.... When Howard Hawks, who directed the 1932 film, and Ben Hecht, who wrote the script, decided to give their Al Capone and his sister the incestuous passions of the Borgias, they were having a nose-thumbing good time. This new film lingers over Tony's possessiveness about his sister, and is so obvious about it that the picture manages to make incest seem dated." (*The New Yorker*, December 26, 1983, p. 50.)

SP: NYPL.

Back Street Universal
Dir: John M. Stahl. SP: Gladys Lehman. Unc: BH and Unc: Gene Fowler. From novel by Fannie Hurst.

With: Irene Dunne, John Boles.

Remade: 1940. Dir: Robert Stevenson, with Charles Boyer and Margaret Sullivan.
1961. Dir: David Miller, with Susan Hayward, John Gavin. A woman's love for a married man; sentimental melodrama.

SP: USC.

1933 *Hallelujah, I'm a Bum.* UA
Pro: Joseph M. Schenck. Dir: Lewis Milestone. SP: S.N. Behrman. Story: BH. Music, lyrics and "rhythmic dialog" by Richard Rodgers and Lorenz Hart. Photo: Lucien Andriot. 82 min.

With: Al Jolson, Frank Morgan, Harry Langdon, Chester Conklin, Edgar Connor, Madge Evans.

Jolson is bum "mayor of Central Park" who returns girl to Mayor of New York. Film was an attempt at a poetic, musical, fairytale. Story shows Hecht at his most whimsical; Hart's lyrics constitute most of the dialogue.
British title: *Hallelujah, I'm a Tramp.*

Topaze RKO
Dir: Harry D'Arrast. SP: BH. Continuity: Charles Lederer from the play by Marcel Pagnol. O Prod: Paris (1928). American Prod: New York (1930) adapt. by Benn W. Levy. Camera: Lucien Andriot. 80 min.

With: John Barrymore, Myrna Loy, Albert Conti, Louis Alberni, Reginald Mason, Jobyna Howland, Jackie Searle, Frank Reicher.

Paramount made a French film from the play, then sold the American rights to RKO. Barrymore does delightful comic transformations as timid professor who takes over his crooked employer's business and mistress. Topaze has a secret vice, the movies, and takes Loy to see *Man, Woman and Sin.* The French version, with Louis Jouvet and directed by Louis Gasnier, was released in this country in 1935.

SP: NYPL, UCLA.

Turn Back the Clock. MGM
Pro: Harry Rapf. Dir: Edgar Selwyn. From O story by: Selwyn and BH. Photo: Harold Rosson. 79 min.

With: Lee Tracy, Mae Clarke, Otto Kruger, George Barbier, Peggy Shannon.

Tracy relives his life in a dream and wakes up happy with the choices he has made.

SP: NYPL, LC.

Design For Living. Paramount
Pro-Dir: Ernst Lubitsch. SP: BH. O Play: Noel Coward. Photo: Victor Milner. 90 min.

With: Fredric March, Gary Cooper, Miriam Hopkins, Edward Everett Horton.

Only line left from original: "Our Immortal Souls."

SP: NYPL.

Queen Christiana. MGM
Pro: Walter Wanger. Dir: Rouben Mamoulian. SP: Salka Viertel and H.M. Harwood. Unc: Ernest Vajda and Claudine West, BH and Gene Fowler. Dial: S.N. Behrman. Story: Viertel and Margaret F. Levine. Photo: William Daniels. 97 min.

With: Greta Garbo, John Gilbert, Ian Keith, Lewis Stone, Elizabeth Young, C. Aubrey Smith, Akim Tamiroff.

The film was a vehicle for Garbo and a lure to keep her at MGM. The script went through many hands under the watchful eye of Irving Thalberg. The film failed to help Gilbert's fading career. Hecht says he and Fowler worked on film as a team.

1934 *Viva Villa.* MGM
Pro: David O. Selznick. Dir: Jack Conway and unc. Howard Hawks. SP: BH from book by Edgcumb Pinchon and O.B. Stade. Photo: James Wong Howe and Charles G. Clark. 112 mins.

With: Wallace Beery, Leo Carillo, Fay Wray, Donald Cook, Stuart Erwin, George E. Stone, Joseph Schildkraut, Katherine DeMille, Henry B. Walthall.

Hecht wrote the original script in fifteen days and later went on location in Mexico where he did revisions and an edited script for Mexican censors. The film shot at same hacienda used by Eisenstein during his abortive movie making venture there. Movie a hit in Mexico after scenes of Villa drunk were deleted by censors. In 1951 the film was banned in Mexico because of scenes showing Villa capturing a town to oblige American newsman, Erwin. (Attack incident has basis in fact, see above Chapter 3, f. 3.) Hecht received Academy Award nomination for best adaptation, 1934.

SP: UCLA, LC, D.

Twentieth Century. Columbia
Pro-Dir: Howard Hawks. SP: BH and Charles MacArthur from their play (1932) based on play *Napoleon of Broadway* by Charles Bruce Milholland. Photo: Joseph August. 91 mins.

With: John Barrymore, Carole Lombard, Walter Connolly, Roscoe Karns, Charles Levison, Etienne Giradot, Dale Fuller, Ralph Forbes, Edgar Kennedy.

Remade as *Streamline Express* (1935) by Mascot. Play: Dir: George Abbott. Pro: Abbott and Phillip Dunning. Remade as stage musical (1978): *On the Twentieth Century.* Dir-Pro: Harold Prince, Book and lyrics: Betty Comden and Adolph Green, Score: Cy Coleman. With: John Collum, Madeline Kahn, Imogene Coca. Original Hecht-MacArthur play alive with contemporary wisecracks and derision; recent musical: aimless nostalgia.

SP: AFI.

Upperworld Warner Bros.
Dir: Roy Del Ruth. SP: Ben Marckson and Unc. Charles Kenyon. Story: BH. Photo: Tony Gaudio. 70 mins.

With: Warren William, Mary Astor, Ginger Rogers, Andy Devine, Dickie Moore.

Hecht story about millionaire William accused of murdering lover Rogers. He looses his empire but is acquitted and returns to simple life with wife Astor.

SP: Acad.

Shoot the Works Paramount
Pro: Albert Lewis. Dir: Wesley Ruggles. SP: Howard J. Green. Dial: Claude Binyon from play *The Great Magoo* by BH and Gene Fowler. Photo: Leo Tover. 82 mins.

With: Jack Oakie, Ben Bernie and Band, Dorothy Dell, Arline Judge, Alison Skipworth, Roscoe Karns, William Frawley.

Orig. title: *Thank Your Stars.* Theme song: "With My Eyes Wide Open I'm Dreaming." Play remade as film *Some Like It Hot* (1939). Has some of the flavor and plot of the play.

190   Appendix A: Filmography

Crime Without Passion Paramount
Pro-Dir-SP: BH and Charles MacArthur. O Story: "Caballero of the Law" (reprinted as "Crime Without Passion") by BH. Photo: Lee Garmes. 70 min.

With: Claude Rains, Margo, Whitney Bourne, Stanley Ridges, Paula Trueman.

Produced at Astoria, Long Island. Montage by Slavko Vorkapich. Hecht and MacArthur appear as reporters. Helen Hayes as extra in hotel lobby.

The President Vanishes Paramount
Pro: Walter Wanger. Dir: William Wellman. Adapt: Lynn Starling. Novel: anonymous (credited to Rex Stout) Co-script: BH and Charles MacArthur (according to Fetherling).

With: Arthur Byron, Edward Arnold, Rosalind Russell, Osgood Perkins, Jason Robards, Andy Devine, Paul Kelly.

Antifacist, antiwar, isolationist film quite outspoken by Hollywood standards. President engineers his own disappearance in order to stem war hysteria.

1935   *The Florentine Dagger* Warner Bros.
Dir: Robert Florey. Adapt: Tom Reed. Dial: Brown Helmes from novel by BH. Photo: Arthur Todd. 69 min.

With: Donald Woods, Margaret Lindsay, C. Aubrey Smith.

Original story recognizable in final film but the fun of playing with dual personalities is gone. A long European prologue and a police subplot have been added.

SP: Acad.

The Scoundrel Paramount
Pro-Dir-SP: BH and Charles MacArthur from play *All He Ever Loved* by BH and Rose Caylor Hecht. Assoc. Dir. and Photo: Lee Garmes. 75 min.

With: Noel Coward, Julie Haydon, Stanley Ridges, Martha Sleeper, Hope Williams, Alexander Woollcott, Rosita Moreno, Lionel Stander, BH and MacArthur (cameos).

O Title: *Miracle on 49th Street*. Character of Mallare patterned loosely after biography of Horace Liveright and personality of Jed Harris. Third film made in Hecht-MacArthur Astoria, New York project. Academy Award: best original story: Hecht and MacArthur.

SP: NYPL, Acad.

Spring Tonic Fox
Pro: Robert T. Kane. Dir: Clyde Brockman. SP: Patterson McNutt and H.W. Hanemann.

Comedy Sequences: Frank Griffin. Adapt: Howard I. Young from play *Man Eating Tiger* (produced: Sept. 1927) by BH and Rose Caylor Hecht.

With: Lew Ayres, Claire Trevor, Walter King, Zasu Pitts, Jack Haley, and Tala Birell.

Girl looking for more adventure than her milquetoast fiancé is providing runs into circus and two escaped lions. Heavy on whimsey, lean on comedy.

The Barbary Coast UA
Pro: Samuel Goldwyn. Dir: Howard Hawks. SP: BH and Charles MacArthur. Source: *The Barbary Coast* by Herbert Asbury. Photo: Edward Curtis. 97 min.

With: Miriam Hopkins, Joel McCrea, Edward G. Robinson, Walter Brennan.

Hecht and MacArthur's return to Hollywood after their Astoria experiment; San Francisco love triangle; the ever present newsman is Col. Marcus Aurelius Cobb; "The dialogue has the wit, the gaudy sentiment and the exuberance of a tipsy poet. [Hecht and MacArthur] write with a demonic gusto that even Hollywood cannot entirely discourage." (Andre Sennwald, *New York Times,* 14 October 1935, 21:1).

1936   *Once in a Blue Moon* Paramount
Pro-Dir-SP: BH and Charles MacArthur. Story: Rose Caylor Hecht. Assoc. Dir-Photo: Lee Garmes. Music: George Antheil. 65 min.

With: Jimmy Savo, Nikita Balieff, Cecelia Loftus, Whitney Bourne, Edwina Armstrong, Sander Szabo, J. Charles Gilbert, Hans Steinke, George Andre, Jackie Borene, Michael Dalmatoff and a cast of 600.

Filmed in 1934 in Astoria and on location in Tuxedo, New York (Aug.–Sept.), but not released until 1936. Edwina Armstrong is Hecht's daughter by first marriage. This fairy tale of circus folks caught in Russian Revolution is, according to Hecht, a "dud."

Soak the Rich Paramount
Pro-Dir-SP: BH and Charles MacArthur. From play by BH and MacArthur. Photo: Charles Shamroy. 85 min.

With: Walter Connolly, Mary Taylor, Alice Duer Miller, Ilka Chase, Lionel Stander, John Howard.

Fourth and last film made in Astoria, Long Island and was produced simultaneously with *Jumbo* by Hecht and MacArthur staged by Billy Rose at the Hippodrome.

1937   *The Hurricane* UA
Pro: Samuel Goldwyn. Dir: John Ford. SP: Oliver H.P. Garrett and Dudley Nichols, and unc. BH. Novel: Charles Nordhoff and James Norman Hall. Photo: Lloyd Noster. Special effects: James Basevi. 110 min.

192 Appendix A: Filmography

With: Dorothy Lamour, John Hall, Mary Astor, C. Aubrey Smith, Thomas Mitchell, Raymond Massey, John Carradine.

Hecht hoped that climactic disaster would get film past censors and audience. The hurricane, at least, was stupendous. Hecht did the rewrite in seventy-two hours for $25,000.

SP: UCLA.

Nothing Sacred UA
Pro: David O. Selznick. Dir: William Wellman. SP: BH; closing sequence: Bud Schulberg, Ring Lardner, Jr., Dorothy Parker Story: "Letter to the Editor" by James A. Street. Wellman says: SP: BH and unc. Ring Lardner, Jr. and unc. George Oppenheimer. Photo: W. Howard Greene. Technicolor. 75 min.

With: Fredric March, Carole Lombard, Walter Connolly, Charles Winninger, Sig Ruman, Frank Fay, Maxie Rosenbloom, Margaret Hamilton, Hedda Hopper, Troy Brown, Hattie McDaniel.

Hecht wrote the script in two weeks on a train and slipped out of Los Angeles before Selznick discovered the film had no usable ending. One of the only thirties comedies made in color.

SP: MOMA, LC, D.

1938   *The Goldwyn Follies* UA
Pro: Samuel Goldwyn. Assoc. Pro: Georgie Haight. Dir: George Marshall. SP: BH, Ritz Brothers and additional comedy sequences by Sam Perrin and Arthur Phillips. Earlier versions: (1936–37) Alice Duer Miller, Bert Kalmer, Harry Ruby, Dorothy Parker and Alan Campbell, Anita Loos and John Emerson. Music: George Gershwin. Lyrics: Ira Gershwin. Songs: Sid Kuller and Ray Golden. Ballet: George Balanchine. Photo: Gregg Toland. Technicolor. 115 min.

With: Adolph Menjou, Ritz Brothers, Vera Zorina, Kenny Baker, Andrea Leeds, Helen Jepsen, Phil Baker, Ella Logan, Bobby Clark, Jerome Cowan, Edgar Bergen and Charlie McCarthy and the American Ballet of the Metropolitan Opera.

Goldwyn's ill-fated attempt at a Ziegfeld annual. Hecht's script, written in two weeks, pokes fun at film producer (Menjou, fresh from the more dignified producer role in *A Star is Born*) who uses a small town philistine, "Miss Humanity" to dictate contents of his next film. Bergen's first film. Songs: "Love Walked In" and "Our Love is Here to Stay." "An American in Paris" choreographed but not used in film.

SP: Acad, UCLA, LC, D.

1939   *Gunga Din* RKO
Pro-Dir: George Stevens. SP: Joel Sayre and Fred Guiol. Story: BH and Charles MacArthur. From poem by Rudyard Kipling. Photo: Joseph H. August. 117 min.

With: Cary Grant, Douglas Fairbanks, Jr., Victor McLaglen, Joan Fontaine, Sam Jaffe.

Honor vs. love with the glorification of male comaraderie so innocent that it seems without dark sexual overtones. Hecht and MacArthur followed the advice they had put on the walls at the Astoria in banners ("Let the Audience in on Your Secret"). "The charm of a movie like *Gunga Din* is that it accepts that its audience is in on the secret, too." (Gerald Weales, *Midway*, Autumn 1967).

SP: AFI, LC.

Wuthering Heights UA
Pro: Samuel Goldwyn. Dir: William Wyler. SP: BH and Charles MacArthur from novel by Emily Bronte. Photo: Gregg Toland. 103 min.

With: Merle Oberon, Laurence Olivier, David Niven, Flora Robson, Donald Crisp, Geraldine Fitzgerald, Hugh Williams, Leo G. Carroll.

Hecht and MacArthur wrote the script on speculation in 1935 and Walter Wanger took an option on it, later selling it to Goldwyn. Hecht says it was written at Alexander Woollcott's country place in eight days. Helen Hayes relates that Hecht and MacArthur wrote spurious scene in which Heathcliff comes to America to fight Indians and rustle cattle in Red Rock Gulch. Woollcott was convinced the scene was written in earnest and protested that they had "raped" Emily Bronte! "She's been waiting breathlessly for years," was MacArthur's retort. Nominated by Academy as Best Picture and for Best Actor (Olivier). Award for Black and White Cinematography: Gregg Toland.

SP: Acad, UCLA, Ind, D. Published: *Twenty Best Film Plays* (1943).

Some Like It Hot Paramount
Pro: William C. Thomas. Dir: George Archainbaud. SP: Lewis R. Foster and Wilkie Mahoney from play *The Great Magoo* by BH and Gene Fowler. Photo: Karl Struss. Songs: Frank Loesser and Burton Lane. 63 mins.

With: Bob Hope, Shirley Ross, Una Merkel, Gene Krupa and Band, Bernard Nedell.

Play earlier adapted as *Shoot the Works* (1934). Story excuse for Krupa numbers for jitterbug fans and for Hope vehicle. Only basic outline of play remains.

SP: Acad.

It's a Wonderful World MGM
Pro: Frank Davis. Dir: W.S. Van Dyke. SP: BH. Story: BH and Herman Mankiewicz. 86 min.

With: Claudette Colbert, James Stewart, Ernest Truex, Frances Drake, Guy Kibbee, Nat Pendleton, Edgar Kennedy.

Title may have come from the headline used by Walter Howie in the Chicago *Examiner* for a MacArthur story (*Charlie*, p. 52–54). In the film it is a line from a poem written by authoress Colbert.

SP: UCLA, LC, D.

Lady of the Tropics MGM
Pro: Sam Zimbalist. Dir: Jack Conway. SP and Story: BH. 92 mins.

With: Robert Taylor, Hedy Lamarr, Joseph Schildkraut, Ernest Cossart, Mary Taylor.

Love with a half-caste on a tropical island.

SP: UCLA, LC. D.

Gone With The Wind MGM
Pro: David O. Selznik. Dir: Victor Fleming. SP: Sidney Howard from novel by Margaret Mitchell. Photo: Ernest Haller. Technicolor. 219 min.

With: Vivian Leigh, Clark Gable.

Oliver Garrett, John Van Druten, and Jo Swerling also worked on the script. Howard wrote early draft. Hecht says he wrote first nine reels in one week for $15,000 with Selznick acting out the parts of Scarlet and her father and Victor Fleming playing Rhett Butler and Ashley. Selznick says Hecht only contributed to the construction of one sequence. John Balderston, Edwin Justus Mayer and Charles MacArthur also contributed according to Gavin Lambert in *GWTW* (1973). Academy Awards: Howard, Best Screenplay (posthumously); Best Actress, Best Supporting Actress.

SP: UCLA, USC, AFI.

Let Freedom Ring MGM
Pro: Harry Rapf. Dir: Jack Conway. SP and Story: BH. 100 min.

With: Nelson Eddy, Virginia Bruce, Lionel Barrymore, Edward Arnold, Victor McLaglen.

Hecht turns Calaveras City into urban Chicago as his Harvard educated journalist hero (Eddy) turns the "hunky" railroad workers against the bosses by exercising freedom of the press. Also titled: *Song of the West* (1940).

SP: UCLA, LC, Ind. D.

1940 *His Girl Friday* Columbia
Pro-Dir: Howard Hawks. SP: Charles Lederer and unc. BH from *The Front Page*. Photo: Joseph Walker. 92 min.

With: Cary Grant, Rosalind Russell, Ralph Bellamy, Gene Lockhart, Abner Biberman, Roscoe Karns, Regis Toomey, John Qualen, Billy Gilbert.

Russell says she had her own gag man supplying her with lines and that the overlapping touches were ad libs. Although its reputation far outshadows Milestone's 1931 film, at the time of its release there was some dissent. Otis Ferguson: "The trouble is that when they made *The Front Page* the first time, it stayed made." (*The New Republic,* 22 Jan 1940).

SP: UCLA, AFI.

Foreign Correspondent UA
Pro: Walter Wanger. Dir: Alfred Hitchcock. O SP: Charles Bennett and Joan Harrison, Add. Dial: James Hilton and unc. BH. Originally to be based on and titled *Personal History* by Vincent Sheean but book shelved. Photo: Rudy Mate. 119 min.

With: Joel McCrea, Laraine Day, Herbert Marshall, Albert Basserman.

Hitchcock wanted Gary Cooper for McCrea role, says he wrote SP with Bennett and made film because of the fake windmills scene. Hecht says he worked on the film (*Playboy,* Nov. 1960).

SP: Acad.

Angels Over Broadway Columbia
Pro: BH. Assoc. Pro: Douglas Fairbanks, Jr. Dir: BH. Co-dir: Lee Garmes, OSP: BH. Photo: Lee Garmes. 78 min.

With: Douglas Fairbanks, Jr., Rita Hayworth, Thomas Mitchell, John Qualen. O Title *Before I Die.*

Academy Award Nomination—Best O SP 1940.

SP: MOMA, AFI, UCLA (as *Before I Die*).

Comrade X MGM
Pro: Gottfried Reinhardt. Dir: King Vidor. SP: BH and Charles Lederer. O Story: Walter Reisch. Photo: Joseph Ruttenberg. 90 min.

With: Clark Gable, Hedy Lamarr, Eve Arden, Felix Bressart.

Academy Award Nomination for O Story.

SP: AFI, D.

The Shop Around the Corner MGM
Pro-Dir: Ernst Lubitsch. SP: Samson Raphaelson and unc. BH from play by Nikolaus Laszlo. Photo: William Daniels. 97 min.

With: Margaret Sullavan, James Stewart, Frank Morgan, Joseph Schildkraut, Sara Haden, Felix Bressart.

Hecht says he plotted movie with Lubitsch. Play adapted into musical *She Loves Me* (1963) Book: Joe Masteroff, Music: Jerry Bock, Lyrics: Sheldon Harnick.

SP: UCLA, AFI, LC.

1941 *Lydia* UA
Pro: Alexander Korda. Dir: Julien Duvivier. SP: BH and Sam Hoffenstein. Story: Duvivier and L. Bush-Fekete. Based on French film *Carnet Du Bal*. Photo: Lee Garmes. 115 mins.

With: Merle Oberon, Edna May Oliver, Alan Marshall, Joseph Cotten, Hans Yaray, George Reeves, Sara Allgood.

O Title: *Illusions*. Oberon made up as a spinster of 60 explains to three old beaus why her passionate love for a seaman kept her from marrying.

1942 *Roxie Hart* Fox
Pro: Nunnally Johnson. Dir: William Wellman. SP: Nunnally Johnson and unc. BH (according to: Kael, Guiles, Fetherling). From play *Chicago* by Maurine Watkins. Photo: Leon Shamroy. 75 mins.

With: Ginger Rogers, Adolphe Menjou, George Montgomery, Lynne Overman, Nigel Bruce, Phil Silvers, Sara Allgood, William Frawley, Spring Byington.

Play was source for Broadway musical, *Chicago*.

SP: LC.

The Black Swan Fox
Pro: Darryl F. Zanuck. Dir: Henry King. SP: BH and Seton I. Miller. Adapt: Miller from novel by Rafael Sabatini. Photo: Leon Shamroy. Technicolor. 85 min.

With: Tyrone Power, Maureen O'Hara, Thomas Mitchell, George Sanders, Anthony Quinn.

War maneuvers chased movie troupe from various coasts during shooting. Pirates in the Caribbean.

Tales of Manhattan Fox
Pro: Boris Moros and S.P. Eagle. Dir: Julien Duvivier. SP and Story: BH, Ferenc Molnar, Donald Ogden Stewart, Samuel Hoffenstein, Alan Campbell, Ladislas Fodor, L. Vadnai, L. Gorog, Lamar Tretti, and Henry Blankfort. 118 mins.

Five sequences,
With: 1) Rita Hayworth, Charles Boyer, Thomas Mitchell.
       2) Henry Fonda, Ginger Rogers.
       3) Elsa Lanchester, Charles Laughton, Victor Franchen and Christian Rub.
       4) Edward G. Robinson.
       5) Paul Robeson, Eddie "Rochester" Anderson, Ethel Waters.

Hecht and Hoffenstein did final script which follows an evening coat through five owners and their stories. A sixth episode starring W.C. Fields was deleted because of time considerations.

SP: AFI, NYPL, LC.

China Girl, Fox
Pro: BH. Dir: Henry Hathaway. SP: BH. O Story: Melville Crossman. Photo: Lee Garmes. 93 min.

With: George Montgomery, Gene Tierney, Victor McLaglen, Lynn Bari, Sig Ruman, Ann Pennington.

McLaglin character: Bull Weed (Gangster in *Underworld,* 1927) O Title: *A Yank in China.*

SP: AFI, LC, D.

1943 *The Outlaw* UA
Pro-Dir: Howard Hughes; unc. dir: Howard Hawks. SP: Jules Furthman and unc. BH. Photo: Gregg Toland. 121 min.

With: Jack Buetel, Jane Russell, Thomas Mitchell, Walter Huston, Mimi Aguglia, Joe Sawyer, Gene Rizzi.

A western that almost burlesques the form, the film is concerned with Billy the Kid, his relationship to Doc Holliday, and the idea that Billy lived on after his supposed death. Censorship problems and publicity campaign selling Buetel as new Muni and Russell as a new Harlow helped the overlong inconsistent film at the box office. *New York Daily News:* "Jules Furthman's suggestive script...does everything possible to inject spirit of bedroom farce into a western." (18 Feb 1948).

SP: UCLA.

1945 *Spellbound* UA-Selznick International
Pro: David O. Selznick. Dir: Alfred Hitchcock. SP: BH. Adapt: Angus McPhail from novel *The House of Dr. Edwardes* by Francis Breeding. Photo: George Barnes. Dream Sequences: Salvador Dali. 110 mins.

With: Ingrid Bergman, Gregory Peck, Michael Chekhov, John Emery, Leo G. Carroll, Rhonda Feming, Bill Goodwin.

Appendix A: Filmography

Hitchcock found book melodramatic and weird; McPhail's treatment was not tight; he valued Hecht's knowledge of psychology. The story of man who thinks he is guilty of a crime was earlier used by Hecht in the novel *The Florentine Dagger* (1923). *New York Herald Tribune;* "The work is a masterful psychiatric thriller." (2 Nov 1945). "Best Film of 1946," *Kolona Cinema Magazine* of Palestine.

SP: AFI, LC, BFI, Published: Best Films of 1945.

1946 *Gilda* Columbia
Pro: Virginia Van Upp. Dir: Charles Vidor. SP: Marion Parsonnet and unc. BH. Adapt: Jo Eisinger. Story: E.A. Ellington. 110 min.

With: Glenn Ford, Rita Hayworth, George Macready, Steven Calleia.

Early straight dramatic role for Hayworth although she does musical numbers including the suggestive "Put the Blame on Mame" sequence. A "Carnival of the double-cross." (*L.A. Times,* 27 Apr 1946).

SP: UCLA, BFI.

Specter of the Rose Republic
Pro-Dir-SP: BH. From story by BH. Co-pro-Dir and Photo: Lee Garmes. 90 mins.

With: Michael Chekov, Judith Anderson, Ivan Kirov, Viola Essen, Lionel Stander.

Hecht wrote the story in 1936 after seeing the ballet of the same name. *Le Spectre de la Rose* was produced in 1911, choreographed by Fokine to music by Carl Weber for Karsavina and Nijinsky. Film story resembles the life and madness of Nijinsky. Hecht planned to give profit shares to seven members of the company beyond their salary from his 50 percent of net profits: Stander, Anderson, Garmes, George Antheil (musical dir.), Ernst Fegte (art dir.), Tamara Geva (choreographer), and Harold Godsoe (ass. dir.). Hecht's attempt at an art film received mixed reactions: Philip Scheuer: "Specter is recommended...to devotees of the different. It is crude but courageous." (*Los Angeles Times,* 15 June 1946).

SP: USC, UCLA (both shooting and continuity scripts).

Notorious RKO
Pro-Dir: Alfred Hitchcock. SP: BH. Story: BH and Hitchcock. Story idea: "The Song of the Flame" from *Saturday Evening Post.* Photo: Ted Tetzlaff. 103 min.

With: Cary Grant, Ingrid Bergman, Claude Rains, Louis Calhern, Madam Konstantin.

Hecht and Hitchcock's interest in uranium and the atom bomb in 1944 confused producers and aroused the interest of the FBI. Selznick claims the film was "entirely his conception."

SP: LC, Ind. D.

1947 *Dishonored Lady.* UA
Pro: Jack Chertock. Dir: Robert Stevenson. SP: Edmund H. North and Unc. BH. Adapt. from play by Edward Sheldon and Margaret Ayer Barnes of same title written for Katherine Cornell. Photo: Lucien Andriot. 85 min.

With: Hedy Lamarr, Dennis O'Keefe, John Loder, Morris Carnovsky (as psychiatrist).

Female editor's past catches up with her when she is accused of murder.

Her Husband's Affairs Columbia
Pro: Raphael Hakim. Dir: S. Sylvan Simon. Story and SP: BH and Charles Lederer. Photo: Charles Lawton, Jr. 83 min.

With: Lucille Ball, Franchot Tone, Edward Everett Horton, Gene Lockhart, Mikhail Rasumny.

Marital comedy with Tone as an advertising executive who gets involved with new inventions. Script burlesques advertising and scientists. Hecht said best jokes were written for Tone but that Ball got all the laughs.

Kiss of Death Fox
Pro: Fred Kohlmar. Dir: Henry Hathaway. SP: BH and Charles Lederer. Story: Eleazar Lipsky. (Extensive outline: Lawrence Blaine, former Ass. D.A. N.Y.C., according to studio publicity release.) Photo: Norbert Brodine. 98 min.

With: Victor Mature, Coleen Gray, Richard Widmark, Brian Donlevy, Karl Malden, Mildred Dunnock.

Hollywood "neorealism" with location filming in New York; Richard Widmark's first important role as psychopath Tommy Udo. Hecht's expressionism, given a realistic base, seemed to suit postwar disbelief in clearcut moral choices in an ominous world.

SP: AFI, UCLA, Fox, LC, D.

Ride the Pink Horse Universal-International
Pro: Joan Harrison. Dir: Robert Montgomery. SP: BH and Charles Lederer. Novel: Dorothy B. Hughes. Photo: Russell Metty. 100 min.

With: Robert Montgomery, Thomas Gomez, Rita Conde, Iris Flores, Wanda Hendrix, Art Smith, Fred Clark.

Location shooting: New Mexico. Montgomery hardbitten type who comes to town to blackmail Clark. Clark fights back but Gomez and Hendrix save Montgomery. The "Pink Horse" is on a carousel. Remade in 1964 for TV as *The Hanged Man* with Robert Culp, Edmund O'Brien and Vera Miles with New Orleans Mardi Gras substituted for New Mexican Fiesta.

The Paradine Case Selznick
Pro: David B. Selznick. Dir: Alfred Hitchcock. SP: Selznick. Novel: Robert Hichens. Adapt: Alma Reville and James Birdie. SP: unc. BH; unc. Hitchcock. Photo: Lee Garmes. 131 min.

With: Gregory Peck, Ann Todd, Charles Laughton, Charles Coburn, Ethel Barrymore, Louis Jourdan, Valli, Leo G. Carroll, Jean Tetzel.

Birdie did his work in London; Hitchcock worked with his wife (Alma Reville) on the script. Selznick rewrote and sent scenes down to the set. Hecht worked on some of the rewrites for Selznick. Much earlier Ethel Borden was given the novel to adapt as a ploy by Louis Mayer to keep her in Los Angeles as a companion to Jean Howard whom he was attempting to woo. Selznick bought the book from MGM who had purchased it in 1933 at Selznick's recommendation when he worked there.

SP: UCLA.

1948 *The Miracle of the Bells* RKO
Pro: Jesse L. Lasky and Walter MacEwen. Dir: Irving Pichel. SP: BH and Quentin Reynolds. Novel: Russell Janney. 120 mins.

With: Fred MacMurray, Alida Valli, Frank Sinatra, Lee J. Cobb.

Hecht's name did not appear on English release. Sinatra's first film role. Religious conferences approved of this film about press agent using a fake miracle to force understanding studio to release film of dead girl from Coal Town, Penn., but general reaction was closer to that of Philip Scheuer: "If you can bring yourself to believe that the release of one movie ... is an event of such solemn import that it requires the possible intervention of God, then you are likely to derive poignant satisfaction from the closing reels." (*Los Angeles Times*, 13 May 1948).

SP: NYPL, UCLA, AFI, LC, D.

Rope Warner Bros.
Pro: Alfred Hitchcock and Sidney Bernstein. Dir: Hitchcock. SP: Arthur Laurents, unc. BH. Adapt: Hume Cronyn from play by Patrick Hamilton. Photo: Joseph Valentine. Technicolor. 80 min.

With: James Stewart, John Dall, Farley Granger, Sir Cedric Hardwicke, Constance Collier.

Story, shot as continuous action in an apartment, is similar to Leopold-Loeb case.

Joan of Arc RKO-Sierra
Pro: Walter Wanger. Dir: Victor Fleming. SP: Maxwell Anderson and Andrew Solt, from *Joan of Lorraine* by Anderson.

With: Ingrid Bergman, Jose Ferrer.

"Hecht and Lederer, who have just completed 'Joan of Arc,' and who were responsible for the scripts of 'Spellbound' and 'Notorious,' will begin work on 'Kiss of Death.'" (publicity release.) Lederer worked on neither *Spellbound* nor *Notorious* and is not listed on *Joan of Arc*.

1949 *Love Happy* UA
Pro: Lester Cowan. Dir: David Miller. SP: Frank Tashlin and Mac Benoff. Unc: BH. Story: Harpo Marx. Photo: William C. Mellor. 82 min.

With: Groucho, Harpo, and Chico Marx, Ilona Massey, Vera-Ellen, Marion Hutton, Raymond Massey, and Marilyn Monroe (in walk-on).

Little is left of *Diamonds in the Pavement,* the original script by Hecht and Tashlin which was intended for Harpo as a sweet clown. Release was delayed in England because of Hecht's association with the film.

Whirlpool Fox
Pro-Dir: Otto Preminger. SP: BH, Andrew Solt (credited to Lester Barstow, Hecht's chauffeur, because of British embargo on Hecht's films) based on novel by Guy Endore. Photo: Arthur Miller. 97 mins.

With: Gene Tierney, Richard Conte, Jose Ferrer, Charles Bickford, Constance Collier.

Suspense melodrama concerns wife of psychoanalyst who is blackmailed by hypnotist and charged with murder. *Time:* "The movie is a Freudian slip." (23 Jan 1950).

SP: Fox, LC, D.

Portrait of Jenny
Pro: David O. Selznick. Dir: William Dieterle. SP: Paul Osborn, Peter Bemeis. Novel: Robert Nathan. Photo: Joseph August. 86 mins.

With: Joseph Cotton, Jennifer Jones, Ethel Barrymore, David Wayne, Lilian Gish, Henry Hull.

Hecht wrote opening titles.

1950 *Perfect Strangers* Warner
Pro: Jerry Wald. Dir: Bretaigne Windust. SP: Edith Sommer. O Play: *Ladies and Gentlemen* (1939) by BH and Charles MacArthur based on play *Twelve in a Box* (1938) by L. Bush-Fekete. Adapt: George Oppenheimer. Photo: Peverell Marley. 88 min.

With: Ginger Rogers, Dennis Morgan, Thelma Ritter, Margalo Gillmore, Alan Reed.

Helen Hayes appeared in the stage version of this juryroom romance.

Where the Sidewalk Ends Fox
Pro-Dir: Otto Preminger. SP: BH (credited to Rex Conner because of British blacklist). Adapt: Victor Trivas, Frank Rosenberg. Robert E. Kent from the novel *Night Cry* by William L. Stuart. 95 min.

With: Dana Andrews, Gene Tierney, Gary Merrill, Craig Stevens, Karl Malden, Bert Freed, Tom Tully.

Psychological crime story shot on location in New York.

SP: UCLA, LC, Fox, BFI.

1951 *The Thing (From Another Planet)* RKO
Pro: Howard Hawks. Dir: Christian Nyby and unc. Hawks. SP: Charles Lederer and unc. BH based on story "Who Goes There?" by John W. Campbell, Jr. Photo: Russell Harlan. 86 min.

With: Margaret Sheridan, Kenneth Tobey, Robert Cornthwaite, Douglas Spencer, James Young, Dewey Martin, James Arness (title role), Sally Creighton.

The film has a good deal of humor for horror picture. James Young plays reporter constantly complaining about freedom of the press. Remade in 1982 by John Carpenter.

SP: AFI, Acad.

Actors and Sin UA
Pro: Sid Keller. Dir-SP-ST: BH. Co-dir and Photo: Lee Garmes. 85 min.

"Actor's Blood" based on BH short story with: Edward G. Robinson, Marsha Hunt, Dan O'Herlihy. "Woman of Sin" based on BH short story: "Concerning on Woman and Sin." (1943)

With: Eddie Albert, Alan Reed, Tracey Roberts, Jenny Hecht.

Film at one point titled *Duo*. Agent Orlando Higgens is protagonist in Hecht's Hollywood comedy mystery *I Hate Actors* (1944).

SP: LC, BFI.

The Secret of Convict Lake. Fox
Pro: Frank P. Rosenberg. Dir: Michael Gordon. SP: Oscar Paul and unc. BH. Adapt: Victor Trivas. Story: Anna Hunger and Jack Pollexfen. 83 min.

With: Glenn Ford, Gene Tierney, Ethel Barrymore, Zachary Scott, Ann Dvorak.

Convicts hiding out in town where there are only women during the 1870s in California.

1952 *The Greatest Show on Earth* Paramount
Pro-Dir: Cecil B. DeMille. SP: Fredric M. Frank, Barre Lyndon, and Theodore St. John. Story: Frank Cavett, Frank and St. John. Photo: George Barnes, J. Peverell Marley, Wallace Kelley. Technicolor. 153 min.

With: Betty Hutton, Cornel Wilde, Charlton Heston, Dorothy Lamour, Gloria Grahame, James Stewart, Emmett Kelly, John Ringling North.

Hecht says he worked on film for three weeks (sitting in conference listening to DeMille talk), but when he revealed he had once been an acrobat in a circus he was dropped from the project.

Monkey Business Fox
Pro: Sol C. Siegel. Dir: Howard Hawks. SP: BH, Charles Lederer and I.A.L. Diamond. Story: Harry Segall. Photo: Milton Krasner. 97 min.

With: Cary Grant, Ginger Rogers, Charles Coburn, Marilyn Monroe, Hugh Marlowe.

O Title: *Darling, I Am Growing Younger.*

SP: Acad, Fox, LC, BFI.

1953 *Roman Holiday* Paramount
Pro-Dir: William Wyler. SP: Ian McLellan Hunter and John Dighton, unc. BH, Dalton Trumbo. Story: Hunter, unc. Trumbo. Photo: Frank F. Planer and Henry Alekan. 118 min.

With: Gregory Peck, Audrey Hepburn, Eddie Albert, Hartley Power, Paoli Carlini, Tullio Carminati, Margaret Rawlings, Alberto Rizzo.

Filmed in Rome. Hunter fronted for the blacklisted Trumbo who wrote the first draft. Hecht wrote the second draft which is closer to his screwball comedies than the final film having: 1) a Chicago gangster instead of Albert to help Peck; 2) a larger measure of Hecht's hard-boiled wisecracking; and 3) a happy ending as boy gets girl. Hunter won Academy Award for Best Motion Picture story; Hepburn won Best Actress. Nominations: Best SP, Best Dir, Supporting Actor (Eddie Albert), Black and White Cinematography.

SP: UCLA, Acad, AFI, Ind.

1954 *Living It Up* Paramount
Pro: Paul Jones. Dir: Norman Taurog. SP: Jack Rose, Melville Shavelson based on stage musical *Hazel Flagg* (1953). Book: BH. Lyrics: Bob Hilliard. Music: Jule Styne, based on *Nothing Sacred* (1937); SP: BH, based on story "Letter to the Editor" by James A. Street. Photo: Daniel Fapp. Technicolor. 94 min.

With: Dean Martin, Jerry Lewis, Janet Leigh, Edward Arnold.

New songs added include: "Champagne and Wedding Cake," "That's What I Like," "Money Burns a Hole in My Pocket." Lewis plays the role of the doomed Hazel, Martin the doctor, and Leigh the sobsister reporter.

SP: Acad, AFI.

1955 *Ulysses.* Paramount
Pro: Dino de Laurentiis and Carlo Ponti in assoc. with William W. Schorr. Dir: Mario Camerini. SP: Franco Brusati, Mario Camerini, Ennio de Concini, Hugh Gray, BH, Ivo Perilli, Irwin Shaw. Dial: Maxwell Weinberg. Based on Homer. Photo: Harold Rossen. Technicolor. 104 min.

With: Kirk Douglas, Silvana Mangano, Anthony Quinn, Rossana Podesto, Sylvie, Daniel Ivernel, Jacques Dumesnil.

Dubbed. Plot fairly faithful to Homer.

SP: Acad.

The Indian Fighter UA
Pro: William Schorr. Dir: Andre de Toth. SP: BH and Frank Davis. Story: Ben Kadish and John Loring (*Variety* 7 February 1955). Photo: Wilfrid M. Cline. Technicolor. 88 min.

With: Kirk Douglas, Elsa Martinelli, Walter Matthau, Diana Douglas, Walter Abel, Lon Chaney, Eduard Franz, Alan Hale, Elisha Cook.

The film has an environmentalist tone with Elisha Cook playing a photographer (newsman?) capturing the Oregon scenery before it is spoiled by settlers.

SP: Ind.

The Court-Martial of Billy Mitchell Warner Bros.
Pro: Milton Sperling. Dir: Otto Preminger. SP and Story: Milton Sperling and Emmet Lavery, unc. BH (worked on courtroom scenes). Color. 100 min.

With: Gary Cooper, Charles Bickford, Ralph Bellamy, Rod Steiger, Elizabeth Montgomery.

"It abounds in historical figures but is singularly lacking in a sense of history itself." (*Saturday Review*, 14 January 1956). There was a suit over story rights. British title: *One Man Mutiny.*

1956 *Miracle in the Rain* Warner Bros.
Pro: Frank P. Rosenberg. Dir: Rudolph Maté. SP and story: BH. 107 min.

With: Jane Wyman, Van Johnson, Peggie Castle, Fred Clark, Alan King.

The film creates a realistic tone but finishes with Wyman greeted in heaven by Van's ghost backed by a choir while down on earth her father returns to the wife he had deserted. Story of wastrel father and subplot of romantic boss-secretary office romance were added to original story to flesh it out and are more in keeping with Hecht's attitudes in the 1950s than the original 1943 morale boosting story of love and faith. Above all, Johnson wants to be a reporter. Unrestrained schmaltz.

SP: UCLA.

1957 *The Iron Petticoat* Romulus-Remus-MGM
Pro: Betty Box. Assoc. Pro: Harry Saltzman. Dir: Ralph Thomas. SP: BH. Story: Harry Saltzman. Photo: Ernest Steward. Vista Vision. 96 min.

With: Bob Hope, Katharine Hepburn, Noelle Middleton, James Robertson Justice.

O title: *Not For Money*. Hecht had his name taken off this British production after he decided that Hope had Hepburn's performance "blow-torched" out of the film. He and Hope exchanged letters in the form of full page ads in *The Hollywood Reporter* (October 1 and 4, 1956). The film is a Cold War *Ninotchka* (or *Comrade X*) with Hepburn as a Russian pilot and Hope as an American Army officer.

SP: USC, LC.

A Farewell to Arms Fox
Pro: David O. Selznick. Dir: Charles Vidor. SP: BH from novel by Ernest Hemingway. Photo: Piero Portalupi and Oswald Morris. Cinemascope. 145 min.

With: Rock Hudson, Jennifer Jones, Vittorio DeSica, Mercedes McCambridge.

Filmed in Italy. John Huston originally contracted to direct; he was fired ten days after shooting began. Hecht and Selznick wrote five drafts in six weeks; the first was completely faithful to the original. Much of novel's dialogue retained in film. 1932 version: Dir: Frank Borzage. With: Helen Hayes, Gary Cooper.

SP: MOMA, UCLA, LC, Ind. BFI.

Legend of the Lost UA
Pro-Dir: Henry Hathaway. SP: BH and Robert Presnell, Jr. 109 min.

With: John Wayne, Sophia Loren, Rossano Brazzi.

O Title: *Tangle*. "Hecht in Hollywood all the way." (*Cue*, 28 Dec 1957) "Sum it up as sex, scenery, skull-digging and skullduggery." (*Los Angeles Times*, 19 Dec 1957).

SP: AFI.

1958 *Queen of Outer Space* Allied Artists
Pro: Ben Schwalb. Dir: Edward Bernds. SP: Charles Beaumont. Story: BH; unc. Walter Wanger. Photo: William Whitley. Cinemascope. 79.5 min.

With: Zsa Zsa Gabor, Eric Fleming, Laurie Mitchell, Paul Birch.

Also titled: *Queen of the Universe*. Hecht did not write the story, but his name on the contract helped raise funds to back the production.

The Fiend Who Walked the West Fox
Pro: Herbert B. Swope, Jr. Dir: Gordon Douglas. SP: Harry Brown and Philip Yordan based on *Kiss of Death* (1947). SP: BH and Charles Lederer. Photo: Joe MacDonald. Cinemascope. 101 min.

With: Hugh O'Brian, Robert Evans, Dolores Michaels.

A cynical combination of horror and western genres.

1959 *John Paul Jones* Warner Bros.
Pro: Samuel Bronston. Dir: John Farrow. SP: Farrow, Jesse Lasky, Jr., and unc. BH (Fetherling). Color. 126 min.

With: Robert Stack, Marisa Pavan, Charles Coburn, Bette Davis, Madonald Carey, Peter Cushing.

Patriotic and inaccurate historical drama.

Hello Charlie Television
Dir: Sidney Lanfield. SP: BH based on *Charlie*. Concerns youth of Charles MacArthur. Hecht wrote a number of television scripts in the 1950s. Most were adaptations of his own plays.

1962 *Billy Rose's Jumbo* MGM
Pro: Joe Pasternak and Martin Melcher. Dir: Charles Walters. Second Unit Dir: Busby Berkeley. SP: Sidney Sheldon. Based on *Jumbo* by BH and Charles MacArthur. Music and Lyrics: Richard Rodgers and Lorenz Hart. Photo: William H. Daniels. Metrocolor. 123 min.

With: Doris Day, Stephen Boyd, Jimmy Durante, Martha Raye, Dean Jaggar.

Five million budget largest for musical at MGM at time. Irving Ravetch and Harriet Frank, Jr. originally to do SP.

1964 *Circus World* Paramount
Pro: Samuel Bronston. Dir: Henry Hathaway. SP: BH, Julien Halevy, James Edward Grant. O Story: Philip Yordan and Nicholas Ray. Photo: Jack Hildyard. Super Technirama-70. 135 min.

With: John Wayne, Rita Hayworth, Claudia Cardinale, Lloyd Nolan, Richard Conte, John Smith, Fran Snygg.

Filmed in Spain. British Title: *The Magnificent Showman.*

SP: Acad. (partial?)

1967 *Casino Royale* Columbia
Pro: Charles Feldman. Dir: John Huston, Kenneth Hughes, Val Guest, Robert Parrish, Richard Talmadge, and Anthony Squire. SP: Wolf Mankowitz, John Law, and Michael Sayers. Unc: 3 drafts by BH, rewritten by Billy Wilder, Joseph Heller, Terry Southern. Peter Sellers and Woody Allen rewrote their own sequences. O Novel: Ian Fleming. Photo: Jack Hildyard with additional photo. by John Wilcox and Nicholas Roeg. 130 min.

With: Peter Sellers, Ursula Andress, David Niven, Orson Welles, Woody Allen, Deborah Kerr, George Raft.

Script began as straight adaptation 12 years before production. BH was working on script at the time of his death.

1969 *Gaily, Gaily* UA
Pro-Dir: Norman Jewison. SP: Abram S. Ginnes based on memoirs by BH. Photo: Richard Kline. Music: Henry Mancini. Color. 106 min.

With: Beau Bridges, Brian Keith, Melina Mercouri, George Kennedy, Hume Cronyn, Margot Kidder.

Only loosely based on *Gaily, Gaily.* Central incident of living in brothel from *Child of the Century;* Resurrection story originally about condemned criminal; Ben's own reformation of girlfriend-prostitute ended when she started doing business at the *Journal;* Keith's Francis Xavier Sullivan based on Sherman Duffy; Bridges's Ben Harvey WASP version of BH. British Title: *Chicago, Chicago.*

SP: UCLA, BFI.

1974 *The Front Page* UA
Pro: Paul Monash. Dir: Billy Wilder. SP: Billy Wilder and I.A.L. Diamond from BH-MacArthur play. Photo: Jordan S. Cronenweth. Panavision. 105 min.

With: Walter Matthau, Jack Lemmon, Carol Burnett, Susan Sarandon, Vincent Gardenia.

SP loaded with period references (BH going to Hollywood; monkey trial; Leopold and Loeb; Hearst and Marion Davies at San Simeon) which only serve to date the film. Critics consensus: "Billy Wilder's brittle, shallow, remake of the legit and film hardly perennial." (*Variety,* 11 Dec 1974).

SP: UCLA.

208   Appendix A: Filmography

Film Projects

Over the years Hecht apparently had a number of assistants who would rough out a project to his specifications. According to Hitchcock Czenzi Ormonde was one of these. She worked with Hitchcock on *Strangers on a Train* (1951). John Lee Mahin also worked for Hecht before he established himself independently. (*Mayer and Thalberg*)

1920   *American Beauty*. Written by BH and Michael Arlen. Story which indicated "that a bright young woman could emerge from three sex affairs and still be fit to marry our hero" was scotched by studio. (*Playboy* Nov 1960)

In "My Testimonial to the Movies" in *Theatre Magazine*, June 1929, Hecht stated he had sold six stories dictated for the movies. This would leave two or three unaccounted for.

Worked on Harlow picture with Paul Bern (d. 1932). Plotted frequently with Edmund Goulding. (*Playboy* November 1960)

Catastrophe sold to Paramount by Hecht and Gene Fowler. Miriam Hokins was to star. (*New York Sun*, 16 January 1933)

Two Thieves. Hecht was to adapt the Manuel Kamroff story for David Selznick. Clark Gable and George Montgomery were suggested as leads. (*Los Angeles Times*, 6 September 1933)

The Prisoner of Zenda. Hecht was to write the fourth adaptation of the work for David Selznick. Roland Leigh, Benn Levy, and John Farrow all had recently worked on the project. There is no indication he did so. The 1937 UA film is credited to Pro: David Selznick, Dir: John Cromwell, W.S. Van Dyke, SP: John L. Balderson. Adapt: Wells Root of stage adapt: Edward Rose of novel by Anthony Hope. Add. Dial: Donald Ogden Stewart. Hecht had just finished work on *Queen Christiana* for Garbo. (New York *Daily Mirror*, 7 December 1933)

Farike the Guest Artist by Hecht and Gene Fowler for W.C. Fields and Marie Dressler. Film was not made because of death of stars according to Hecht. Dressler died in 1934, Fields in 1946. (*Playboy* November, 1960)

Murder at 21 to have been written by BH for Paramount. (*New York Times*, 12 December 1935).

Sweet Land of Liberty (musical about WPA Federal Theatre Project) and *The Duchess of Broadway* were both to be done under contract to Samuel Goldwyn signed while *To Quito and Back* was in rehearsal. (*New York Times*, 13 July 1937)

1939   Hecht conferred with Mayor LaGuardia about plan to make film in New York City. (*New York Times*, 14 November 1939)

The Mating Call. Hecht was to write a screenplay of Lois Montross's story for producing firm of Loew and Lewin. Film was to be about the advertising business and Carole Lombard was a possibility for the role. (New York *Herald Tribune*, 20 June 1941)

A Life of Sarah Bernhardt was prepared by BH in 1949 at David Selznick's request for Ingrid Bergman. She felt herself unsuited for the part and the project collapsed. (*Selznick,* 1970)

1955 Hecht, Gene Fowler, and Westbrook Pegler were collaborating on *The Life and Death of Al Capone* according to Pegler in his newspaper column. Fetherling believes it was an unfinished film project.

Appendix B

New York Theatre Productions

1917 *The Hero of Santa Maria* by BH and Kenneth Sawyer Goodman. On third bill of Washington Square Players. (*New York Times*, 14 February 1917)

1922 *The Egotist*, a three act comedy by BH. An aging theatrical lothario has never actually cheated on his wife but she believes his reputation and leaves him. With: Leo Dietrichstein. John Corbin: "What is presented as a comedy of character during three acts of clever straining is wrenched into a final curtain of pathos." (*New York Times*, 31 December 1922) Played in Chicago prior to New York under title: *Under False Pretenses*. Opened (New York): 25 December 1922, played six weeks.

1925 *The Stork* by BH, a three act comedy adapted from Hungarian original by Laszlo Fodor. Dir: Frederick Stanhope. Pro: Schwab and Mandel. With: Geoffrey Kerr, Katherine Alexander. Young man caught between marital duties and the Premiership of France. Some good comedy. "Mildly amusing, but of the kind called risque." (*New York Times*, 27 January 1925) Opened: 25 January 1925.

1927 *Man Eating Tiger* by BH and Rose Caylor Hecht. Play about girl leaving dull fiance for the circus played in Allentown PA but Philadelphia opening was postponed. Later became the basis for film *Spring Tonic* (1935). (*New York Times*, 25 September 1927, VIII, 4:8).

1928 *The Front Page* by BH and Charles MacArthur. 3 acts. Dir: George Kaufman. Pro: Jed Harris. With: Lee Tracy, Osgood Perkins. 276 performances.
    1929: Los Angeles production: "Despite their screen training the authors have told their play in theatrical terms throughout, and the whole thing is generally regarded hereabouts as a triumph for the motion picture writing craft." (*New York Times*, 6 January 1929)
    1946: Revived: Dir: MacArthur. With: Lew Parker and Arnold Moss. 76 perf.
    1968: Revived: Dir: Harold J. Kennedy. With: Robert Ryan, Bert Convy, Helen Hayes, Peggy Cass, Charles White, John McGiver. 222 perf.

1932 *The Great Magoo* by BH and Gene Fowler. 3 acts. Dir: George Abbott. Pro: Billy Rose. With: Paul Kelly, Claire Carleton, Victor Killian, and Harry Green. Backstage love story of two Coney Island losers. "The formula of these picaresque slumming parties is now thrice familiar and maggoty talk is no longer a fine theatrical virtue.... And for a pair of men of the world their hokum and sentimentalities are astonishingly naive." (*New York Times*, 3 December 1932). Opened: 2 December 1932. 11 perf. 1982: Revived by Hartford Stage Company November 12-December 19. Dir: Mark Lamos.

Twentieth Century by BH and Charles MacArthur based on *Napoleon of Broadway*, a play by Charles Milholland. 3 acts. Dir: George Abbott. Pro: Abbott and Philip Dunning. With: Moffat Johnston, Eugenie Leontovitch, William Frawley, Granville Bates.

Opened: 29 December 1932. 152 perf.
Revived: 1950. Dir: Jose Ferrer with Ferrer and Gloria Swanson. Pro: ANTA. 233 perf.
Remade: 1978 as Musical *On the Twentieth Century*. Book and Lyrics: Betty Comden and Adolph Green. Music: Cy Coleman. Pro-Dir: Harold Prince. With: John Cullum, Madeline Kahn, Imogene Coca.

Groucho Marx played Jaffe during the week of August 13, 1934 at the Lakewood Theatre, Maine. Ruth Johnson, his wife, played Anita Highland.

1935   *Jumbo* by BH and Charles MacArthur. Music and Lyrics: Richard Rodgers and Lorenz Hart. Production staged by John Murray Anderson. Book dir: George Abbott. Pro: Billy Rose. With: Jimmy Durante, Arthur Sinclair, W.J. McCarthy, Donald Novis, Gloria Grafton. The imperfect wedding of the circus and musical comedy with former in total command. Rivalry between two circus owners solved when their children fall in love. Opened at Hippodrome 16 November 1935 after two years of planning and postponement. Hecht and MacArthur were simultaneously directing in Astoria. 233 perf.

1937   *To Quito and Back* by BH. 2 acts. Pro: The Theatre Guild. Dir: Philip Moeller. Pro: Theresa Helburn, Lawrence Langner and Moeller for Theatre Guild. With: Sylvia Sidney, Leslie Banks, Joseph Buloff. Writer running away from wife and life with lover joins revolution. Brooks Atkinson: "Mr. Hecht's brave salute to the cause of revolution quickly dwindles away into a sham battle of words and fine phrases." (*New York Times*, 7 October 1937). Opened: 6 October 1937. 46 perf.

1939   *Ladies and Gentlemen* by BH and Charles MacArthur, comedy in two acts. From play by Ladislaus Bush-Fekete. Dir: MacArthur and Lewis Allen. Pro: Gilbert Miller. With: Helen Hayes, Philip Merivale. Hayes largely responsible for success of juryroom romance. Opened: 17 October 1939. 105 perf. First played: Santa Barbara, San Francisco and Los Angeles.

1939   *Fun to Be Free* by BH and Charles MacArthur, pageant. Pro: Billy Rose at Madison Square Garden for Red Cross War Bond Drive.

1942   *Lily of the Valley* by BH. Three Acts. Dir: BH. Pro: Gilbert Miller. With: Myron McCormick, Siegfried Rumann, Clay Clement, Minnie Dupree. Corpses in the county morgue discuss their lives. Some good writing in sharp scenes. Good acting but play had no ultimate goal and rambled. Brooks Atkinson: "The loose ends are dyed in bold colors, but they are never tied into a coherent play." (*New York Times*, 27 January 1942). Opened 26 January 1942. 8 perf.

Appendix B: New York Theatre Productions 213

1943   *We Will Never Die: A Memorial Service to the Two Million Jewish Dead of Europe* by BH. Pro: Billy Rose. Based on BH story "Remember Us." Dir: Moss Hart, Music: Kurt Weill. Sponsored by The Emergency Committee to Save the Jewish People of Europe. March 9, 1943. Two perfs. Madison Square Garden. Toured: Washington, Philadelphia, Boston, Chicago, St. Louis, and Los Angeles.

Tribute to Gallantry.

1944   *The Common Man*, a one-act play by BH produced on April 19, 1944 by Stage for Action as part of Roosevelt reelection campaign. Hecht champions the common man who is not fooled by the Republican side show although a soldier is lured off stage by a hootchie-coochie dancer. The second of the three plays on the program was *That They May Win* by Arthur Miller which attacked inflation under the current administration.

Seven Lively Arts. Pro: Billy Rose. Music and Lyrics: Cole Porter. Ballet music: Igor Stravinsky. Sketches: Moss Hart, George Kaufman, Robert Pirosh, Joseph Schrank, Charles Sherman. Doc Rockwell's comments by BH. With: Rockwell, Beatrice Lilly, Bert Lahr. Opened 7 December 1944. 183 perf.

1946   *Swan Song* by BH and Charles MacArthur based on story by Ramon Romero and Harriett Hinsdale. Dir: Joseph Pevney. Pro: John Clein. With: David Ellin, Theo Goetz, Jacqueline Horner, Marianne Stewart, Scott McKay. Psychological melodrama about neurotic pianist bent on murder of his rival. Unexceptional. Despite negative notices the play found an audience and enjoyed a decent run. Out of town title: *Crescendo.* Opened 15 May 1946.

A Flag is Born by BH. Pageant. Music: Kurt Weill. Dir: Luther Adler. Pro: Jules J. Leventhal for American League for a free Palestine. With: Paul Muni, Celia Adler, Marlon Brando, Quentin Reynolds. Pageant follows dispossessed survivors Muni and Celia Adler as they travel from Europe to Israel. Jewish history is expounded and a case is made for armed revolt against the British. Despite script weaknesses and adverse criticism both for cheapening suffering and for exposing it at all, production was very successful fund raiser for American League. Principals contributed their services. Muni's performance called one of the great ones of his career by Brooks Atkinson, "Without sentimentality, without heroics he is speaking for the Jewish race with an actor's eloquence." (*New York Times*, 7 September 1946) Luther Adler took over when Muni left show. 120 performances in New York before nationwide tour. Opened 5 September 1946.

1953   *Hazel Flagg.* Book BH. Musical satire in three acts. Based on story by James A. Street and film *Nothing Sacred* (1937). Music: Jule Styne. Lyrics: Bob Hilliard. Presented by Styne and Anthony Farrell. Book dir: David Alexander. With: Helen Gallagher, John Howard, Thomas Mitchell, Benay Venuta. Gallagher is singing and dancing Hazel brought to New York by Howard's magazine to enjoy her last days before radium poisoning sets in. Walter Connolly part of editor now a woman (Venuta). Opened 11 February 1953. 125 perf.

1958 *Winkelberg* by BH. Two Acts. Pro-Dir: Lee Falk. With: Mike Kellin, James Mitchell, Sondra Lee, Frances Chaney. Harmonica accompaniment by John Sebastion. Based on life of Maxwell Bodenheim murdered in Greenwich Village in 1954 and a friend of Hecht's from his Bohemian days in Chicago before World War I. Winkelberg arrives in heaven but is sent back to earth to find a worthy part of his life. Incidents of his life are then traced. He remains both a figure of conscience and an obstinate fool intent on self-destruction. The play was produced in the Village at the Renata Theatre on Bleeker Street and never found a substantial audience. Jenny Hecht played the part in a 1963 Los Angeles production by the Stage Society.

1962 *Simon* by BH from play *The Dreams of Simon Marchand* by Bertolt Brecht and Leon Feuchtwanger. Young girl dreams she is Joan of Arc and incites town to rebel against Nazis. With: Jenny Hecht. Opened: Cleveland Playhouse, 31 January 1962.

Unrealized Projects

Once Upon a Night to be rewritten by Hecht and MacArthur for Lee Shubert and Lawrence Schwab. Schwab had collaborated on script with Milton Lazarus which tried out in Wilmington in 1938. MacArthur was to direct. (*New York Times,* 23 July 1939)

Musical of *Underworld* (life of Dion O'Bannion) to be written with Ted Yates, Jr. and produced by Michael Wettach and Lew Gallo. (*New York Times,* 18 June 1959)

Appendix C

Bibliography of Works by Hecht

While the following bibliography does not pretend to be complete, it does include all major and most minor publications by Hecht. A few articles by Hecht which may be pertinent have also been included.

Anderson, Margaret, ed. *The Little Review Anthology.* Hermitage House, 1953. Contains some of Hecht's contributions to the journal.
BH and Maxwell Bodenheim. "The Master Poisoner," in Bodenheim, Maxwell. *Minna and Myself.* New York: Pagan, 1918.
Erik Dorn. 1921; rpt. New York: Boni and Liveright, 1924.
Fantazius Mallare: A Mysterious Oath. Chicago: Covici-McGee, 1922. Reprinted: Harcourt Brace Jovanovich, 1978.
Gargoyles. New York: Boni and Liveright, 1922.
1001 Afternoons in Chicago. New York: Covici-Friede, 1922.
"Literature and the Bastinado," in *Nonsenseorship.* Ed. G.P. Putnam. New York: G.P. Putnam, 1922.
The Florentine Dagger. New York: Boni and Liveright, 1923.
Humpty Dumpty. New York: Boni and Liveright, 1924.
Tales of Chicago Streets. Girard, Kansas: Halderman-Julius, 1924.
The Kingdom of Evil: A Continuation of the Journal of Fantazius Mallare. Chicago: Pascal Covici, 1924. Reprinted: Harcourt Brace Jovanovich, 1978.
BH and Mawell Bodenheim. *Cutie—A Warm Mama.* Chicago: Hechtshaw Press, 1924.
BH and Kenneth Sawyer Goodman. *The Wonder Hat and Other One-Act Plays.* New York: London D. Appleton, 1925. Contains: *The Wonder Hat; The Two Lamps; The Hero of the Shops; The Hand of Siva; The Hero of Santa Maria.*
Broken Necks: Containing More "1001 Afternoons." Chicago: Pascal Covici, 1926.
Count Bruga. New York: Boni and Liveright, 1926.
Infatuation and Other Stories of Love's Misfits. Girard, Kansas: Halderman-Julius, 1927.
Jazz and Other Stories of Young Love. Girard, Kansas: Halderman-Julius, 1927.
The Unlovely Sin, and Other Stories of Desire's Pawns. Girard, Kansas, Halderman-Julius, 1927.
BH and Charles MacArthur. *The Front Page.* New York: Covici-Friede, 1928. rpt. Samuel French, 1950.
"My Testimonial to the Movies: The Frank Confession of a Literary Man Who Puts Into Words What Others Have Only Dared Think." *Theatre Magazine,* June 1929.
The Champion from Far Away. New York: Covici-Friede, 1931.
A Jew in Love. New York: Covici-Friede, 1931.
BH and Charles MacArthur. *The Twentieth Century.* New York: Samuel French (Unpublished). Prod: 1932.

BH and Gene Fowler. *The Great Magoo: A Love Sick Charade in Three Acts and Something Like Eight Scenes, Recounting the Didoes of Two Young and Amorous Souls, Who Nigh Perished When They Weren't in the Hay Together.* New York: Covici-Friede, 1933.
To Quito and Back. New York: Covici-Friede, 1937.
A Book of Miracles. New York: Viking, 1939.
Gassner, John, and Dudley Nichols, eds. *Twenty Best Film Plays.* New York: Crown, 1943. Contains *Wuthering Heights.*
BH and Charles MacArthur. *Ladies and Gentlemen.* New York: Samuel French, 1941.
1001 Afternoons in New York. New York: Viking, 1941.
Concerning a Woman of Sin, and Other Stories. New York: Editions for the Armed Services, 1943.
"Remember Us." *Reader's Digest,* February 1943.
Miracle in the Rain. New York: Knopf, 1943.
A Guide for the Bedeviled. New York: Scribners, 1944.
I Hate Actors. New York: Crown, 1944.
The Collected Stories of Ben Hecht. New York: Crown, 1945.
Gassner, John, and Dudley Nichols, eds. *Best Film Plays of 1945.* New York: Crown, 1946. Contains *Spellbound.*
Monroe, Marilyn and Ben Hecht (uncredited). *My Story.* New York: Stein and Day, 1974.
A Child of the Century. New York: Simon and Schuster, 1954.
Charlie: The Improbable Life and Times of Charles MacArthur. New York: Harper, 1957.
The Sensualists. New York: Julian Messner, 1959.
A Treasury of Ben Hecht: Collected Stories and Other Writings. New York: Crown, 1959.
"If Hollywood is Dead or Dying as a Moviemaker, Perhaps the Following Are Some of the Reasons." *Playboy,* November 1960, Vol. 7, No. 1.
Perfidy. New York: Julian Messner, 1961. Written with Samuel Tamir.
Gaily, Gaily. Garden City: Doubleday, 1963. Of the nine chapters, portions of six appeared in *Playboy Magazine* (1962-63) and one was published in *Argosy* (1963).
Letters from Bohemia. Garden City: Doubleday, 1964.
"The Incomplete Life of Mickey Cohen." *Scanlan's,* March 1970.

Notes

Preface

1. The material was actually written in the early 1950s.
2. Norman Mailer, *Marilyn: A Biography* (New York: Grosset & Dunlap, 1973), P. 18.
3. Ben Hecht, *A Child of the Century* (New York: Simon and Schuster, 1954), p. 335.

Chapter 1

1. Doug Fetherling, *The Five Lives of Ben Hecht* (Canada: Lester and Orpen, 1977).
2. Gary Fincke, "The Fiction of Ben Hecht: A Study of Polarity," Diss. Kent State 1974. Ronald Roberts, "The Novels of Ben Hecht," Diss. Baylor 1970.
3. Ben Hecht, *A Child of the Century* (New York: Simon and Schuster, 1954), p. 2.
4. Fred Guiles, *Hanging On in Paradise* (New York: McGraw-Hill, 1975), p. 195.
5. Ben Hecht, dir., *The Specter of the Rose,* Republic, 1946.
6. *Child,* p. 393.
7. Ibid., p. 119.
8. Ibid., p. 87.
9. Ibid., pp. 190-91.
10. Ibid., p. 127.
11. Ibid., p. 158.
12. Ibid., pp. 142-43.
13. Ibid., p. 143.
14. Ibid., p. 191.
15. Ibid.
16. Ibid.
17. Ibid.
18. Ibid., p. 119.
19. Ibid., p. 147.
20. Ben Hecht, *Gaily, Gaily* (Garden City: Doubleday, 1963) pp. 31-32.
21. *Child,* p. 260.

22. Ibid., p. 149.
23. Ibid., p. 266.
24. Ibid., p. 250.
25. Ibid., p. 253.
26. Henry Justin Smith, *Deadlines* (Chicago: Covici-McGee, 1922), p. 47.
27. Ibid.
28. Ibid., 81-82.
29. Harry Hansen, *Midwest Portraits* (New York: Harcourt, Brace, 1923), p. 327.
30. David Karsner, *Sixteen Authors to One* (New York: Lewis Copeland, 1928), p. 243.
31. Ibid., p. 244.
32. Ibid.
33. *Child*, p. 269.
34. Ibid., p. 273.
35. Ibid., p. 275.
36. Ibid., p. 281.
37. Ibid., p. 282.
38. Ibid., p. 315.
39. Ibid., p. 270.
40. Ben Hecht, *Letters from Bohemia* (Garden City: Doubleday, 1964), p. 137.
41. *Letters*, p. 138.
42. Ibid., pp. 138-39.
43. *Child*, p. 127.
44. *Letters*, p. 142.
45. Malcolm Cowley, ed., *After the Genteel Tradition: American Writers 1910-1930* (Carbondale: Southern Illinois Univ. Press, 1964), p. 3.
46. Ibid., p. 17.
47. *Child*, p. 216.
48. Ibid., p. 234.
49. Hansen, p. 327. Years later, in *Design for Living* (1933), Hecht gave Miriam Hopkins, a Margaret Anderson-like critic of her friends' work, the epithet "Rotten" to fling at them whenever there was something she did not like.
50. *Child*, p. 169.
51. Bernard Duffy, *The Chicago Renaissance in American Letters: A Critical History* (East Lansing: Michigan State Univ. Press, 1956), p. 247.
52. Ibid.

53. Ibid., p. 248.
54. *Letters*, p. 4.
55. Ibid., p. 1.
56. *Child*, p. 203.
57. Ibid.
58. Hansen, p. 330.
59. Ben Hecht, *1001 Afternoons in Chicago* (New York: Covici-Friede, 1922), p. 12.
60. Ibid., p. 13.
61. Karsner, p. 240.
62. Smith, p. 49.
63. Hansen, p. 315.
64. Ibid., p. 317.
65. Ibid., p. 342.
66. *Child*, p. 327.
67. Ibid., p. 330.
68. Ibid., p. 331.
69. Ibid., p. 333.
70. *Gaily*, p. 142.
71. Ibid.
72. Ibid., p. 146.
73. Hansen, p. 325.
74. *Child*, p. 227.
75. *Gaily*, p. 152.
76. In *Child of the Century* Hecht says this occurred in the spring of 1925 but he also says he spent the summer of that year in Florida. It is likely that he went to Hollywood in 1926 even possibly in 1927. The first script Hecht wrote after being on the job only four days was *Underworld* for Paramount. It took a week to write. The third draft of the scenario by Robert Lee is dated March 1927.
77. Ibid., p. 466.

Chapter 2

1. Ben Hecht, *A Child of the Century* (New York: Simon and Schuster, 1954), pp. 466-67.
2. Ben Hecht, *Charlie: The Improbable Life and Times of Charles MacArthur* (New York: Harper, 1957), p. 159.
3. *Theatre Magazine*, pp. 18, 62.
4. *Child*, p. 252.

220   Notes for Chapter 3

5. Ibid., p. 474.
6. Rudy Behlmer (ed.), *Memo from David O. Selznick* (New York: Viking, 1972), p. 70.
7. Harry Geduld, *The Birth of the Talkies* (Bloomington: Indiana University Press, 1975), p. 266.
8. Donald McCaffrey, *The Golden Age of Sound Comedy* (New York: A.S. Barnes, 1973).
9. Pauline Kael, *The Citizen Kane Book* (Boston: Little, Brown, 1971), p. 18.
10. Ibid., p. 19.
11. Robert Littel, *Theatre Arts Monthly*, March 1929, in Barnard Hewitt, *Theatre U.S.A.* (New York: McGraw Hill, 1959), p. 378.
12. Lewis Jacobs, *The Rise of the American Film* (1939; 2nd ed. New York: Teachers College Press, 1957), p. 508.
13. Ibid., p. 532.
14. Ibid., p. 536.
15. Ibid., p. 535.
16. Robert Sklar, *Movie Made America* (New York: Random House, 1975), p. 187.
17. Molly Haskell, *From Reverence to Rape* (Baltimore: Penguin, 1974), p. 91.
18. Sklar, p. 188.
19. Gerald Mast, "Preston Sturges and the Dialogue Tradition," in *Film Theory and Criticism*, ed. Gerald Mast and Marshall Cohen (New York: Oxford, 1974), p. 555.
20. Siegfried Kracauer, *Theory of Film: The Redemption of Physical Reality* (New York: Oxford, 1960), p. 103.
21. Kael, pp. 15-16.

Chapter 3

1. Pauline Kael, *The Citizen Kane Book* (Boston: Little, Brown, 1971), p. 13.
2. Steven Scheuer, ed., *Movies on TV* (New York: Bantam, 1977), p. 18.
3. This episode actually has some basis in fact—but it was for a movie studio rather than for a newspaper that Villa rearranged his battle plans. According to Terry Ramsaye in *A Million and One Nights* (1926), Villa signed a contract with the Mutual Film Corporation. Mutual agreed to bankroll the revolution in return for filming privileges and other compensations which included the promise by Villa that, whenever possible, he would attack in the daytime when the light was good for filming. The studio planned to incorporate the battle footage into a feature film about the Mexican war directed by D.W. Griffith in California.
4. Kael, p. 20.
5. Alex Barris, *Stop the Presses!* (New York: Bantam, 1977), p. 18.
6. On one occasion Hecht scooped MacArthur by solving a murder case MacArthur had been investigating for his paper. He was responsible for the arrest and conviction of Carl Wanderer, and both he and MacArthur were present at his execution.
7. Ben Hecht, *A Child of the Century* (New York: Simon and Schuster, 1954), p. 391.

8. Ben Hecht, *Letters From Bohemia* (Garden City: Doubleday, 1964), p. 197.
9. Ibid., p. 197.
10. Ibid.
11. Ben Hecht, *The Improbable Life and Times of Charles MacArthur* (New York: Harper, 1957) p. 135.
12. Ben Hecht and Charles MacArthur, *The Front Page* (New York: Samuel French, 1950), p. 139.
13. Ibid., p. 65.
14. This male group orientation was shared by Howard Hawks who directed a number of Hecht and Hecht-MacArthur films, including *The Twentieth Century* (1934) and *His Girl Friday* (1940).
15. *Front Page*, p. 36.
16. Ibid.
17. Ibid., p. 35.
18. Ibid., p. 31.
19. Ibid., p. 141.
20. Brooks Atkinson, *New York Times*, 15 Aug. 1928, p. 19, col. 2.
21. *Front Page*, pp. 114-15.
22. Ibid., p. 102.
23. Walter Kerr, *New York Times*, 25 May 1969, Sec. II, p. 1, col. 1.

Chapter 4

1. Brooks Atkinson, *New York Times*, 25 Jan. 1933.
2. Noel Coward, *Design for Living* (Garden City: Doubleday, 1933), III, 2, p. 138.
3. *The London Times*, 26 Jan. 1939.
4. *New York Times*, 25 Jan. 1933.
5. Frank Swinnerton, *The Georgian Scene* (New York: Farrar and Rinehart, 1934), pp. 448-49.
6. Milton Levin, *Noel Coward* (New York: Twayne, 1968), p. 106.
7. George Jean Nathan, "Several Writers for the Theatre," in George Jean Nathan, *Passing Judgments* (New York: Knopf, 1935), pp. 147-58.
8. Fred Lawrence Guiles, *Hanging On in Paradise* (New York: McGraw-Hill, 1975), p. 26.
9. Herman G. Weinberg, *The Lubitsch Touch* (New York: Dover, 1977), p. 14.
10. *The Shop Around the Corner* is one of the films Hecht is said to have worked on, but Raphaelson talks at length about writing the film with Lubitsch without mentioning Hecht. Hecht says he and Lubitsch plotted *Shop Around the Corner* together. On the other hand, in *The Lubitsch Touch* Herman Weinberg also discusses Walter Reisch's screenplay for *Comrade X*, a film officially credited to Hecht and Charles Lederer with only the story by Reisch.

11. Ben Hecht, "Collaborating with Mr. Lubitsch," in Weinberg, pp. 270-71.
12. "An Interview with Samson Raphaelson," in Weinberg, pp. 232-33.
13. Weinberg, p. 271.
14. Ed Lowry, *Design for Living*, "Cinema Texas Program Notes," 15 Sept. 1976, Vol. II, no. 1.
15. Richard Corliss, *Talking Pictures* (New York: Penguin, 1975), p. 13.
16. Alistaire Cooke, "The Film of *Design for Living*," *London Observer*, Sun. 23 Sept. 1933.
17. Doug Fetherling, *The Five Lives of Ben Hecht* (Canada: Lester and Orpen, 1977), p. 58.
18. Coward, *Design for Living*, II, 3, p. 102.
19. Noel Coward, *Play Parade* (Garden City: Doubleday, 1933), p. xvii.
20. Coward, *Design for Living*, I, 1, pp. 10-11.
21. *New York Times*, 25 Jan. 1933.
22. *Talking Pictures*, p. 13.
23. Molly Haskell, *From Reverence to Rape* (Baltimore: Penguin, 1974), p. 99.
24. Ibid., p. 100.
25. Ibid., p. 102.

Chapter 5

1. Ben Hecht, *Charlie: The Improbable Life and Times of Charles MacArthur* (New York: Harper, 1957), p. 89.
2. Ibid., p. 89-90.
3. Ibid., p. 91.
4. *New York Times*, 30 Dec. 1932, p. 15, col. 1.
5. Ben Hecht and Charles MacArthur, *The Twentieth Century* (unpublished manuscript), Act I, Scene 4, p. 49. Subsequent references to pagination will be abbreviated as they appear in the original, *e.g.* 1-4-49.
6. *Charlie*, p. 54.
7. *Front Page*, p. 31.
8. *Twentieth Century*, 1-4-50.
9. Ibid., 2-30.
10. Ibid., 1-2-27.
11. Ibid., 1-4-43.
12. Ibid., 2-26.
13. Ibid., 2-39.
14. *New York Times*, 12 Feb. 1933, Sec IX, p. 1, col. 1.
15. The name is a thinly veiled reference to Percy Hammond, critic for the *New York Tribune* from 1921-1936. Hammond was particularly noted for his attacks on vulgarity in the theatre.

16. *Twentieth Century,* 1-1-17.
17. Ibid., 1-3-38.
18. *New York Times,* 30 Dec. 1932, p. 15, col. 1.
19. *Twentieth Century,* 2-34.
20. Mordaunt Hall, *New York Times,* 4 May 1934, p. 24, col. 2.
21. Thornton Delehanty, *New York Post,* no date.
22. Pauline Kael, *The Citizen Kane Book* (Boston: Little, Brown, 1971), p. 48.
23. Ibid., p. 48.
24. Ibid., p. 48.
25. Andrew Sarris, "The World of Howard Hawks," in *Focus on Howard Hawks,* ed. Joseph McBride (Englewood Cliffs: Prentice Hall, 1972), p. 48.
26. *Hollywood Journal,* 9 June 1935.
27. "A discussion with the Audience at the 1960 Chicago Film Festival," in McBride, p. 21.
28. Manny Farber, "Howard Hawks," in McBride, p. 28.
29. Ted Sennet, *Lunatics and Lovers* (New Rochelle: Arlington House, 1973), p. 14.
30. Donald McCaffrey, *The Golden Age of Sound Comedy* (New York: A.S. Barnes, 1973), p. 132.
31. Richard Corliss, *Talking Pictures* (New York: Penguin, 1975), p. 17.
32. McCaffrey, p. 133.
33. Based on the play *Chicago* by Maurine Watkins (which is also the source of the recent Broadway musical), the screenplay is credited to Nunnally Johnson, but Doug Fetherling and Pauline Kael (at least according to "Cinema Texas Program Notes," Vol. III, no. 1, 15 Sept. 1976) credit Hecht as well. Either Hecht or Johnson were capable of the style of the film.
34. Otis Ferguson, *Film Criticism of Otis Ferguson* (Philadelphia: Temple University Press, 1971), p. 257.
34. Herman Weinberg, *The Lubitsch Touch* (New York: Dover, 1977), p. 149.
36. Fred Lawrence Guiles, *Hanging On in Paradise.* New York: McGraw-Hill, 1975, p. 185.

Chapter 6

1. Ben Hecht, *Charlie: The Improbable Life and Times of Charles MacArthur* (New York: Harper, 1957), p. 183.
2. Ibid., p. 189.
3. Helen Hayes, *On Reflection* (New York: M. Evans, 1968), p. 177.
4. Ben Hecht, *A Child of the Century* (New York: Simon and Schuster, 1954), p. 475.
5. Fred Lawrence Guiles, *Hanging On in Paradise* (New York: McGraw-Hill, 1975), p. 119.
6. *Charlie,* p. 185.

Notes for Chapter 6

7. Ibid., pp. 183-85.
8. Ibid., p. 186.
9. Ibid., pp. 186-87.
10. Ibid., p. 190.
11. Ibid., p. 189.
12. Ibid., p. 188.
13. Ibid., p. 187. Only technically accurate. This was Claude Rains's second film, but since he was either invisible or swathed in bandages in his first movie (*The Invisible Man*, 1933) Hecht is truthful after his fashion.
14. *Child*, p. 484.
15. Charles Higham, *Hollywood Cameramen: Sources of Light* (Bloomington: Indiana University Press, 1970), p. 44.
16. Guiles, p. 115.
17. "Crime Without Passion," in *A Treasury of Ben Hecht* (New York: Crown, 1959), p. 214.
18. *Child*, p. 376.
19. Ibid., p. 392.
20. Ibid., p. 377.
21. Guiles, p. 110.
22. *Variety*, 4 Sept. 1934.
23. Richard Watts, *New York Herald Tribune*, 9 Sept. 1934.
24. Eileen Creelman, *New York Sun*, 11 Sept. 1934.
25. *London Times*, 10 Sept. 1934.
26. *Charlie*, p. 185. Hecht's ignorance of Vorkapich's work is open to question. Vorkapich had done a montage earlier that year for *Viva Villa*, a film Hecht wrote. In *Viva Villa*, however Vorkapich's efforts were confined to montages which condensed action while in *Crime Without Passion* his sequences combined a symbolic set of images with the subjective neuroticism of the central character. To achieve these effects Vorkapich had to construct his images as well as edit them.
27. Higham, *Hollywood Cameramen*, p. 44.
28. *Variety*, 4 Sept. 1934.
29. Herman Weinberg, "Coffee Brandy and Cigars," Autumn 1965, in *Saint Cinema* (New York: Dover, 1973), p. 241.
30. *Variety*, 8 May 1935.
31. *New York Post*, 22 May 1935.
32. Ibid.
33. *Variety*, 8 May 1935.
34. Ben Hecht, *A Jew in Love* (New York: Covici-Friede, 1931), p. 212.

35. *Child*, p. 496.
36. Ibid.
37. *New York Times*, 3 May 1935.
38. Ibid.
39. John Reddington, *Daily Eagle*, 12 May 1935.
40. *Time*, 13 May 1935.
41. *New York Herald Tribune*, 3 May 1935.
42. Letter to the author, 27 October, 1977.
43. Regina Crewes, *New York American*, 3 May, 1935.
44. *Guiles*, pp. 124-25.
45. *Variety*, 9 Dec. 1936.
46. *Charlie*, p. 189.
47. Frank Nugent, *New York Times*, 5 Feb. 1936.
48. Higham, p. 24.

Chapter 7

1. Ben Hecht, *Guide for the Bedeviled* (New York: Scribners, 1944), p. 57.
2. Ibid., p. 77.
3. Ibid., p. 160.
4. Ibid., pp. 56-57.
5. Martin Gottfried in his book *Jed Harris: The Curse of Genius* (Boston: Little, Brown, 1984) says Boshere, described as "The Comet" in *A Jew in Love,* is "a thinly disguised portrait of Jed Harris, 'The Meteor.'" Gottfried says that Hecht "recorded Harris's behavior with the acuity of a superlative reporter" and filled the book with his own attitude towards Harris "a mixture of fascination and hatred." While Gottfried calls the novel "vicious" he also says that "feverish though Hecht's images may seem to a modern ear, in 1928 it was not so odd to view and even live life in purple." pp. 90-91.
6. Ben Hecht, *A Jew in Love* (New York: Covici-Friede, 1931), p. 3.
7. Leslie Fiedler, *The Jew in the American Novel* (New York: Herzl Institute, 1959), pp. 22-23.
8. Fiedler, p. 22. Fiedler points out that Budd Schulberg was also accused of anti-Semitism a decade later because of his portrait of an ambitious Jewish Hollywood writer, Sammy Glick, in *What Makes Sammy Run?* (1941)—an attitude, said Fiedler, that failed to consider either the work as a whole or the intentions of the author.
9. Sol Liptzin, *The Jew in American Literature* (New York: Bloch, 1966), p. 188. Philip Roth today often suffers the same kinds of attacks and even confronts the issue of Jewish self-analysis and its critical response in *The Ghost Writer* (1979).
10. *Guide*, p. 91.
11. Ibid., p. 93.

Notes for Chapter 8

12. Ibid., p. 254.

13. Ibid., p. 240.

14. For a detailed account of Allied reaction to the Holocaust see: Arthur D. Morse's *While Six Million Died: A Chronicle of American Apathy* (New York: Random House, 1968) and Walter Laquerer's *The Terrible Secret: Suppression of the Truth About Hitler's "Final Solution"* (New York: Penguin, 1982). Laquerer outlines reactions that vary from disbelief to disinterest to active suppression by Allied Governments and fear of making the situation worse by Jewish authorities. Among many other examples he outlines this policy by the Planning Committee of the British Ministry of Information (MOI) which in July of 1941 decided "That while a certain amount of horror was needed in British propaganda, this was only to be used sparingly and 'must always deal with the treatment of indisputedly innocent people. Not with violent political opponents. And not with Jews.'" (p. 91, MOI memorandum, 25 July 1941, INF 1/251).

15. *Guide*, p. 119.

16. Among prominent men attracted to the work of the Committee were Senator Guy M. Gillette of Iowa, William Randoph Hearst, Secretary of the Interior Harold Ickes, Van Wyck Brooks, and Louis Bromfield. Arthur Morse calls Bergson an "extraordinary firebrand who had sparked a series of fullpage advertisements in leading newspapers calling attention to United States apathy in the face of the Nazi extermination program.

    "Bergson's zeal often proved disconcerting to his supporters and his plan to organize a Hebrew army and set up an embassy in Washington representing the Jewish State diminished some of his effectiveness. But his attention getting techniques were in dramatic contrast to those of the more conventional Jewish spokesmen." (Morse, p. 77).

17. *P.M.*, February 1943, p. 19.

18. Ben Hecht, *A Child of the Century* (New York: Simon and Schuster, 1954), p. 589.

19. The *S.S. Ben Hecht* was seized by the Israeli government and became the subject of wrangling and court suits into the early 1950s.

20. *Child*, p. 618.

Chapter 8

1. Ben Hecht, *A Guide for the Bedeviled* (New York: Scribner, 1944), p. 202.

2. Ibid., p. 514.

3. Otto Preminger, *Preminger: An Autobiography* (Garden City: Doubleday, 1977), p. 149. Preminger also comments that during this period Hecht had a problem with the drug Demoral, a residue of his recovery from surgery.

4. Richard Griffith, *The Film Till Now* (Middlesex: Hamlyn, 1967), p. 467.

5. François Truffaut, *Hitchcock* (New York: Simon and Schuster, 1967), pp. 121-22.

6. Donald Spoto, *The Art of Alfred Hitchcock* (New York: Hopkinson and Blake, 1977), p. 161.

7. Truffaut, p. 122.

8. Ben Hecht, *A Child of the Century* (New York: Simon and Schuster, 1954), p. 626.

9. Raymond Durgnat, *The Crazy Mirror* (New York: Delta, 1972), p. 189.

10. Ben Hecht, *Roman Holiday* (Paramount file copy SF 83316), C-4, p. 38.
11. *Saturday Review*, 5 Sept. 1953.
12. American Film (Vol. III, No. 6, April 1978), pp. 67-68.
13. Durgnat, p. 189.
14. *Roman Holiday*, F-6, p. 92.
15. Ibid., B-2, p. 25.
16. Ibid., B-1, p. 20.
17. Preminger, p. 148.
18. *Child*, p. 514.

Bibliography

Books

Adamson, Joe. *Groucho, Harpo, Chico and Sometimes Zeppo.* New York: Simon and Schuster, 1973.
Agee, James. *Agee on Film,* Vol. I. New York: Grosset & Dunlap, 1967.
Alpert, Hollis. *The Barrymores.* New York: Dial, 1964.
_____. *The Dreams and the Dreamers: Adventures of a Professional Movie Goer.* New York: Macmillan, 1962.
Anderson, Margaret. *My Thirty Years' War.* New York: Covici-Friede, 1930.
Asbury, Herbert. *The Barbary Coast: An Informal History of the San Francisco Underworld.* New York: Knopf, 1933.
Barris, Alex. *Stop the Presses! The Newspaperman in American Film.* New York: A.S. Barnes, 1976: New York: Bantam, 1977.
Bauer, Yehuda. *American Jewry and the Holocaust: The American-Jewish Joint Distribution Committee 1939-1945.* Detroit: Wayne State University Press, 1981.
Baxter, John. *The Cinema of Josef von Sternberg.* New York: A.S. Barnes, 1971.
_____. *The Gangster Film.* New York: A.S. Barnes, 1970.
_____. *Hollywood in the Thirties.* New York: A.S. Barnes, 1970.
Begin, Menachem. *The Revolt: Story of the Irgun.* Tel Aviv: Havar, 1964.
Bell, J. Bowyer. *Terror Out of Zion: Irgun Zvai Leumi, LEHI, and the Palestine Underground, 1929-1949.* New York: St. Martin's Press, 1977.
Behlmer, Rudy, ed. *Memo from David O. Selznick.* New York: Viking, 1972.
Bluestone, George. *Novels into Film: The Metamorphosis of Fiction into Cinema.* Berkeley: Univ. of California Press, 1968.
Bobker, Lee R. *Elements of Film.* New York: Harcourt Brace, 1974.
Bode, Carl. *Mencken.* Carbondale: Southern Illinois Univ. Press, 1969.
Bodenheim, Maxwell. *Duke Herring.* New York: Horace Liveright, 1931.
Brownlow, Kevin. *The Parade's Gone By.* New York: Ballantine, 1970.
Cohen, Mickey, as told to Nugent Peer. *Mickey Cohen: In My Own Words.* Englewood Cliffs: Prentice-Hall, 1975.
Corliss, Richard (ed). *Hollywood Screenwriters.* New York: Avon, 1972.
_____. *Talking Pictures: Screenwriters in the American Cinema.* Woodstock, 1974; rpt. New York: Penguin, 1975.
Coward, Noel. *Design for Living: A Comedy in Three Acts.* Garden City: Doubleday, 1933.
_____. *Play Parade.* Garden City: Garden City, 1933.
Cowley, Malcolm, ed. *After the Genteel Tradition: American Writers 1910-1930.* Carbondale: Southern Illinois Univ. Press, 1964.
Duffy, Bernard. *The Chicago Renaissance in American Letters: A Critical History.* East Lansing: Michigan State Univ. Press, 1956.
Durgnat, Raymond. *The Crazy Mirror: Hollywood Comedy and the American Image.* 1970; rpt. New York: Delta, 1972.

_____. *The Strange Case of Alfred Hitchcock.* Cambridge: MIT Press, 1974.
Ferguson, Otis. *Film Criticism of Otis Ferguson.* Philadelphia: Temple Univ. Press, 1971.
Fetherling, Doug. *The Five Lives of Ben Hecht.* Canada: Lester and Orpen, 1977.
Fiedler, Leslie A. *The Jew in the American Novel.* New York: Herzl Institute Pamphlet No. 10, 1959.
Fincke, Gary. "The Fiction of Ben Hecht: A Study in Polarity." Dissertation, Kent State, 1974.
Fishbein, Morris. *Morris Fishbein, M.D.: An Autobiography.* New York: Doubleday, 1969.
Fort, Charles. *New Lands.* New York: Boni and Liveright, 1923.
Fowler, Gene. *Good Night, Sweet Prince: The Life and Times of John Barrymore.* New York: Viking, 1944.
_____. *Skyline: A Reporter's Reminiscence of the 1920s.* New York: Viking, 1961.
Fulton, Albert R. *Motion Pictures: The Development of an Art from Silent Films to the Age of Television.* Norman: Univ. of Oklahoma Press, 1960.
Gabree, John. *Gangsters: From Little Caeser to the Godfather.* New York: Pyramid, 1973.
Gassner, John. *Dramatic Soundings.* New York: Crown, 1968.
Garcia-Granados, Jorge. *The Birth of Israel: The Drama As I Saw It.* New York: Knopf, 1949.
Geduld, Harry M., ed. *Authors on Film.* Bloomington: Indiana Univ. Press, 1972.
_____. *The Birth of the Talkies: From Edison to Jolson.* Bloomington: Indiana Univ. Press, 1975.
Gessner, Robert. *The Moving Image: A Guide to Cinematic Literacy.* New York: Dutton, 1968.
Gilmer, Waller. *Horace Liveright: Publisher of the Twenties.* New York: Davis Lewis, 1970.
Gottfried, Martin. *Jed Harris: The Curse of Genius.* Boston: Little, Brown, 1984.
Griffith, Richard. *The Film Till Now.* Middlesex: Hamlyn, 1967.
Guiles, Fred Lawrence. *Hanging On in Paradise.* New York: McGraw-Hill, 1975.
Hansen, Harry. *Midwest Portraits: A Book of Memories and Friendships.* New York: Harcourt, Brace, 1923.
Haskell, Molly. *From Reverence to Rape: The Treatment of Women in the Movies.* Baltimore: Penguin, 1974.
Hayes, Helen. *On Reflection.* New York: M. Evans, 1968.
Hecht, Marie Armstrong. *My First Husband.* New York: Greenberg, 1932.
Herman, Lewis. *A Practical Manual of Screen Playwriting for Theatre and Television Films.* New York: Meridian, 1952.
Hewitt, Barnard. *Theatre U.S.A..* New York: McGraw-Hill, 1959.
Higham, Charles. *Hollywood Cameramen: Sources of Light.* Bloomington: Indiana Univ. Press, 1970.
Higham, Charles, and Joel Greenberg. *Hollywood in the Forties.* New York: A.S. Barnes, 1968.
Hoffman, Frederick, Charles Allen, and Carolyn F. Ulrich. *The Little Magazine: A History and a Bibliography.* Princeton: Princeton Univ. Press, 1947.
Houseman, John. *Run-Through.* New York: Simon and Schuster, 1972.
Hurt, James, ed. *Focus on Film and Theatre.* Englewood Cliffs: Prentice-Hall, 1974.
Jacobs, Lewis. *The Rise of the American Film: A Critical History.* New York: Teachers College Press, 1967.
Kael, Pauline. *The Citizen Kane Book.* Boston: Little, Brown, 1971.
_____. *Deeper Into Movies.* Boston: Little, Brown, 1973.
_____. *I Lost It at the Movies.* Boston: Little, Brown, 1965.
_____. *Kiss Kiss, Bang Bang.* Boston: Little, Brown, 1968.
_____. *Reeling.* Boston: Little, Brown, 1976.
Karpf, Stephen Louis. *The Gangster Film: Emergence, Variation and Decay of a Genre 1930-1940.* New York: Arno, 1973.
Karsner, David. *Sixteen Authors to One.* New York: Lewis Copeland, 1928.
Katz, Shmuel (Samuel). *Days of Fire.* New York: Doubleday, 1968.

Knight, Arthur. *The Liveliest Art: A Panoramic History of the Movies.* New York: Macmillan, 1959.
Kracauer, Siegfried. *Theory of Film: The Redemption of Physical Reality.* 1960; rpt. New York: Oxford, 1976.
Lambert, Gavin. *GWTW: The Making of Gone with the Wind.* Boston: Little, Brown, 1973.
Langer, Laurence. *The Magic Curtain.* New York: Dutton, 1951.
Laquerer, Walter. *A History of Zionism.* New York: Holt, Rinehart & Winston, 1972.
———. *The Terrible Secret: Suppression of the Truth about Hitler's "Final Solution."* New York: Penguin, 1982.
LaValley, Albert J., ed. *Focus on Hitchcock.* Englewood Cliffs: Prentice-Hall, 1972.
Lawson, John Howard. *Film: The Creative Process: The Search for an Audio-Visual Language and Structure.* New York: Hill and Wang, 1964.
Levin, Milton. *Noel Coward.* New York: Twayne, 1968.
Lipsky, Louis. *A Gallery of Zionest Profiles.* New York: Farrar, Straus and Cudahy, 1956.
Liptzin, Sol. *The Jew in American Literature.* New York: Block, 1966.
McArthur, Colin. *Underworld U.S.A.* New York: Viking, 1972.
McBride, Joseph, ed. *Focus on Howard Hawks.* Englewood Cliffs: Prentice-Hall, 1972.
McCaffrey, Donald W. *The Golden Age of Sound Comedy: Comic Films and Comedians of the Thirties.* New York: A.S. Barnes, 1973.
Madsen, Axel. *William Wyler.* New York: Crowell, 1973.
Mailer, Norman. *Marilyn.* New York: Grosset and Dunlap, 1973.
Mander, Raymond, and Joe Mitchenson. *Theatrical Companion to Coward.* London: Rockliff, 1974.
Marx, Samuel. *Mayer and Thalberg: Make-Believe Saints.* London: W.H. Allen, 1976.
Mast, Gerald. *A Short History of the Movies.* Indianapolis: Bobbs Merrill, 1971.
Mast, Gerald, and Marshall Cohen, eds. *Film Theory and Criticism: Introductory Readings.* New York: Oxford, 1974.
Meredith, Scott. *George S. Kaufman and His Friends.* New York: Doubleday, 1974.
Mersand, Joseph. *Traditions in American Literature: A Study of Jewish Characters and Authors.* New York: Modern Chapbooks, 1939.
Moore, Jack B. *Maxwell Bodenheim.* New York: Twayne, 1970.
Morse, Arthur D. *While Six Million Died: A Chronicle of American Apathy.* New York: Random House, 1968.
Nathan, George Jean. *Passing Judgments.* New York: Knopf, 1935.
Oppenheimer, George, ed. *The Passionate Playgoer.* New York: Viking, 1958.
Parish, James Robert, and Michael R. Pitts. *The Great Gangster Pictures.* Metuchen, N.J.: Scarecrow, 1976.
Pinchon, Edgcumb. *Viva Villa! A Recovery of the Real Pancho Villa—Peon... Bandit... Soldier... Patriot.* New York: Harcourt, Brace, 1933.
Powdermaker, Hortense. *Hollywood: The Dream Factory.* Boston: Little, Brown, 1950.
Preminger, Otto. *Preminger: An Autobiography.* Garden City: Doubleday, 1977.
Ramsaye, Terry. *A Million and One Nights: A History of the Motion Picture.* New York: Simon and Schuster, 1926, Vol. II.
Roberts, Marc. "The Novels of Ben Hecht." Dissertation, Baylor, 1970.
Rotha, Paul, and Richard Griffith. *The Film Till Now: A Survey of World Cinema.* Middlesex: Hamlyn, 1967.
Scheuer, Steven, ed. *Movies in T.V.* New York: Bantam Books, 1977.
Schulberg, Budd. *What Makes Sammy Run?* New York: Random House, 1941.
Sennet, Ted. *Lunatics and Lovers: A Tribute to the Giddy and Glittering Era of the Screen's "Screwball" and Romantic Comedies.* New Rochelle: Arlington House, 1973.

Sherman, Stuart. *Critical Woodcuts.* New York: Scribner's, 1926.
Sklar, Robert. *Movie Made America: A Cultural History of American Movies.* New York: Random House, 1975.
Smith, Henry Justin. *Deadlines: Being, The Quaint; The Amusing; The Tragic; Memoirs of a News-Room.* Chicago: Covici-McGee, 1922.
Spewack, B.C., and Samuel Spewack. *Boy Meets Girl; Spring Song.* New York: Random House, 1936. Also in *Best Plays of 1935-36.*
Spoto, Donald. *The Art of Alfred Hitchcock: Fifty Years of His Motion Pictures.* New York: Hopkinson and Blake, 1977.
Swinnerton, Frank. *The Georgian Scene.* New York: Farrar and Rinehart, 1934.
Teichmann, Howard. *George S. Kaufman: An Intimate Portrait.* New York: Dell, 1972.
Thomas, Bob. *Selznick.* New York: Doubleday, 1970.
Todorov, Tzvetan. *The Fantastic: A Structural Approach to a Literary Genre.* Trans. Richard Howard. Cleveland: Case Western Reserve Univ. Press, 1973.
Truffaut, François. *Hitchcock.* New York: Simon and Schuster, 1967.
Tyler, Parker. *Magic and Myth of the Movies.* New York: Simon and Schuster, 1947.
von Sternberg, Josef. *Fun in a Chinese Laundry: An Autobiography.* New York: Macmillan, 1965.
Wagner, Geoffrey. *The Novel and the Cinema.* Rutherford: Fairleigh Dickenson, 1974. Contains chapter on *Wuthering Heights.*
Waldau, Roy S. *Vintage Years of the Theatre Guild 1928-1939.* Cleveland: Case Western Reserve, 1972.
Weinberg, Herman G. *Josef von Sternberg: A Critical Study.* New York: Dutton, 1967.
⎯⎯⎯. *The Lubitsch Touch: A Critical Study.* New York: Dover, 1977.
⎯⎯⎯. *Saint Cinema: Writings on the Film 1929-1970.* 1970; rpt. New York: Dover, 1973.
Wellman, William A. *A Short Time for Insanity: An Autobiography.* New York: Hawthorne, 1974.
Wells, Samuel E. (Junius Junior, pseud.). *Pseudorealists.* New York: Outsider Press, 1931. A comparison between *A Jew in Love* and Faulkner's *Sanctuary.*
Willis, Donald C. *The Films of Howard Hawks.* Metuchen, N.J.: Scarecrow, 1975.
Wilson, Robert, ed. *The Film Criticism of Otis Ferguson.* Philadelphia: Temple Univ. Press, 1971.
Winston, Douglas Garrett. *The Screenplay as Literature.* Cranbury: Associated Univ. Presses, 1973.
Wollen, Peter. *Signs and Meaning in the Cinema.* Bloomington: Indiana Univ. Press, 1972.
Wood, Robin. *Howard Hawks.* New York: Doubleday, 1968.

Articles

American Film. Vol. III, No. 6, April 1978.
Belton, John. "Monkey Business." *Film Heritage,* Winter 1970-71, Vol. 6, No. 2, pp. 19-26.
Brown, Geoff. "'Better Than Metro Isn't Good Enough!' Hecht and MacArthur's Own Movies." *Sight and Sound,* Summer 1975.
Brown, Geoff, and Andrew Nichols. "Hecht and MacArthur." *British Film Institute National Film Theatre,* Apr/May 1975. Notes to showings of Hecht-MacArthur films.
Cooke, Alistaire, "The Film of *Design for Living.*" *London Observer,* 23 Sept. 1933.
Diehl, Digby. "New Monroe Book From Old Memoirs." *Los Angeles Times,* 15 April 1974.
Fuller, Stephen. "Ben Hecht: A Sampler." *Film Comment,* Winter 1970-71, Vol. 6, No. 4, pp. 32-39. Contains filmography prepared by Fuller and Rose Caylor Hecht.
Hamill, Pete. "A Rose for Ben Hecht." *New York Post,* 28 February 1973.
Hayes, Alfred. "The Pair From Paramount." *New Theatre,* March 1936, pp. 14-15, 33.
Houston, Penelope. "Scripting: The Return of Hecht." *Sight and Sound,* August-September 1951, pp. 21, 30.

Katz, Shlomo. "Ben Hecht's *Kampf.*" *Midstream: A Quarterly Jewish Review*, Winter 1962. An essay review of *Perfidy*.
Kauffmann, Stanley. "Take Two: *Roman Holiday.*" *American Film*, April 1978, Vol. III, No. 6.
Leon, William T. "The Scoundrel." *Films in Review*, March 1975, Vol. 26, No. 3, pp. 143-49.
Lowry, Ed. "Cinema Texas Program Notes." *Design for Living*, 15 Sept. 1976, vol. II, no. 1.
Sarris, Andrew. "The Sex Comedy Without the Sex." *American Film*, March 1978, Vol. III, No. 5.
Schrader, Paul. "Notes on Film Noir." *Film Comment*, Vol. VIII, Spring 1972, pp. 8-13.
Thomas, Sam. "Memories of Ben." *Performing Arts*, September 1973, Vol. 7, No. 9.
Weales, Gerald. "The End of *Gunga Din* OR Why I'm Not Happy at the Movies Any More." *Midway*, Autumn 1967, pp. 73-81.

Index

Abbott, George, 80
Actor's Blood, 169
Actors and Sin, 115, 169-71
Adler, Celia, 158
Adler, Luther, 158
Albert, Eddie, 171, 178
All He Ever Loved, 126
All the President's Men, 42
Alpert, Hollis, 134
Altalena, 157
American Film Institute Catalogue, 41
American League for a Free Palestine, The, 157
Anderson, Margaret, 14, 69
Anderson, Sherwood, 14, 15, 22, 23, 67
Angels Over Broadway, 115, 122, 143-49, 163
Antheil, George, 66, 137, 171
Arden, Eve, 106
Armstrong, Edwina, 137
Art of Alfred Hitchcock, The, 166
Atkinson, Brooks, 50, 59, 74, 81, 84, 87
Awful Truth, The, 30, 64

Barbary Coast, 2, 42, 94, 110
Bari, Lynn, 153
Barris, Alex, 44
Barry, Philip, 34
Barrymore, John, 15, 84, 90
Barstow, Lester, 159
Bazin, André, 39
Begin, Menachem, xii, 158
Belasco, David, 80-81
Bell, Edgar Price, 11
Bellamy, Ralph, 91, 95-96
Belle of the Nineties, 37
Benchley, Robert, 143
Bennett, Charles, 143
Bennett, Joan, 91
Bergman, Ingrid, 79, 163-64
Bergson, Peter, 155-58
Bialik, 149
Birth of the Talkies, The, 29

Bluestone, George, xiii
Bodenheim, Maxwell, 14, 15, 22, 23, 24, 67, 129, 169, 181
Bogart, Humphrey, 79
Bombshell, 45
Book of Miracles, A, 132
Book of the Damned, The, 132
Bourne, Whitney, 113, 120, 137
Boy Meets Girl, ix
Brandeis, Louis, 149
Brando, Marlon, 158
Brecht, Bertolt, 181
Bressart, Felix, 106
Brice, Fanny, 128
Bringing Up Baby, 30, 84
British Cinematograph Exhibitor's Association, The, 159
Brooklyn Daily Eagle, 133
Brown, John Mason, 125

Cabellero of the Law, 116
Cagney, Jimmy, 38
Capra, Frank, 176
Carroll, Leo G., 163
Casablanca, 79, 178
Chaplin, Charles, 143
Charlie: The Improbable Life and Times of Charles MacArthur, 162
Chekov, Michael, 169
Chicago Daily News, xii, 1, 9, 15, 17, 21, 28, 152, 178, 181
Chicago Herald-Examiner, 2
Chicago Journal, 1, 4, 6-8, 28
Chicago Literary Times, The (Ben Hecht's Chicago Literary Times), 1, 17, 21
Chicago Renaissance in American Literature, The, 15
Child of the Century, A, 10, 162
China Girl, 115, 143, 153-55, 160
Circus World, 5, 148, 179
Citizen Kane Book, xii

Index

Citizen Kane, 32, 42
Clark, Mae, 38
Coburn, Charles, 174
Colbert, Claudette, 31, 106
Comden, Betty, 134
Committee for a Jewish Army of Stateless and Palestinian Jews, The, 156
Comrade X, 29, 30, 42, 106-8, 139, 142, 143
Concerning a Woman of Sin, 162, 171
Confessions of a Nazi Spy, 143
Connelly, Marc, 33
Connolly, Walter, 84, 98-104, 137
Cooper, Gary, 57, 63, 76
Corliss, Richard, xii, 2, 62, 75, 103
Cormack, Bartlett, 34
Cossart, Ernest, 129, 133
Count Bruga, 24, 169
Covici, Pascal, 18
Coward, Noel, 57-60, 61-77, 80, 113, 125, 130, 133, 134, 140
Cowley, Malcolm, 13
Crazy Mirror, The, 171
Crewes, Regina, 134
Crime Without Passion, 61, 110-40, 147
Crossfire, 153
Cutie—A Warm Mama, 21

Dadaism, 12-13, 21, 66, 67
Dali, Salvador, 164
Darrow, Clarence, 20
Day, Laraine, 143
De Palma, Brian, xii
Deadlines, 9
Delehanty, Thornton, 90
Dell, Floyd, 14
Dennis, Charles, 11
Design for Living, xiii, 29, 30, 54, 56, 57-77, 80, 84, 95, 133
Diamond, I.A.L., 176
Dietrichstein, Leo, 17, 24
Dighton, John, 176
Dishonored Lady, 162
Divorcee, The, 34
Douglas, Kirk, 179
Dracula, 123
Dregs, 23
Duffy, Bernard, 15
Duffy, Sherman, 7-8
Durante, Jimmy, 52, 139
Durgnat, Raymond, 171, 178

Eastman, John C., 6
Easy Living, 30, 31
Egoist, The, 17, 24
Eisenstein, Sergei, 39
Emergency Committee to Save the Jewish People of Europe, The, 156

Erik Dorn, 1, 17, 19, 55, 150
Erwin, Stuart, 42
Evening Standard, 159
Every Day's a Holiday, 37

Fairbanks, Douglas, Jr., 55, 143-48, 163
Fantazius Mallare, 1, 17, 20, 126
Farber, Manny, 94
Farewell to Arms, A, 3, 27
Faulkner, William, 3
Ferguson, Otis, 106
Fetherling, Doug, 2, 159
Feuchtwanger, Leon, 181
Fiedler, Leslie, 150
Fields, W.C., 32
Fight for Freedom, 152, 158
Fitzgerald, F. Scott, 3
Flag is Born, A, 2, 158
Florentine Dagger, The, 17, 20, 169
Fontaine, Joan, 55
Fontanne, Lynn, 57, 58, 72
Ford, Glenn, 167
Foreign Correspondent, 10, 42, 142, 143
Fort, Charles, 132
Four's a Crowd, 91
Fowler, Gene, xii, 22, 33, 67
Freedom of the Press, 41
Frenzied Fricassee, 23
Frohman, Charles, 81
From Reverence to Rape, 37
Front Page, The, xiii, 2, 4, 6, 25, 29, 34, 41-56, 57, 58, 71, 75, 77, 81-83, 100, 102, 108, 171, 181
Fun to be Free, 152

Gable, Clark, 5, 30-31, 44, 106, 108
Gaily, Gaily, 162
Garbo, Greta, 108
Gargoyles, 17, 20
Garmes, Lee, 113, 122, 133, 137, 139, 143, 153, 169
Geduld, Harry, 29
Gentleman's Agreement, 153
Gentlemen of the Press, 41
Georgian Scene, The, 59
Gilda, 148, 166, 167
Gilliatt, Penelope, 134
Gingham, Elizabeth, 14
Goin' to Town, 37
Golden Age of Sound Comedy, The, 79
Goldwyn, Samuel, 110
Gone with the Wind, 1
Goodman, Kenneth Sawyer, 22-23
Grant, Cary, 31-32, 47, 91, 95-96, 164-67, 174-76
Great Dictator, 143
Great Magoo, The, xii

Index   237

Green Berets, The, 42
Green, Adolph, 134
Greenberg, Hayim, 155
Griffith, Richard, 164
Grimaces, 20
Grosz, George, 12, 67
Guide for the Bedeviled, A, 155, 161, 162
Guiles, Fred, xii, 3, 60, 61, 108, 116, 117, 134, 182
Gullan, Campbell, 58
Gunga Din, 55, 147

Haganah, 2
Hall, Mordaunt, 90
Hammond, Percy, 125, 133
Hanging On in Paradise, xii, 3, 60
Hangmen Also Die, 153
Hansen, Harry, 10, 18, 20, 182
Harlow, Jean, 37
Harris, Jed, 50, 150, 151
Harrison, Joan, 143
Hart, Moss, 33, 156
Hartford Stage Company, xii
Haskell, Molly, 37-38, 61, 75-76
Hawks, Howard, xii, 2, 84-96, 112, 176, 179
Hay Fever, 58
Haydon, Julie, 128, 134
Hayes, Helen, 111, 133
Hayward, John, 139
Hayward, Leland, 109, 171
Hayworth, Rita, 145-48, 166, 179
Headlines, 41
Hecht, Jenny, 161, 171, 181
Hecht, Joseph, 5
Hecht, Marie Armstrong, 18, 19
Hecht, Rose Caylor, 18, 19, 21, 24, 110, 117, 126, 134, 149, 152, 156, 161
Hecht, Sarah Swernofsky, 5
Hemingway, Ernest, 86, 106
Henreid, Paul, 79
Hepburn, Audrey, 176
Hepburn, Katharine, xii, 31-32
Hero of Santa Maria, The, 23
Hilton, James, 143
His Girl Friday, xiii, 2, 29, 30, 34, 54, 79, 90-96, 108
Hitchcock, Alfred, 10, 21, 52, 112, 143, 163-67
Holiday, 34
Hollywood Screenwriters, The, xii
Homecoming, The, 23
Hope, Bob, 159
Hopkins, Miriam, 57, 63, 76
Horton, Edward Everett, 64
Howard, Sidney, 33
Howie, Walter, 6
Hughes, Howard, 52
Humpty Dumpty, 24

Hunter, McClellan, 176
Hutchens, Martin, 6

I Hate Actors, 162
I'm No Angel, 37
Idyll of the Shops, An, 23
Indian Fighter, The, 179
Irgun, xii, 2, 141-60
Iron Petticoat, The, 159
It Ain't No Sin, 37
It Happened One Night, 31, 44, 77, 84, 176
It's a Wonderful World, 29, 30, 106-8

Jabotinsky, Vladimir, 156
Jacobs, Lewis, 34-37
Jaffe, Sam, 56
Jew in American Literature, The, 150
Jew in Love, A, 4, 25, 117
Jewish Frontier, The, 155
Joy of Living, The, 30
Judaism, 141-60
Jumbo, 5, 139

Kael, Pauline, xii, 33, 39, 41, 42, 91
Karns, Roscoe, 84
Karsner, David, 10, 18
Kauffmann, Stanley, 178
Kaufman, Beatrice, 46
Kaufman, George, 30, 33, 45, 46, 47
Kaun, Alexander, 14
Keller, Walter, 139
Kennedy, Joseph, 153
Kerr, Walter, 52
Kirov, Ivan, 169
Kiss of Death, 162
Kracauer, Siegfried, 39

Lady Eve, The, 30
Lamarr, Hedy, 106
Lardner, Ring, 33
Lardner, Ring, Jr., 105
Last of Mrs. Cheney, The, 34
Lawrence of Arabia, 42
Lederer, Charles, 94, 95, 106, 111, 176
Legend of the Lost, 148, 179
Legion of Decency, The, 61
Lemmon, Jack, 51
Let Freedom Ring, 42, 142
Letters From Bohemia, 67, 162
Levant, Oscar, 111
Levin, Milton, 60
Levin, Shmarya, 149
Liptzin, Sol, 150
Literary Review (Chicago), 3
Littel, Robert, 34
Little Caesar, 34
Little Review, 14

Liveright, Horace, 129, 150
Living Theatre, 181
Lombard, Carole, xii, 84, 90, 100-104
Loren, Sophia, 179
Lou Grant, 42
Love Happy, 159
Love Parade, The, 57, 76
Lowry, Ed, 61
Loy, Myrna, 37
Lubitsch, Ernst, 57, 60-77, 84, 108, 112, 156
Lulu Belle, 80
Lunatics and Lovers, 96
Lunt, Alfred, 57, 58, 72

McCaffrey, Donald, 32, 57, 79, 98, 105
McCrea, Joel, 143
McLaglen, Victor, 153
MacArthur, Alfred, 20
MacArthur, Charles, xi, xiii, 2, 20, 22, 25, 33, 42, 41-56, 61, 67, 79-96, 109-40, 143, 152
MacMurray, Fred, 42, 179
Macready, George, 166, 167
Mailer, Norman, xiv
Mankiewicz, Herman, xii, 4, 15, 24, 33, 106
March, Fredric, 57, 63, 76, 98-105
Margo, 119, 123
Martinelli, Elsa, 179
Marx Brothers, 32
Marx, Harpo, 111
Mast, Gerald, 39
Master Poisoner, The, 23
Mature, Victor, 162
Mayer, Louis B., 28
Menjou, Adolph, 54, 106
Merrily We Go to Hell, 34
Midnight, 30
Midwest Portraits, 18
Mielziner, Jo, 34
Milestone, Lewis, 51, 52
Milholland, Charles, 80
Miracle in the Rain, 179
Miracle of the Bells, 42, 105, 179
Mitchell, Thomas, 145-48, 163
Moisse, 20
Monkey Business, 2, 174-76
Monroe, Marilyn, xiv, 174
Montgomery, George, 106, 153
Moon Is Down, The, 153
Moonshooter, The, 46
Moreno, Rosita, 126
Morgan, Helen, 52
Mortal Storm, The, 143
Moscow Art Theater, 21
Movie Made America, 37
Muni, Paul, 158
My Favorite Wife, 30

My Man Godfrey, 30
My Story, xiv

Nagel, Conrad, 91
Napoleon of Broadway, The, 80
Nathan, George Jean, 60, 74, 111, 133
New York American, 134
New York Herald Tribune, 125, 158
New York Post, 90
New York Times, 125, 130, 137
Nichols, Dudley, 33
Night Ride, 41
Ninotchka, 108
Nothing Sacred, xiii, 3, 23, 27, 29, 30, 42, 79, 80, 90, 96-108
Notorious, 47, 148, 163-67
Novels into Film, xiii
Nugent, Frank, 137

O'Brien, Pat, 51, 54, 103
Once in a Blue Moon, 5, 109, 115, 137-39
One Thousand and One Afternoons in Chicago, 17, 152
Oppenheimer, George, 33

P.M., 152, 156
Paradine Case, The, 162
Paris Underground, 153
Paris-Bound, 34
Parker, Dorothy, 33
Peck, Gregory, 163, 176
Perfidy, 159, 181
Perrin, Nat, 33
Philadelphia Story, The, 30, 31, 34, 42
Playboy, 162, 181
Players' Workshop, 14, 23
Poem of David, The, 23
Point Valaine, 133
Powell, William, 37
Power of the Press, 45
Preminger, Otto, 163, 182
Price, Vincent, 169
Provincetown Players, 23
Public Enemy, The, 34, 38

Qualen, John, 145-48
Queen of Outer Space, The, xiii

Racket, The, 34
Rains, Claude, 79, 119-25, 140, 166-67
Raphaelson, Samson, 60, 61
Reader's Digest, The, 155
Reddington, John, 133
Reed, Alan, 171
Reisch, Walter, 106
Remember Us, 155
Revisionist Party, 156

Rice, Elmer, 34
Ride the Pink Horse, 162
Ridges, Stanley, 128, 133
Rise of the American Film, The, 34
Roadhouse Nights, 29, 41, 52
Robinson, Edward G., 34, 42, 169
Rogers, Ginger, 106, 174-76
Roman Holiday, 42, 174-79
Roosevelt, Franklin, 153
Roosevelt, Theodore, 14-15
Rose, Billy, 139, 152, 156
Roxie Hart, 29, 30, 42, 106
Ruggles of Red Gap, 30
Ruggles, Charles, 52
Russell, Rosalind, 91, 95-96
Ryskind, Morrie, 33

St. Johns, Adela Rogers, 91
S.S. Ben Hecht, 157
Sandburg, Carl, 9
Sarris, Andrew, xii, 91
Saturday Review, 178
Savo, Jimmy, 113, 134
Scarface, The, xii, 2, 3, 27, 29, 32, 34
Scheuer, Steven, 42
Schulberg, Budd, 105
Scoundrel, The, 61, 109-40, 150, 151
Selden, Harry, xiv
Selznick, David, 28, 105, 111, 112
Sennet, Ted, 96
Sennwald, Andre, 130
Sensualists, The, 162
Sex Comedy Without the Sex, The, xii
Shamroy, Leon, 139
Shanghai Express, 113,
She Done Him Wrong, 37
Sheldon, Edward, 80
Sheridan, Margaret, 176
Shop Around the Corner, The, 60
Sinatra, Frank, 179
Sklar, Robert, 38-39, 57
Smart Set, The, 17
Smiling Lieutenant, The, 57, 76
Smith, Henry Justin, 1, 9, 12, 15, 182
Smith, Wallace, 8
Soak the Rich, 109, 133, 134, 137
Song of Russia, 153
Specter of the Rose, 115, 133, 167, 169
Spellbound, 21, 163-64
Spewack, Bella and Samuel, xi
Spoto, Donald, 166
Stallings, Laurence, 33
Stander, Lionel, 129, 133, 137, 169
Star Reporter, The, 41
Stevens, Ashton, 2
Stewart, James, 106
Stiles, Gordon, 11

Stop the Presses, 44
Street Scene, 34
Sturges, Preston, xii, 39
Swinnerton, Frank, 59
Szabo, Sander, 137
Szulaski, Stanislau, 14

Talking Pictures, xii
Taylor, Mary, 137
Telling the World, 41
Temple, Shirley, 31
Thalberg, Irving, 54, 112
Theatre Arts Monthly, 34
Theatre Guild, 142, 152
Theatre Magazine, 27
Theatre of Blood, 169
They Knew What they Wanted, 33
Thin Man, The, 30, 32, 37
Thing, The (From Another Planet), 2, 42, 176
Tierney, Gene, 153
Time, 133
To Quito and Back, 142, 152, 154
Tobey, Kenneth, 176
Too Many Husbands, 30
Topaze, 29, 176
Topper, 30
Tracy, Lee, 45
Trouble in Paradise, 57
Trueman, Paula, 121, 123
Truffaut, Francois, 166
Trumbo, Dalton, 176
Twentieth Century, The, xii, xiii, 2, 4, 25, 27, 29, 30, 34, 44, 54, 55, 79-91, 96, 105, 108, 169, 171

Ulric, Lenore, 80
Underworld, 25
Upperworld, 121

Variety, 123, 125, 137
Vidor, Charles, 166
Visions of Simone Marchand, The, 181
Viva Villa, 2, 28, 42, 55, 90
Von Doehman, Karl, 12
Von Gleichen, Count Russworn, 11
Vorkapich, Slavko, 122
Vortex, The, 58

Wanger, Walter, 116
Watts, Richard, 121
Wayne, John, 179
We Will Never Die, 156
Wedding Present, 91
Weill, Kurt, 156
Weinberg, Herman, 61, 108, 123
Wellman, William, 105
West, Mae, 37, 61
Where the Sidewalk Ends, 159, 162

Whirlpool, 159, 162
Widmark, Richard, 162
Wilder, Billy, 33, 51
Williams, Hope, 128
Winkelberg, 181
Winninger, Charles, 98
Wonder Hat, The, 23
Woolcott, Alexander, 33, 113, 117, 129

Wuthering Heights, xiii, 3, 27
Wyler, William, 176, 179

Young Man in Manhattan, 41

Zanuck, Darryl, 112
Zionism, 149, 155-60